# Handbook of Legal Tech

AF896083

EDITED BY COLIN S. LEVY

**Commissioning editor**
Alex Davies

**Managing director**
Sian O'Neill

***The Handbook of Legal Tech***
**is published by**

Globe Law and Business Ltd
3 Mylor Close
Horsell
Woking
Surrey GU21 4DD
United Kingdom
Tel: +44 20 3745 4770
www.globelawandbusiness.com

*The Handbook of Legal Tech*

ISBN 978-1-78742-967-3
EPUB ISBN 978-1-78742-968-0
Adobe PDF ISBN 978-1-78742-969-7

© 2023 Globe Law and Business Ltd except where otherwise indicated.

The right of the contributors to be identified as authors of this work has been asserted by them in accordance with sections 77 and 78 of the Copyright, Designs and Patents Act 1988.

All rights reserved. No part of this publication may be reproduced in any material form (including photocopying, storing in any medium by electronic means or transmitting) without the written permission of the copyright owner, except in accordance with the provisions of the Copyright, Designs and Patents Act 1988 or under terms of a licence issued by the Copyright Licensing Agency Ltd (www.cla.co.uk). Applications for the copyright owner's written permission to reproduce any part of this publication should be addressed to the publisher.

DISCLAIMER
This publication is intended as a general guide only. The information and opinions which it contains are not intended to be a comprehensive study, or to provide legal advice, and should not be treated as a substitute for legal advice concerning particular situations. Legal advice should always be sought before taking any action based on the information provided. The publisher bears no responsibility for any errors or omissions contained herein.

# Contents

# Foreword

The legal industry stands at the precipice of a technological revolution. As legal professionals, it is incumbent upon us to comprehend this confluence of law and technology to maintain our competitive edge and relevance in today's rapidly evolving world. This book serves as an outstanding resource for those in the legal profession who aspire to broaden their understanding of legal technology, from the rationale behind it to its practical implementation, and the wider implications of burgeoning legal tech trends.

Part I delves into the rationale underpinning legal tech. The authors not only raise the question, "Why legal tech?" but also furnish persuasive arguments to demonstrate the indispensability of legal tech for the future of the legal industry. Moreover, they scrutinize the intricate relationship between technology and law, examining the ways for technology to enhance various aspects of legal practice, and the ramifications of the escalating influence of technology on the legal sector.

Part II provides a deep dive into the practical aspects of legal tech, proffering pragmatic advice and insights into diverse legal technologies. Ranging from document automation to litigation analysis, the authors furnish invaluable guidance on capitalizing on legal tech to achieve superior legal outcomes. The book encompasses a wide array of legal technologies, such as eDiscovery, legal research, legal operations, contract management, and artificial intelligence. Furthermore, the authors probe the potential role of blockchain and NFTs in the realm of legal practice.

Part III investigates broader issues pertaining to legal tech that extend beyond its practical applications. The authors analyze the ethical dimensions of legal tech and the ramifications of technology on access to justice. They also delve into the challenges of embracing legal tech in a field that has historically been resistant to change and provide valuable insights into the trajectory of the industry.

With enough knowledge and experience under their belts, the innovators who contributed chapters to this book have crafted a compelling book that provides informative and inspiring reading for legal professionals who wish to remain at the vanguard of legal tech. They impart invaluable insights into the most recent legal technologies, practical advice on harnessing these technologies for optimal benefit, and thought-provoking contemplations on the wider implications of legal tech. This book also includes suggestions for supplementary reading and learning more, making this book a solid resource for those keen on delving deeper into legal tech.

This book represents the diversity of thought and experience that defines the legal tech space. The stories, the experiences, the lessons learned in each chapter together will help you enrich your comprehension of the nexus between law and technology. As I have long written about and spoken about, legal tech is for everyone. Technology should be something to be embraced and not feared. It is my sincere hope that this book and its insights will help you welcome technology and use it to help you work smarter and not harder.

**Colin S. Levy**

# Executive summary

Technology is everywhere. Its presence is undeniable. The legal industry, steeped in history and tradition, is not immune to the changes brought about by technological advancement. No facet of the legal industry can escape or ignore the increasingly important role of technology in the practice of law. Yet, technology can overwhelm, confuse, or downright intimidate many.

The *Handbook of Legal Tech* provides guidance from many of the leading figures within the legal tech space on the different parts of law practice being enhanced and improved by technology. This book is aimed at lawyers both in-house and in private practice globally who have an interest in legal tech and wish to learn more about how it will impact and enhance their work.

Technological advancement and innovation accelerate at an unprecedented pace and so the legal profession is faced with an urgent need to adapt to the rapidly digitizing world. While legal tech itself is not new, the speed of change has created a sense of urgency for the industry. Our opening chapter, by legal innovation and NewLaw strategist, Naomi Thompson. delves into why it is imperative for the legal sector to prioritize digital transformation in order to redefine its value proposition, both as in-house legal counsel and in practice. By embracing legal tech, legal professionals can position themselves as strategic advisors to help organizations navigate the evolving business landscape and to seize the opportunities presented by the digital era.

Zack Barnes then takes us through the history and evolution of legal tech, from the pre-technology era through to digitalization to automation and algorithmic intelligence. In chapter two, and by looking to the past to bring us to the future, Zack brings us to the present day, and Part II.

Part II looks at the how of legal tech and begins with a chapter on eDiscovery by Cat Casey, chief growth officer at Reveal Brainspace. Cat tracks the evolution of Discovery to eDiscovery and beyond, breaking down the amendments to the Federal Rules of Civil Procedure that helped build eDiscovery. She then demystifies the eDiscovery process and electronically stored information, followed by a breakdown of the tools of the eDiscovery trade, from the most basic to AI-powered and cutting edge. She then digs into legal and ethical considerations with a focus on specific case law and eDiscovery mistakes and how to avoid them. The chapter concludes by looking to the future of eDiscovery.

In chapter four, Josh Blandi, CEO and co-founder of UniCourt, discusses why law firms and legal departments should care about legal data, legal research, and legal analytics. Josh argues that firms and in-house counsel should be taking advantage of advances in legal data, legal research, and legal analytics because it is in their own best business interest and because their clients and business partners expect them to be looking to the future of law to remain relevant, competitive, and capable of providing strategic, data-driven legal services. He begins the chapter by laying out a common set of definitions for these legal terms of art, and then details prominent use cases for each, including leveraging legal data in the insurance industry, the impact of legal research on online businesses, and using legal analytics for business development and risk management. Josh closes out the chapter by detailing the vibrant legal ecosystem that law firms and legal departments have at their fingertips, concluding that those who invest in improving their data infrastructure now will be better positioned to succeed in the evolving business of law.

Chapter five, on contract lifecycle management (CLM), is a breakdown of contract processes and systems using a practical lens informed by real world experience. Tony Thai, CEO and chief engineer at HyperDraft, goes through the steps of how to analyze an organization's need for a system, the scoping and design of a system for a particular use case, and the ultimate implementation of a system. Without performing a deep dive into every phase, the goal is for readers to walk away with a basic framework they can use for their organization. There is no one-size-fits-all approach to analysis, design, or implementation of a CLM system, but this is a good place to start.

Chapter six looks at document automation. Dorna Moini, CEO and founder of Gavel, discusses how document automation has transformed from a critical internal law firm technology to a way to build client-facing legal products that transform a law firm's practice. The chapter starts with a brief history of document automation, which explains how the technology has been critical for internal operations and the rise of its use over the years. She then explains the tactical components of automating legal documents within a firm, spelling out the toolkit you have as you automate your practice. This section will be critical for any firm that is starting out with document automation or upgrading to a more robust tool. Finally, Dorna discusses the client-facing features that a document automation tool can have and the rise of the "legal product". This discussion is critical in the face of a growing gap in access to justice across the United States and beyond and encourages legal professionals to deliver legal services to the masses in a scalable way for their practice.

Chapter seven is on alternative dispute resolution (ADR) and is authored by Rich Lee, CEO and co-founder of New Era ADR. One of the most dynamic areas in legal technology is the world of alternative dispute resolution, he argues. As a much-needed alternative to our overburdened court systems, there are substantial opportunities to improve the process and technology behind ADR as it exists today. Doing so can bring about wide-ranging positive change that saves people and organizations massive amounts of time, money, and acrimony while bringing many positive societal benefits, from greater accessibility of our justice systems to less acrimonious disputes.

Chapter eight then looks at lessons from a legal tech start-up. Daniel Farris, founder of NMBL Technologies, examines legal industry trends that have led to the rise of legal ops and the increased adoption and reliance on technology products in the legal industry. Using the prior decade as a guide, Daniel identifies the key trends and drivers that guided him and his co-founders in NMBL Technologies to create Proxy, a legal workflow management SaaS product. Primarily, though, this chapter focuses on lessons learned by Daniel and the NMBL Technologies team in creating Proxy and bringing it to market. Concepts like Last Best Experience, the value of Integrations, Minimum Viable Product, and how to sell to lawyers are explained and the chapter provides anyone seeking to enter the legal technology space or build a new product with a useful guide and some valuable recommendations to increase the likelihood of success.

Chapter nine, by Tom Stephenson, vice president, Legal.io, looks at legal operations. The modern era of the corporate legal operations profession has witnessed a significant transformation in recent years, with companies increasingly recognizing the need for a more strategic and proactive approach to managing their legal functions. As a result, the role of legal operations professionals has become increasingly crucial in ensuring that legal departments operate efficiently and effectively. Corporate legal operations' six core functional elements include people operations and strategic planning, knowledge and risk management, outside counsel and external initiatives, financial planning and spend analysis, technology and data analytics, and project management and practice operations. Overall, the profession represents an exciting and dynamic field, with a wide range of opportunities for legal professionals to contribute to the success of their organizations. This chapter explores these core functional elements of legal operations, examining their importance, the skills required to succeed in each area, and the latest trends and best practices. Tom also explores legal operations professionals' challenges and opportunities in the modern business world and the skills and expertise required to succeed in this critical function.

Chapter ten, on Artificial Intelligence, is penned by Joshua Walker, CEO at System.Legal. Joshua argues there are three primary functions of AI to the practicing lawyer (and, for that matter, for anyone impacted by law). These are:

1. Information extraction;
2. Analytics and predictive modeling; and
3. Generation.

Information extraction is the leveraging of AI to figure out what has happened in the past – whether in legal policy, doctrine (e.g., case law), procedure (e.g., litigation), and/or relations (e.g., contracting). Analytics and predictive modeling leverages that empirical (and attendant doctrinal) data to detect patterns and model risks (positive or negative). Generative AI includes tools that generate legal text. For example, these are tools that can create contracts, pleadings, summaries, briefs, etc. For some reason, #3 is rarely rooted appropriately in #1 and #2. This chapter introduces all three legal AI forms, documents what can go wrong, and provides tactical advice for optimizing legal results.

In chapter 11, Olga V. Mack, vice president and CEO at Parley Pro, looks at blockchain and blockchain-enabled applications in law. Blockchain is a distributed database that allows for secure, transparent, and tamper-proof transactions between two or more parties in a peer-to-peer (P2P), without an intermediary, manner. Its applications are endless, and it has the potential to revolutionize many industries, including law. Olga's chapter acts a guide for lawyers who want to understand blockchain, how it could be applied in law, and how it can enhance law practice. First, it explains blockchain, how it works, and why you want to use it. Second, the chapter examines the following application: much more intelligent contracts and contract analysis, streamlined payments in legal instruments and litigation and settlement, intellectual property, a chain of custody, and DAOs. This exciting new industry can allow you to completely change your career and become a leader in this unexplored territory. Keep an eye on blockchain, says Olga. It just might be the next big thing in the legal industry.

Part III concludes the book by looking at broader issues in legal tech.

Chapter 12 on legal tech ethics is by Jan L. Jacobowitz, founder and owner of Legal Ethics Advisor. As the legal profession continues to emerge from the pandemic environment, technology remains an integral part of the practice of law. Many lawyers continue to work remotely, and video conferencing has become a core component of lawyering. But what are the legal ethics implications of all this technology? Lawyers who do not understand the connection between ethics rules such as competence, communication, and the use of technology in a law practice may find themselves tripping on ethical landmines. Conversely, lawyers who understand both the rules and the benefits of technology can employ it to contribute to the competent, successful practice of law. Jan's chapter explores legal ethics and technology in the contexts of individual use, outsourcing, and social media to provide a roadmap to assist lawyers in ethically embracing technology, employing its benefits, and avoiding ethical landmines.

Chapter 13, by Natalie Anne Knowlton, co-founder of Access to Justice Ventures, looks at technology's role in legal justice. The justice system, says Natalie, was designed for use by attorneys. The majority of people navigating the system today, however, are without legal assistance. This chapter discusses the critical role of legal technology in efforts to increase access to justice for the many who need it. It begins by setting out the broader context of the justice gap and by exploring the amorphous terms "access to justice" and "legal technology". Then, the chapter explores select trends in the evolution of access to justice technology tools, including the shift to accessible and deployable legal information, the emergence of end-to-end case management tools, and the productization of legal services. Finally, the chapter considers some of the challenges in designing tomorrow's tech-enabled justice system. Here, Natalie discusses deepening digital divides, limitations on market-based technology solutions, and regulatory uncertainties.

In chapter 14, Zach Abramowitz, founder of Killer Whale Strategies, explores the rise of law firm tech businesses and the advantages they have over traditional legal tech start-ups. He argues that starting as a people business, such as a law firm, provides a significant advantage in terms of having a built-in client base and go-to-market strategy, as well as minimal change to customer habits. Zach discusses the importance of focusing on customer outcomes rather than pushing new technology on lawyers who may be hesitant to adopt it. He acknowledges that there are some who are skeptical of law firms venturing outside their core competencies, but he points out that start-up founders often have to do things that don't scale in order to get to a point where scaling becomes possible. Overall, Zach is optimistic about the future of law firm tech businesses and believes they are built on solid foundations.

Chapter 15, by the book's editor, Colin Levy, takes a look at legal tech adoption. The legal tech landscape continues to shift, thanks to technology. However, many technological investments end up underutilized, leading to financial, resource-based, and trust-related consequences. To overcome the challenges of shelfware and resistance to change, legal professionals must embrace innovation and adapt to new methods, while also considering the human element in technology adoption. Encouraging change starts with establishing trust and understanding the perspectives of users and stakeholders. By focusing on the human impact of technology, demonstrating its benefits to individuals, and providing necessary support, legal professionals can encourage the adoption of legal tech. Creating a culture of innovation, prioritizing open communication, and celebrating small wins can also facilitate better adoption and lead to a more efficient and effective workplace.

Our final chapter is by Richard Tromans, founder of Artificial Lawyer. This chapter looks at how the legal innovation ecosystem has evolved and what has been driving this development, before the book concludes with a short section on further reading and resources.

# About the authors

**Zach Abramowitz** is the founder of Killer Whale Strategies and an investor in disruptive legal start-ups. Killer Whale Strategies works with Am Law 100 firms, Fortune 500 legal departments, and other organizations looking to capitalize on the current wave of disruption sweeping the legal industry. Zach writes longform essays for Legal Evolution, publishes webinars twice monthly, and maintains an active newsletter on legal technology start-ups that reaches thousands of attorneys and entrepreneurs. He is regularly quoted in industry news on legal disruption and wrote a regular column for Above the Law from 2015-2019. Zach is an NYU Law trained attorney who practiced as an M&A associate at Schulte Roth & Zabel before leaving to launch a start-up. Prior to starting his legal career, Zach worked as a stand-up comedian and a producer for ESPN Radio.

The process of turning invention into something valuable is innovation and it relies on facilitators looking for ways to make hard parts of adoption work better, easier, more efficiently. **Zack Barnes**' career has focused on the creative solutions at the nexus of academia, industry, technology, and particularly law to help drive R&D teams towards the next solution.

**Josh Blandi** is the CEO and co-founder of UniCourt, a Legal Data as a Service (LDaaS) company that provides real-time court data and legal analytics you can trust. UniCourt's mission is to make court data more organized, accessible, and useful for Am Law and Fortune 500 companies. UniCourt's API-first approach empowers the combination of internal data with external litigation data to find new business opportunities, optimize litigation strategies and outcomes, and power innovative solutions. Josh is featured in the Class of 2023 Legal Rebels by the *ABA Journal* and the ABA Center for Innovation and is a Fastcase50 honoree. Under his leadership, UniCourt has received numerous awards including the Technology Award of the American Legal Technology Awards and has been recognized as the Overall LegalTech Data Solution Provider of the Year at the LegalTech Breakthrough Awards. As part of Josh's strategic vision to provide Legal Data as a Service, he has assembled a diverse, global team across the US and India to unlock the potential of legal data.

**Cat Casey** is chief growth officer at Reveal Brainspace, helping lead innovation for legal technology solutions, and a zealous advocate for AI in legal. She is a thought leader and outspoken advocate of legal professionals embracing technology to deliver better legal outcomes. She has two decades of experience assisting clients with complex eDiscovery and forensic needs that arise from litigation, expansive regulation, and complex contractual relationships. Cat is a published author, keynote speaker, podcaster, and all-around advocate for upskilling legal professionals facing the dawn of an AI renaissance in law.

**Daniel Farris** is founder and CEO of NMBL Technologies, Inc., a legal technology company specializing in legal workflow management and automation. He is also an attorney at global Am Law 100 firm Norton Rose Fulbright, where he serves as partner-in-charge of the Chicago office and specializes in technology transactions, privacy and data security, intellectual property licensing, and commercial contracting. Daniel has a Masters of Science in Information Systems from DePaul University and a Juris Doctor from Loyola University Chicago School of Law. Before entering the practice of law, Daniel was a software engineer and network administrator. He now counsels companies large and small on technology creation, implementation, adoption, licensing, and use. His practice is highly technology-enabled, focused on client experience, efficiency, people, and process. As a legal tech founder, Daniel is working to enable the adoption of legal ops and support digital transformation in the legal industry.

**Jan L. Jacobowitz** is a legal ethics, social media, and technology expert who is the founder and owner of Legal Ethics Advisor. Jan provides legal ethics consulting, expert testimony, opinion letters, and CLE training to law firms and legal organizations. She is a past president of the Association of Professional Responsibility Lawyers and the co-chair of its Future of Lawyering Committee. For over a decade, Jan was the director of the Professional Responsibility and Ethics Program (PREP) at the University of Miami's School of Law. Under her direction, PREP was a 2012 recipient of the ABA's E Smythe Gambrell Award – the leading national award for a professionalism program. She continues to teach professional responsibility as an adjunct professor at Miami Law. Prior to devoting herself to legal ethics consulting and legal education, Jan practiced law for over 20 years. She began her career as a legal aid attorney in the District of Columbia, prosecuted Nazi war criminals at the Office of Special Investigations of the US Department of Justice, and was in private practice with general practice and commercial litigation firms in Washington and Miami.

**Natalie Anne Knowlton** is the founder of Access to Justice Ventures, LLC, empowering entrepreneurs who are developing scalable access to justice solutions. She formerly served as a regulatory advisor and the director of special projects at IAALS, the Institute for the Advancement of the American Legal System. She is committed to bringing deep empathy to the court users' experience and in pursuit of that goal employs legal and empirical research and analysis, facilitates collaboration among stakeholders, and engages in national outreach and advocacy. Natalie is in the 2023 class of American Bar Association (ABA) Legal Rebels, and is listed among the ABA Legal Technology Resource Center's 2022 Women of Legal Tech. She sits on the Justice Technology Association Board of Advisors, was a judge for the American Legal Technology Awards (2021-2023; Access to Justice), and co-founded the Denver chapter of Legal Hackers.

**Rich Lee** is the CEO and co-founder of New Era ADR and is the former general counsel of two fast-growing VC-backed technology companies, Civis Analytics and Livevol.

**Colin S. Levy** is an experienced lawyer and legal tech expert. Throughout his career, Colin has seen technology as a key driver in improving how legal services are performed. Because his career has spanned industries, he has witnessed myriad issues, from a systemic lack of interest in technology to the high cost of legal services barring entry to consumers. Now, his mission is to bridge the gap between the tech world and the legal world, advocating for the ways technology can be a useful tool for the lawyer's toolbelt rather than a fear-inducing obstacle to effective legal work. Colin is a sought-after writer and speaker. He is often asked to be a guest on legal tech podcasts, contribute to articles, blog posts, and other types of content published on various law outlets, and enjoys interviewing leading leaders in the legal and legal tech spaces.

**Olga V. Mack** is the vice president at LexisNexis and CEO of Parley Pro, a next-generation contract management company that has pioneered digital negotiation technology. Olga embraces legal innovation and has dedicated her career to improving and shaping the future of law. She is convinced that the legal profession will emerge even stronger, more resilient, and more inclusive than before by embracing technology. She shares her views in her columns on Above the Law, Forbes, Bloomberg Law, Association of Corporate Counsel (ACC) Docket, MIT Computational Law Report, Newsweek, and Venture Beat. Olga is also an award-winning general counsel, operations professional, start-up advisor, public speaker, adjunct professor, and entrepreneur. Olga co-founded SunLaw, an organization dedicated to preparing women in-house attorneys to become general counsels and legal leaders, and WISE to help female law firm partners become rainmakers. She lectures at Berkeley Law and has received numerous awards for her work, including the Silicon Valley Women of Influence, ABA Women in Legal Tech, Make Your Mark, Corporate Counsel of the Year, and Women Leaders in Technology Law. She is a fellow of CodeX, the Stanford Law Center for Legal Informatics, and a fellow of the College of Law Practice Management.

**Dorna Moini** is the CEO and founder of Gavel, a no-code platform for building document automation and client-facing web applications for the law. Prior to starting Gavel, Dorna was a litigator at Sidley Austin. There, in her pro bono practice, she worked with legal aid organizations to build a web application for domestic violence survivors to complete and file their paperwork, which led to the idea for Gavel. Dorna is on the Legal Services Corporation Emerging Leaders Council and is a member of LAFLA's advisory board. She was named an ABA Legal Rebel and a Fastcase 50 honoree. She also teaches the Legal Innovations Lab at USC Law School.

**Tom Stephenson** is vice president and legal operations evangelist at Legal.io, an enterprise marketplace for legal talent and technology. He has spent over a decade focusing on helping legal departments run smarter and faster during periods of hyper-growth while implementing right-sized technology to provide meaningful data about how legal teams work. As well as working alongside global law firms, legal tech vendors, and corporate law departments, Tom is passionate about education and advocacy within the corporate legal operations ecosystem. A graduate with a Master of Legal Studies from the University of Illinois, Tom regularly speaks as an authoritative voice on innovative legal operations strategies that drive efficiency, innovation, and transparency within an organization, including at Harvard Law School.

**Tony Thai** is the CEO and chief engineer of HyperDraft, a technology company that powers law firms and legal departments with AI-powered document and workflow automation software. Tony is a veteran attorney who has practiced at many of the world's most prestigious law firms and in-house at multiple large technology companies. Prior to his legal career, he was an enterprise software engineer and serial entrepreneur. He was recently recognized as a Fastcase 50 Honoree, serves as an adjunct professor at USC Gould School of Law, and is a legal and business advisor to a variety of technology companies.

**Naomi Thompson** is a legal innovation strategist working at the intersection of business, law, data, and technology, published author and prolific speaker. Naomi is a results-driven and strategic-minded professional who has held several influential roles throughout her career. Naomi started as a corporate in-house lawyer and transitioned to strategy implementation and business operations in emerging markets, including as chief of staff in a leading, pan-African investment firm. Naomi's strategic objective is to use her business and legal experience to lead and accelerate the transformation of the legal industry. She has a wealth of experience in developing and executing legal transformation strategies. Naomi was appointed to deliver PwC's regional NewLaw strategy and, prior to joining PwC, Naomi was senior vice president for Exigent Group's regional EMEA Legal Solutions offering, advising both local and global organizations on legal department transformation initiatives. Naomi now consults with multi-national organizations on all aspects of their legal transformation strategies. Naomi serves on several boards, has a Master of Business Administration from Hult International Business School and a Bachelor of Laws degree (LLB).

**Richard Tromans** has worked in the legal sector for over 22 years. He started in journalism before moving into management consulting in 2008 with a focus on market change and providing strategic advice to the legal sector. Since 2016 he has had a focus on legal innovation and that year started Artificial Lawyer, the globally-read legal tech and innovation news and information site. He strongly believes that we have only just begun the journey of transforming the legal profession.

**Joshua Walker** is a serial entrepreneur and IP attorney. Previously, he co-founded CodeX: The Stanford Center for Legal Informatics and, subsequently, Lex Machina – where he served as CEO, chief legal architect, and chairman. He also led legal for Airbus SE, Silicon Valley, as general counsel and co-founder of A^3, while leading advanced contract AI development. Now, as CEO of System.Legal, Josh continues to develop AI enterprise systems across legal, finance, risk, and governance for select clients. Josh received his A.B. degree, m.c.l., from Harvard College (Special

Concentration in Conflict Studies) and his J.D. from the University of Chicago Law School, where he was a cornerstone scholar. Prior to law school, he served as analyst at the Office of the Prosecutor, International Criminal Tribunal for Rwanda, where he helped deploy its first working database.

Part I:

# The why of legal tech

# Chapter 1: **Introduction**

*By Naomi Thompson, legal innovation and NewLaw strategist*

As digital transformation continues at pace across the legal industry – and legal technology fundraisers follow suit – there will be a greater need for legal industry leaders and participants to effectively evaluate the tools that best enable their teams to devise and apply technology-enabled solutions to client and business challenges.

The legal industry and profession are also at a juncture of looking inward. At the core of the case for legal tech as an innovation and improvement imperative is redesign. Legal industry participants are required to rethink and redefine an effective value proposition, measurable service levels and output measurements beyond just the quality metric. As client expectations evolve and market movements dictate greater shifts in work distribution, legal is moving to measurement in value, not time.

## The why of legal tech

*The Handbook of Legal Tech* enters the conversation at this critical juncture. The *Handbook* explores various aspects of legal technology and aims to provide actionable insights for readers and legal tech users to navigate this rapidly evolving field, while also exploring the benefits and broader implications of legal tech for the legal profession. Legal tech is not new to the legal landscape, but the advent of generative artificial intelligence (AI) and foundational models for legal application has injected a necessary urgency into the conversation and will shape how lawyers and sector participants engage with legal tech conceptually and in practice. The legal sector has long been regarded as ripe for technological disruption, with AI and other innovative tools tapped to transform the way legal services are delivered.

Purpose-built legal AI tools powered by large language models (commonly "LLMs") and natural language processing capabilities continue to provide proofs of concept for both the use of technology in substantive areas of legal practice, as well as the criticality of lawyers within this process. Across eDiscovery, contract analysis, due diligence, and legal research, legal tech has arguably demonstrated its ability to significantly free up valuable time, improve governance and collaboration approaches, and support the creation of enhanced work product and a transformed value proposition. These tools' ability to analyse, cluster, and review dense legal language and unprecedented volumes of data are saving lawyers countless hours of manual review time and reporting on contract terms, case law, court proceedings, legislation, and discovery. Additionally, diligent curation of these tools forms part of supervised machine learning and over time supports broader knowledge management and risk mitigation efforts. Users of legal tech must of course apply a precise reasoning lens to identify limitations and avoid opaque outcomes.

The proliferation of legal tech solutions available to the legal industry is bringing about a revolution in the way lawyers work, communicate, and manage their practices. Use cases across the spectrum reveal that the application of legal tech can streamline routine tasks such as document generation, document and contract review, data entry and research, freeing up valuable time for lawyers to focus on higher-level analysis involving legal strategy, negotiation, and client management. AI-powered contract analysis, document automation, e-discovery, and machine learning offer a range of tools designed to make the legal process more efficient, more cost-effective, and enhance the delivery of legal services.

### The client experience

Yet efficiency gains should not be the only consideration for lawyers to adopt legal tech. At the center of digital strategy is the client experience. Technology should be seen as a strategy to prioritize the client experience and deliver improved, consistent results and outcomes for clients. A legal tech strategy does not exist in a vacuum; it encompasses the entire operating model to future-proof the business.[1] This shift makes legal services more accessible to a wider range of individuals, putting clients at the forefront of legal transformation.

In a world that is exponentially changing, companies and organizations face mounting pressure to adapt. With growing client expectations, there is increasing demand for more value and innovation but without the willingness to pay more for the product or service.[2] Compounded by the increased frequency and complexity of regulatory changes, organizations across the world are leveraging digital technologies and data to ensure their survival. Legal is no exception. The growth of legal tech has been driven by the need to keep up with an increasingly digitized world, where legal services are no longer solely about providing legal advice but about finding effective and efficient solutions to problems using technology.

This business imperative provides in-house legal teams with a unique opportunity, not just to change the way they deliver legal services, but to become strategic advisors and expand their impact and influence across the organization.[3] The legal function is vital to driving the overall transformation of organizations. For example, businesses that seek to invest and adopt new technology can only proceed as quickly as their legal team can evaluate the risks associated with said technology, namely contractual risk, cybersecurity, data privacy, operational resilience, etc. By seizing this opportunity, in-house legal teams can position themselves as valuable business partners and help their organizations to thrive.

Legal tech can further enforce in-house lawyers' position as strategic advisors and help them stay abreast of legal trends and developments, keeping pace with evolving regulatory changes and requirements and proactively advising businesses on ways to stay ahead of their competitors. This can be especially important for in-house legal teams, which are typically required to have expertise in a wide range of areas to ensure that their organizations comply with relevant laws and regulations.

Legal tech encompasses a wide range of tools and solutions that in-house legal teams can use to enhance their advisory role and stay updated on legal trends, and efficiently manage compliance, leverage contract management tools to surface and manage obligations and risks, access knowledge databases, conduct effective legal research, and monitor regulatory changes.

Legal research and analytics tools provide in-house legal teams with real-time updates on legal trends through proactively scanning the landscape for regulatory changes relevant to their industry. These tools can analyse vast amounts of legal data and highlight key insights, enabling in-house lawyers to stay informed and proactively advise their organizations on potential legal implications and strategies. This further enhances the function's strategic capabilities, allowing in-house legal teams to proactively ensure that their organizations are compliant, resolve issues, identify commercial opportunities, and focus on more strategic work.

Legal departments are also embracing the challenge of identifying repetitive tasks in the delivery of legal services and utilizing process design and workflows to standardize and automate their processes. By adopting legal tech and optimising workflows, legal empowers the business with self-service tools, provides the business with quick access to critical information and documents, and enables legal to achieve more with their available resources.

By leveraging legal collaboration platforms, data integration, and analytics, legal can improve collaboration between the legal department and other functions, enabling organizations to enhance their responsiveness to legal issues and challenges and contribute to a more cohesive and agile organizational response to legal matters. Improved collaboration between the legal department and other functions within the organization enhances legal's performance, ultimately transforming the experience and support provided to internal business stakeholders.

Law firms, on the other hand, are facing a more dynamic and highly competitive environment where traditional competitors are no longer the only players in the game, and the expectations of customers and stakeholders continue to evolve. The application of technology in the legal field has rapidly transformed from a niche concept to a crucial aspect of modern-day legal practice. The rapid pace and complexity of technological advancements mean that digital transformation must be a top priority for law firms more than any other type of organizational change.

## Adopting legal tech

The adoption of legal tech is not to simply identify tools that can enhance the practice of law, reach the finish line, and switch off the engines.[4] It requires a commitment to ongoing learning, pivoting, and testing and a willingness to adapt and embrace change in a traditionally change-resistant sector. Legal leaders are apt to navigate complexity and therefore apply that approach to legal tech with a focus on innovation as a continuous improvement process. As leaders and law firms learn to adapt to this new reality, they will be better positioned to succeed in the long-term and stay ahead of the competition.

The legal profession is at a critical crossroads, driven by complex regulatory change, global economic pressures, digitization, increased competition, and changing client expectations. Integrated effectively, legal tech can augment processes in practice and in business and play a critical role in responding to these changes becoming a component of success for both in-house legal teams and law firms alike.

Demonstrating the effective "why" of legal tech, *The Handbook of Legal Tech* is a timely, practical, and important entry to an area of increasing importance for everyone within, and interacting with, the legal industry.

*References*

1 Parker, I. (2021) *Successful digital transformation in law firms: A question of culture*. London: Globe Law and Business.

2 State of the Corporate Law Department: Managing risk, mitigating litigation and controlling costs (2023). Thomson Reuters Institute. www.thomsonreuters.com/en-us/posts/legal/state-of-the-corporate-law-department-2023/.

3 PricewaterhouseCoopers (2023) Legal transformation for business growth. From guardian of risk to enabler of transformation: why investing in legal pays. www.pwc.co.uk/services/legal/insights/transform-legal-transform-business.html.

4 Hill, L.A., Cam, A.L. and Menon, S. (2022) Where can digital transformation take you? insights from 1,700 leaders, HBS Working Knowledge. Available at: https://hbswk.hbs.edu/item/leading-in-the-digital-era-where-can-digital-transformation-take-you.

# Chapter 2:
# Tech and law – looking back to move forwards

*By Zack Barnes*

## In the beginning...

...was the command line, with apologies to Neal Stephenson whose essay-turned-book of that title should be required reading for law school. The legal industry and its technology and software application coevolution predates computer processors.[1] From clay to paper to typewriters (still paper) to personal computers (still paper too) and well into the digital age, legal services remained a highly manual industry.

The use of computer technology and software applications ("legal tech") to improve and streamline legal processes, research, document management, analysis, discovery, and client services has been implemented in the span of a single generation's career. Actually, to blame a single event, the emergence of personal computers led to the accelerated legal tech developments the industry has experienced in the past decade and a half. Legal tech encompasses tools focused on driving work product quality, increased efficiency, reduced costs, and improved access to legal services for clients. Given the diversity of legal workflows, there are a growing variety of products for case management systems, e-discovery, contract management platforms, virtual legal assistants, and increasingly analytical tools for a variety of niche applications. Automated document review, predictive analytics, and online dispute resolution systems are just starting to change how legal professionals work, enabling them to handle larger volumes of cases or focus more on high-value tasks requiring human judgment. This legal tech evolution is driving client demands for improved accuracy and quality, accelerated production times, and faster, more transparent communications and invoicing.

It's easy to shrug off each incremental improvement as "good enough", but new developments are coming at shrinking intervals. For attorneys and clients, understanding the historical evolution of technology and legal services through the current state of the art towards the future is useful at this increased development pace. Specifically, the challenges that the legal industry faced in the pre-technology era and how the core solutions address them. Moreover, the historical context of this coevolution helps in assessing the impact of legal technology we may take for granted in today's work. This experience highlights the risks associated with and the potential opportunities of technology-driven legal services. Finally, reviewing our current tools with an eye toward the next challenge or the next thing that could be just a little bit better, we may reasonably predict (ok, take a scientifically wild guess at) the future of technology and solutions development.

Admittedly, we can't cover the minutiae of every technology's impact on every practice area – such a treatise would be immense and immediately obsolete. Thus we aim for a high-level review of the past, the digital revolution, and the legal tech applications of automation, computer intelligence, and analytics to serve as a review of how far the industry has come and a jumping off point for how the industry continues to incorporate what comes next.

## Pre-technology era

In the prehistoric – rather, the pre-technology – era of law, legal practice was manual paper management. Skipping over the quill-calligraphy on parchment to typewriter revolutions for brevity, even as computer-word processors became increasingly advanced, a vast majority of legal work remained paper-based. The reliance on forests-full of documents, correspondence, and physical files also required an army of professional manual labor to move it around, and we're not talking about lumberjacks. These paper-pushing processes both entrenched that army of professionals and represented a constraint to efficient legal service; simple contracts took a couple weeks, complex transactions several months, and disputes or litigation took years simply due to the number of people that had to physically handle a document. While the latter might not have accelerated much (for other reasons), banks and other legal-bound business moved at the pace of the legal review and the legal system.

The most obvious place for this was paper work-products – from document preparation including drafting, transcription into a typed format, revising or negotiation, and eventual finalization for agreements. Let us not even get into patent writing in the paper era. While professional typists and paralegals may have done the preliminary documents, timekeeper attention and redrafting resulted in significant billable hours to clients' invoices.

Moving on to what happens next in the legal process, filings, document processing, and communication all produced considerable delays. Correspondence between lawyers, clients, and courts primarily relied on postal mail, which even before deregulation added delays in exchanging information and documents. This resulted in legal proceedings that could be prolonged due to the time required for document mailing, receipt, recordation, processing, and notification, leading to inefficiencies and extended timelines for resolution.

Among the contributing factors to this comparatively glacial pace was limited access to legal information. Publishers were the aggregators of laws, decisions, precedents, and other opinions. Any legal research required physical presence in law libraries and relied on the availability of relevant legal texts and resources from those publishers. Subscribing to these resources was a financial barrier but collating and storing regular updates to those volumes often required dedicated office space and a paralegal, if not a legal librarian, for large multidisciplinary business firms.

Setting aside the possession or alternative accessibility of the organized volumes, finding the relevant legal text, and gathering materials for a client matter at hand required significant resources. Firm professionals and junior lawyers would spend considerable billable time conducting library research, combing indexes and summaries to identify the specific volume that may contain relevant legal information. The identified passages would either be bookmarked or photocopied (again, we've skipped past the hand- and typewritten transcription era here), inserted in the file or otherwise brought to a handling attorney. Even these passages would be organized and paraphrased for that attorney's attention, taking additional time. Thus, even in rare cases where a company had a general counsel that had at least some legal library, they rarely had the time nor other means to comb these resources, and an individual layperson was left lost.

Beyond legal research for precedent, litigation and discovery took hours of combing through boxes of photocopies and print-outs. Even as some of those documents were supplied in digital formats, they were generally printed out for searching and flagging. Not that litigation was ever an efficient process, but the number of human resources for this was significant.

Moving out of the trees, geographically, clients were limited to the law firms that were nearby their homes or corporate headquarters. Aside from telephones there were few ways to share information quickly, especially documents. Clients had to expend considerable resources to identify the (closest) firm that had expertise in their issue at hand and then await conflicts clearance. Documents had to be sent by registered mail or couriers to ensure delivery.

Finally, in this pre-technology era, clients lacked transparency regarding the resources used, costs associated with them, timelines, and how that made it to an invoice from counsel. Firms with longtime client relationships tended to bill more predictably. However, for other clients the variability in those costs and timelines made it hard to budget for expenses and make business plans accordingly. Even so, individuals and businesses of all sizes came to rely on firms.

With our permissible hindsight, the pre-technology era of legal services moved at the speed of paper. Manual labor, document analysis and processing times, and poor client communications were just the accepted cost of business. Contributing challenges included access to legal information, geographical constraints, and the resulting unpredictable actual legal costs. As computer technology began to make its way into businesses and even homes, clients began to ask for solutions to these challenges. It was this inquiry that began to drive the development, adoption, and in-housing of legal technology.

## Along came digitalization

And then, Steve Jobs invented the personal computer and Al Gore invented the internet. Tongue firmly in-cheek (neither did), these two developments in personal computing and connectivity changed society, business, and of course the legal services industry. Early computer advancements weren't specifically focused on legal and business was faster at adopting the use of computers for broad purposes. However, for legal it was eliminating printed documents that led to a revolution in all legal workflows.

The catalyst for the first changes was the introduction of word processors, which replaced manual typewriters. The adoption of word processors in the legal industry was not as fast as in other industries, as there were professional staff that had been generating and handling the documents that had to evolve as well. These programs and later software like Microsoft Word enabled lawyers to draft and edit documents efficiently. Also with word processors, lawyers could now benefit from features such as automatic spell-check, copy-pasting text, and the ability to easily make and track revisions, without relying on a professional typist. Sidebar: As much as we might pretend the industry has advanced, most legal professionals have a colleague (or three) that prints documents, reads them, marks changes with a pen, and then hands it off to someone else to make the changes. Print, revise, recycle, reprint, rinse, repeat – but these are the exception rather than the rule. This centralizing of the document drafting process allowed for efficient lawyer-centric formatting, drafting, and revising of legal documents.

And as much as legal work is all in new digital documents, there are likely to be warehouses of paper legal documents under the lock and care of the government, law firms, and private entities for eternity. However, digitization – the process of converting physical legal documents into digital formats, a manual process itself for scanning, indexing, and then storing documents electronically – is ongoing and will be into the middle of the 21st century. But in converting these to digital documents, those warehouses, filing cabinets and bankers' boxes were less necessary, and reduced overhead for attorneys. More importantly, when combined with the new documents, a central document management system with searchable, centralized work-product and a document repository is created. Firm lawyers could easily store, retrieve, share, and create uniformity in legal documents. Moreover, these document management systems enabled lawyers to implement robust version control, collaboration features, and advanced search capabilities, further improving productivity and streamlining workflows. Finally, these storage systems became early databases of at least partially sorted information.

As telephone modems gave way to high-speed internet for all, how legal professionals access information changed. With the advent of the internet, a vast amount of legal information became readily available online. Attorneys and their teams can now search and analyze case law, statutes, and legal opinions, saving time in document preparation and client responses. Aggregators that specialized in organized, digital, legal information introduced remotely accessible subscription databases such as Westlaw and LexisNexis. These internet-accessible collections of legal information, including case law, statutes, regulations, and legal commentary were more valuable than physical libraries in their facilitation of faster and more comprehensive legal research. The attorney never had to be in the presence of books, or know exactly in which volume a precedent could be found, as these databases all had search functions built-in, all through the internet.

And with the internet came a new communication called electronic mail – "email". This paragraph buried in this chapter is a disservice to the significance of disruption this technology has brought to everything. Or maybe that is a testament to how commonplace and ordinary it has become to us. Either way, among legal professionals just reading the word email can trigger involuntary anxiety pangs to check the latest email response (go ahead, look, we'll wait). Without equal, email has gutted the postal and courier industries by entirely eliminating the need for paper letters. While legal documents occasionally required ink signatures, email revolutionized communication, allowing lawyers, clients, courts, and opposing parties to instantly exchange documents, valuable information, and appointments (tee times included).

And then with the digital documents, internet and email came the ability of clients to be geographically removed from their legal counsel. This allowed clients to find and retain the best attorneys for their needs, not to mention to compare attorney billing rates to meet their cost needs. The benefit was not all for clients, as the internet has also facilitated remote work and virtual law practice. Lawyers can now access document management case files, client information, and legal resources from anywhere, thanks to the internet.

However, this transition from physical to electronic document management came at the expense of the professional legal staff. The subsequent emergence of legal operations as a strategic function within the business of law saw the evolution of other professional roles in the legal industry. Paralegals and other staff began to perform document creation, templating, and research tasks. This freed up attorneys to spend more time on complex legal analysis, strategy development, and client counseling. The adoption of technology in legal processes boosted attorney efficiency, lowered response times to business needs, and clients began expecting more, faster. This shifted focus to quality and efficiency to deliver improved client service, satisfaction, and legal cost reductions.

Finally, digitalization, the internet, and email catalyzed the emergence of the legal tech industry. To deliver fast, accurate, quality, legal advice, attorneys need a wide range of software, tools, and platforms to address clients' needs. And where there are unmet needs, there are solutions (and vendors).

## Automate everything

From that perspective, document-based workflows represented a significant opportunity to reduce manual labor in repetitive, tedious tasks, while improving quality of legal advice. The digital era has provided options in solutions for automating the preparation, management, and analysis of documents, reducing previously time-consuming or labor-intensive tasks. This automation reduces unproductive (read: unbillable) time for attorneys and legal professionals and speeds client delivery.

First, proofreading and formatting tasks in the legal field were time-consuming and labor-intensive, relying on eyeballs-on-text scrutiny and adherence to complex style guides. Early versions of automated proofreading tools focused on basic grammar and spell checks, offering limited assistance to legal professionals. As context recognition algorithms advanced, these tools evolved to understand the intricacies of legalese, enabling the tools to identify and correct errors specific to legal terminology. Moreover, the integration of formatting rules and styles have improved these tools, allowing for consistency, including headings, numbering, citations, and formatting conventions, through a document. Lawyers can seamlessly incorporate these tools within their document workflows, saving proofreading and formatting time while reducing the risk of errors. As text recognition algorithms and large language models advance, it is expected that automated legal tech tools for proofreading and formatting will become even more sophisticated and provide faster assistance for document workflows.

Second, with consistent formatting and context recognition, legal documents are easier to manage. For the in-house attorney, contract management tools have grown to automate the lifecycle of contracts, from version control during negotiation to execution and renewal. These tools automatically centralize contract storage, organization, and automate tasks such as contract tracking, deliverables, and deadlines. This automated contract management legal tech increases efficiency, reduces risks, and improves governance. For the firm attorney, case and transaction management software applications facilitate the organization, tracking, and management of the documents involved in complex legal disputes and transactions. These legal tech solutions automate document management, including document collating, storage, calendaring, task completion, progress, and inter-party communications. By centralizing and automating these administrative processes, these solutions enhance efficiency and reduce overhead. As legal tech tools continue to integrate legal industry-specific artificial intelligence, large language models, and machine learning functionalities, it is expected that these contract and case management tools will be so efficient that many in-house legal teams will prefer to use them, rather than relying on outside counsel.

Despite continuing developments in legal industry computer intelligence functionalities, document database analysis will remain a firm-centered workflow. Specifically, due diligence legal professionals need to review and analyze large volumes of documents to identify potential risks, liabilities, and compare them against other filings. Legal tech solutions for automatically categorizing and extracting relevant information from documents, flagging potential issues, and providing a comprehensive overview are still evolving to reduce the risk of missing critical details during increasingly complicated due diligence processes. And when that diligence breaks down, such that investigations and litigation proceed, e-discovery teams use similar tools. These e-discovery platforms leverage automation and computer intelligence for identifying, collecting, and reviewing electronic documents. These tools are evolving with new search algorithms, data analytics, and computer learning models to sift through large volumes of electronic data, including emails, documents, and even metadata stored by software programs, to identify relevant evidence faster and more accurately.

While deeper discussions of these topics follow, simple automation advances the next generation of legal tech tools by leveraging computer intelligence. These automation tools continuously learn and improve, adapting to the nuances of legal writing through the applications of artificial intelligence, machine learning techniques, and large language models.

## Algorithm intelligence

This leads us to the computer in the room. Many electrons and much ink have been spilled already and more is coming as computer intelligence evolves as the disruptor of all industries, including legal services. Artificial Intelligence (AI), Machine Learning (ML), and Large Language Models (LLMs) have emerged as powerful if misunderstood computer intelligence tools. Often used incorrectly and interchangeably, there is still confusion as to the practical definition of those terms and what they "do". And as used herein, AI refers to software systems developed to perform sometimes abstract tasks that appear to require human intelligence. ML is a type of AI that uses algorithms and statistical models that enable computers to learn from data to make predictions that a human could not practically compile and interpret. LLMs are ML language models trained on vast amounts of text data (like, all of the internet) and that generate human-like text responses to queries.

At the highest level, AI systems were designed to categorize information, extract and organize it as data, analyze vast amounts of that data for patterns or anomalies, and finally sort that data based on priority. While this sorting of the data represents a deductive reasoning that seemingly requires human intelligence and judgment, it is the application of a human-defined set of rules that leads to the outcome. Following that ruleset creates the reasoning path to the output. Changing the parameters of those rules then results in a different output or conclusion. This type of AI is particularly useful for converting certain laws or due diligence processes into the rules and processing data against those rules. Once the rules are applied, missing information or anomalies in the dataset can be identified and prioritized by where in the deductive sequence the error was noted. Applications for this deductive AI include tax codes and securities filing needs, and continue to evolve in due diligence, e-discovery, and other legal workflows.

As computer processor power continues to increase, the volume of information a computer can process has exceeded human capabilities entirely (as in every human on earth combined could not process the volume of data a computer can in the same amount of time). It has become possible to create algorithms that analyze disorganized information and organized datasets for statistical evaluation and back comparison for accuracy, relevance, and other parameters in the results. While this required manual inputs of good and bad results to the application at the beginning, this machine learning is credited with underpinning the generative AI that is filling news feeds today. Over time, applications improve their own performance with increasing data being incorporated, analyzed, and results output. As a statistical analysis intelligence, machine learning has grown from finding small anomalies in large datasets, be they auditing accounting records, mergers and acquisitions, transactional values, or trends in court decisions, into a much more powerful tool.

While we might be forgiven for stopping there, it is impossible not to address the leap in advancement of large language models (LLM). Historically, as AI engineers worked on natural language processing (NLP), the nuances of language, and especially the intricacies of legalese, exceeded rule-based and statistical algorithms capabilities. However, incorporating ML analysis in to a significantly large number of parameters (as in, hundreds of billions) allows the model to classify words and phrases, determine context, and predict the next word, tense, and meaning in a phase or sentence. While still in its infancy, applications in legal research, validation against case law and precedent, and document creation are rapidly evolving.

The intense attention being paid to these tools is driving their development at higher velocities than previous software applications. Even as these tools have demonstrated capabilities that exceed human capabilities in a number of areas, the primary resistance for adoption remains the perception of the computer missing a critical piece of information or in its interpretation of information and data. While legal professionals should critically evaluate the outputs of tools using AI, ML, and LLM, these technologies offer vast improvements in efficiency, accuracy, alternative solutions to client challenges, and new analysis methods for lawyers.

## Predictive analytics

Beyond just finding and analyzing the existing data, the capability of computer intelligence to extrapolate forward requires mentioning. While this may have fit under the previous section, we've split it off here because it's the "next step" and an area of computer technology that attorneys are extremely hesitant to trust. However, computer intelligence tools can analyze historical data, current events, and other factors, and constantly update this to identify patterns and trends, and output predictions. These potential outcomes allow legal teams to move proactively to position their clients and optimize their teams for success.

Obvious applications include legislative and judicial predictions and case management for clients. By constantly analyzing historical case data, including regulatory statutes, legal precedents, and past outcomes these tools help attorneys understand the changing state of legislation and predict next steps in order to better advise their clients in strategic business decisions. Additionally, as court decisions and regulation enforcements evolve, predictive analytics tools allow attorneys to advise their clients of recommended paths, potential outcomes, and the risks in pursuing those actions. This analysis enables lawyers to develop strategies based on their clients' goals, assess the strengths and weaknesses of different legal advising, and build a strategy to achieve that goal.

Perhaps less obvious but equally important to a legal team's operations are workflow sharing and resource allocation applications. Legal firms can analyze their internal data, such as lawyer productivity, matter complexity and duration, client need and financial sensitivity, and their own financial goals to optimize the team working on the project. Additionally, these applications permit rapid re-allocation and sharing of information among the team and the clients. By identifying the most effective allocation of lawyers, support staff, and other resources, firms can increase efficiency, reduce costs, and improve overall client satisfaction. This data-driven approach helps ensure that the right resources are assigned to each case, resulting in better outcomes for clients and a more profitable practice for the firm.

Beyond just internal workflow, as computer intelligence improves with the growth in legal data, legal teams leveraging predicative analytics will be able to provide clients better options to proceed with their projects and thus more satisfactory outcomes. Additionally, they will also differentiate themselves for future work.

## The future

If we engage in futurist speculation, in the next generation of attorneys, it's likely that the legal industry faces the following challenges:

- Distributed, self-executing, ledgers or blockchain technology will lead to the commoditization of legal contracts, digital identity verification, and intellectual property rights, and reshape the way legal agreements are formed and enforced;

- The emergence of AI-based legislation, legal assistants, and court systems will change the way certain regulations are created or modified, enforced, and adjudicated; and
- Augmented reality, if not virtual, court systems.

However, in the near future, as clients demand more cost effective and predictable legal costs, the industry faces its largest disruption – the loss of its protected status in the world's largest economy. As legal services are increasingly able to be provided by non-lawyers and alternative legal service providers, the firms, and in-house attorneys alike, are going to have to address increased competitive pressure. For firms that will entail value-based rather than hourly billing and a drive for increased internal efficiency to deliver a profit under that model. In-house legal teams will have to acquire technology to efficiently manage more of their workflows, rather than outsourcing it to firms. Thus, the primary means to remain competitive will be through mitigating risk in rapid trial and adoption of computer software technologies, such as automation, computer intelligence, and predictive analytics.

This should not be considered an indictment of the legal industry. After all, it has evolved from paper to digital, and the integration of these technologies has required legal professionals to acquire new skills and adapt to changing roles. Detailed ideas of how to do that follow.

*References*

1 https://en.wikipedia.org/wiki/In_the_Beginning..._Was_the_Command_Line

Part II:

# The how of legal tech

# Chapter 3:
# eDiscovery

*By Cat Casey, chief growth officer, Reveal Brainspace*

## Introduction

Welcome to the wild(ish) world of electronic discovery (eDiscovery) – the detective work of the legal world. It's the process of identifying, collecting, processing, reviewing, and producing electronic documents and data in the context of legal proceedings.

Discovery, as it was known before the "e" was added, consisted of bankers' boxes, more papercuts than one should ever have to imagine, and a very manual approach to uncovering information.

Discovery is the process by which parties to a legal dispute exchange information and evidence relevant to the case. It can involve a wide range of activities, such as document requests, depositions, and interrogatories. The goal of discovery is to ensure that all parties have access to the relevant information and evidence necessary to prepare for trial. It's kind of like a legal version of an Easter egg hunt, except instead of candy and plastic eggs, you're searching for legal evidence and information!

### Gimme an "E"

In today's digital age, we leave a digital footprint with everything we do. From sending emails to creating spreadsheets, our electronic documents and data can provide critical evidence in legal cases. And that's where eDiscovery comes in, using sophisticated software and tools to help legal professionals sift through this mountain of data and uncover the evidence needed to build their case.

As with any detective work, there are challenges and considerations that come with eDiscovery. Privacy concerns, ethical considerations, and the sheer volume of data can all make the eDiscovery process a real nail-biter. However, with the right tools and expertise, eDiscovery can help legal professionals navigate this digital minefield and find the evidence they need to make their case.

In the past, the legal discovery process was about as fun as a root canal.

You'd sit in a dimly lit room for hours on end, sifting through piles of paper documents with only a highlighter and a cup of coffee to keep you company. Thanks to the introduction of legal technology, we've upgraded from highlighters to cutting-edge eDiscovery software and can now breeze through millions of electronic documents in record time.

Of course, as with any new technology, eDiscovery comes with its own set of challenges and considerations. There are legal and ethical issues to consider, as well as the potential for human error when dealing with vast amounts of electronic data. But with the right tools and know-how, eDiscovery can be a game-changer for legal professionals.

## From bankers' boxes to hard drives – the evolution of eDiscovery

Previously, legal professionals were forced to sift through mountains of paper documents to build their cases. It was a grueling process that required highlighters, paperclips, and the patience of a saint. But then, in the late 1990s, along came the internet, and everything changed.

The eDiscovery process, once rife with bankers' boxes full of documents, expanded dramatically with the advent of the internet and email. The velocity in the development of innumerable data types, sizes, and formats has not stopped.

Now, in a single minute, over 400,000 apps are downloaded, 20 million texts and hundreds of millions of emails sent,[1] in addition to over 750,000 hours of Netflix[2] binge-watched. This volume of creation and consumption has grown dramatically just in the last few years.

So, what is a digital detective to do? Where should law firms, in-house, and legal service providers look to uncover potentially relevant electronically stored information (ESI)?

As people started to communicate more and more through email, text messages, and other digital channels, legal professionals realized that electronic data could be a goldmine of evidence in legal cases. However, they also quickly realized that they needed a new set of tools and techniques to deal with this digital evidence. So, eDiscovery was born.

In the early days of eDiscovery, legal professionals were forced to use basic search and retrieval tools to find electronic evidence. As the volume of electronic data exploded, eDiscovery tools and software evolved to keep pace. Today, we have cutting-edge tools and techniques like predictive coding, machine learning, and artificial intelligence to help us sort through massive amounts of data and find the evidence we need.

There have been challenges and setbacks along the way. Legal professionals have had to navigate privacy concerns, ethical considerations, and constantly evolving technology. But through it all, eDiscovery has remained a critical player in the legal world, helping legal professionals uncover digital evidence and build strong cases. So, there you have it, the history of eDiscovery – a tale of innovation, perseverance, and (of course) digital clues.

## Civil procedure gets digital

Since the early 2000s, there have been several amendments to the Federal Rules of Civil Procedure (FRCP)[3] that have had a significant impact on eDiscovery. Below are some of the key amendments.

### 2006 FRCP amendments

This one was a bit of a wake-up call for the legal profession, which was still getting to grips with the challenges of managing electronic information in legal disputes. It was like a referee blowing the whistle and saying, "Hey, everyone, this eDiscovery stuff is serious business now, so let's get our act together and figure out how to deal with it!"

The first major eDiscovery amendment to the FRCP was made in 2006. This amendment included changes to Rules 16, 26, 33, 34, 37, and 45, which were intended to address the unique challenges posed by ESI. Among other things, the amendments clarified the parties' obligations to preserve, collect, and produce ESI, and set forth a framework for addressing eDiscovery disputes.

- *Rule 16.*[4] This required the parties to discuss the discovery of ESI early in the litigation process. The rule clarifies that the court may issue an order regarding the discovery of ESI and emphasizes the importance of cooperation between the parties in resolving eDiscovery issues.
- *Rule 26.*[5] This required parties to disclose certain ESI in their initial disclosures. The rule also clarified that parties must meet and confer regarding ESI discovery issues and provided guidance on how to handle disputes related to the form of production of ESI.
- *Rule 33.*[6] This clarified that a party may serve on any other party a request to produce ESI in addition to traditional paper documents. The rule also established a procedure for objecting to a request for ESI.
- *Rule 34.*[7] This clarified that ESI may be subject to discovery requests and provided guidance on how to handle disputes related to the form of production of ESI. The rule also established a procedure for objecting to a request for ESI.

- *Rule 37.*[8] This established sanctions for failure to preserve or produce ESI. The rule provided guidance on the factors that a court may consider when determining whether to impose sanctions and clarified that the sanctions may include an adverse inference instruction, an order striking pleadings, or an order dismissing the action.
- *Rule 45.*[9] This clarified that subpoenas may be issued for the production of ESI and provided guidance on how to handle disputes related to the form of production of ESI.

## 2015 FRCP amendments

This one was all about proportionality. It's like the legal system finally realized that not every case requires the same level of eDiscovery firepower. It was like saying, "Hey, let's stop throwing nuclear missiles at every legal dispute and start using a bit of common sense and proportionality when it comes to eDiscovery."

The most recent eDiscovery amendments to the FRCP were made in 2015. These amendments included changes to Rules 1, 4, 16, 26, 30, 31, 33, 34, 37, and 55, and were intended to address the ongoing challenges of managing eDiscovery in an increasingly digital world. The amendments emphasized the importance of proportionality in eDiscovery and clarified the scope of discovery and the requirements for asserting objections to discovery requests.

- *Rule 1.*[10] This emphasized the importance of cooperation between the parties and their lawyers in conducting litigation. The rule emphasizes that the parties and their counsel should work together to achieve a just, speedy, and inexpensive resolution of the case.
- *Rule 4.*[11] This clarified the requirements for serving a summons and complaint, particularly when serving an individual in a foreign country. The rule also added provisions regarding the use of electronic means to serve process.
- *Rule 16.*[12] This emphasized the importance of early and active management of cases by the court. The rule encourages courts to issue scheduling orders early in the case and requires the parties to confer in good faith to discuss the case management plan, including the discovery of ESI.
- *Rule 26.*[13] This clarified the scope of discovery to include only information that is proportional to the needs of the case and required the

parties to meet and confer regarding the preservation and production of ESI.

- *Rule 30.*[14] This limited the number of depositions that a party may take without leave of the court and clarified the procedures for obtaining such leave.
- *Rule 31.*[15] This made similar changes to Rule 30, limiting the number of written interrogatories that a party may serve without leave of the court.
- *Rule 33.*[16] This made several changes to the procedures for serving and responding to requests for production of documents, including ESI. The rule requires parties to specify the form in which ESI will be produced and provides additional guidance on the procedure for objecting to a request.
- *Rule 34.*[17] This made similar changes to Rule 33, requiring parties to specify the form in which ESI will be produced, and providing additional guidance on the procedure for objecting to a request.
- *Rule 37.*[18] This imposed several changes to the sanctions that a court may impose for failure to preserve or produce ESI. The rule provides guidance on the factors that a court may consider when imposing sanctions and clarifies that sanctions may include an adverse inference instruction, an order striking pleadings, or an order dismissing the action.
- *Rule 55.*[19] This clarified the procedure for default judgments and added a new subsection addressing the availability of default judgment in certain circumstances.

The 2015 amendments to the FRCP were designed to address the evolving nature of litigation, including the increasing use of technology in the discovery process. These amendments emphasized the importance of early and active management of cases by the court and encouraged the parties to work together to achieve a just, speedy, and inexpensive resolution of the case.

### Other amendments

These amendments were like a new coat of paint on an old house. They were necessary updates to the rules to make sure they were keeping up with the times. It's like saying, "Hey, let's put some new technology into this old legal system and see if we can make it work a bit better".

In addition to the eDiscovery-specific amendments, there have been other changes to the FRCP that have had an impact on eDiscovery. For example, in 2018, amendments were made to Rule 23,[20] which governs class actions. These amendments were intended to address issues related to the use of technology in managing and administering class actions, including eDiscovery.

While there are still challenges and uncertainties surrounding eDiscovery, the amendments to the FRCP have helped to provide some much-needed clarity and guidance in this complex and rapidly evolving area of the law.

## Demystifying the eDiscovery process

eDiscovery is like being a high-tech detective, but instead of a magnifying glass and a trench coat, you have a laptop and a cup of coffee. Legal professionals use fancy software and tools to dig through electronic documents and data, hunting for clues that can make or break a case. As with any good mystery, there are twists and turns along the way. Privacy concerns, ethical considerations, and the sheer volume of data can all make eDiscovery a rollercoaster but with the right set of skills and tools, legal professionals can navigate this digital jungle and come out on top. They can find that one email, that one spreadsheet, that one piece of evidence that turns the case in their favor. It's like a game of cat and mouse, but instead of a mouse, you're chasing down digital evidence.

Figure 1 shows a quick breakdown of what happens in each step along the way.

- *Identification*. Find whose electronically stored Information (ESI) you want to look at and where it lives.
- *Preservation*. Prevent people from altering or destroying this data.
- *Collection*. Have experts use technology to copy and document the ESI itself and data about the data (metadata).
- *Processing*. Turn 1s and 0s of ESI into a reviewable format and get rid of garbage data.
- *Review*. Use humans and tech to look at and categorize data by relevance and issues, get rid of more garbage.
- *Analysis*. Build your case using insights from the review.
- *Production*. Share the non-garbage data relevant to the matter with interested parties.

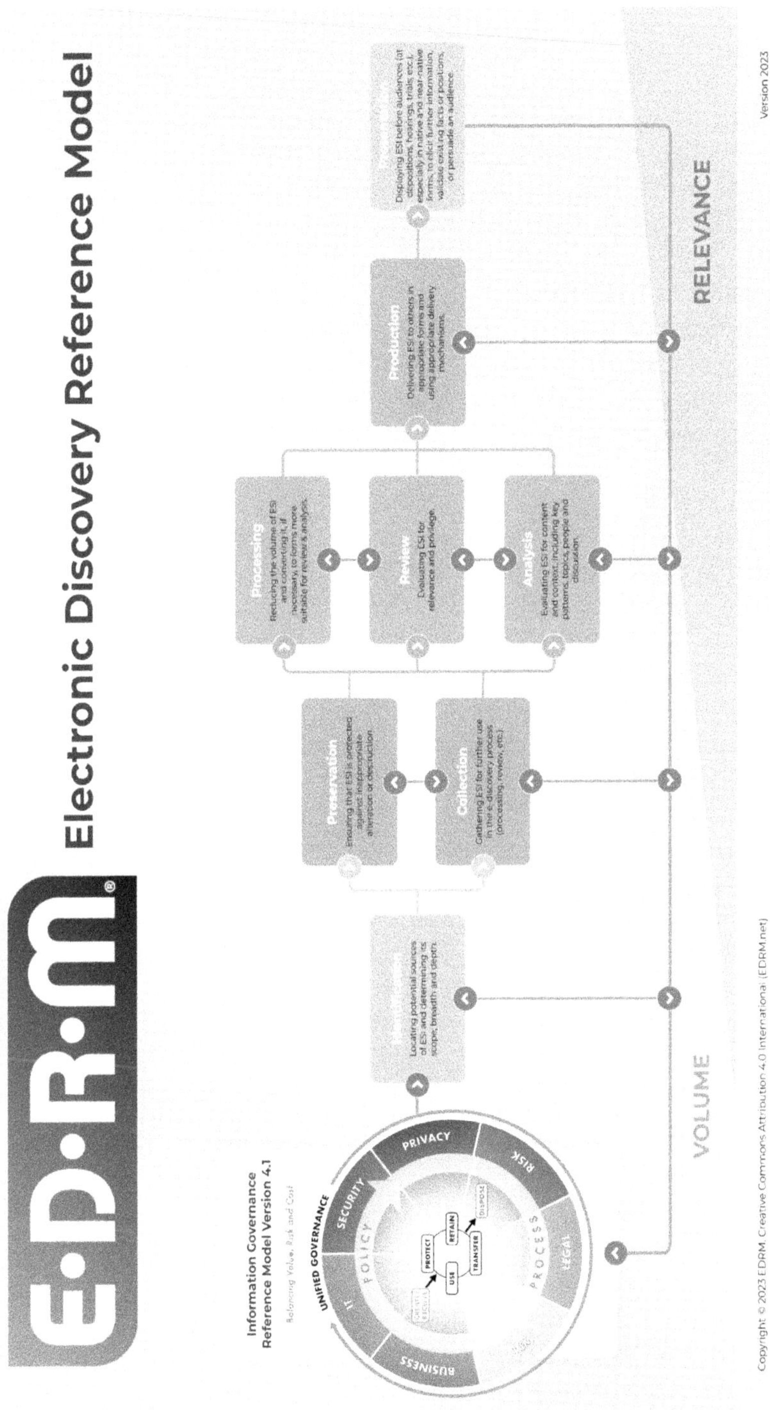


*Figure 1: Electronic Discovery Reference Model.*[21]

Fear not if your eDiscovery matter does not neatly follow this great workflow – few do in real life. In practice, the eDiscovery process may be much messier – you may have any number of things that cause you to backtrack, repeat a step, or even start the process over. This is completely normal. Just be sure to diligently document your process throughout and work with technology that is designed to adapt along with you.

## What does ESI mean?

Pretty much anyone in the eDiscovery space understands that ESI is electronically stored information, and yet this question packs an increasingly interesting punch. In an era of collaboration tools, ephemeral (self-destructing) messaging apps, the internet of things, and now Elon Musk's proposed Neuralink chip[22] embedded inside a human brain, answering this question is significantly more complicated.

What is potentially relevant has evolved substantially since the "e" was added to discovery. The world has fundamentally shifted, and we are using a wide array of new and legacy technologies to communicate, work, and interact. This paradigm shift has brought a veritable deluge of potentially relevant information to scour.

The simple answer is that ESI for the purposes of eDiscovery is a moving target that will continue to evolve with the tools we utilize to conduct business and interact with each other. The key to not drowning in this sea of data is twofold. First, talk with custodians early to understand how and via what technology they communicate and conduct business. Second, prioritize and triangulate your data sources by digging into the richest sources first and using insights from each successive data source to refine and narrow the scope of review in subsequent ones.

Key categories today that should be discussed in any custodial interview or while scoping an eDiscovery matter include the following:

- Electronic or hard copy documents (spreadsheets, presentations, documents, PDFs, etc.).
- Email (Gmail, Outlook).
- Instant messaging (Jabber, Yammer, Facebook messenger).
- Collaboration tools (Slack, Teams).
- Text/SMS.
- Messaging apps (WeChat, WhatsApp).
- Social media (Facebook, Instagram, Twitter, LinkedIn, Snapchat, TikTok).

- Ephemeral messaging (Signal, Wikr, Telegram).
- Internet of things (Smart devices like Fitbits, smart watches, Alexa, Nest).
- Emerging tech (ChatGPT, Metaverse, Dalle).

## Finding relevant data

Initially, the transition from discovery to eDiscovery simply meant shifting from filing cabinets to desktop computer files and Outlook folders. Factors like cloud computing, the proliferation of bring-your-own-device (BYOD) policies, and third-party hosted applications have complicated the process of data identification. The rapid post-COVID-19 shift to remote work has also created a Zoom boom[23] and opened new data sources and locations to investigate.

Data architecture differs from organization to organization and the proliferation of third party managed and hosted applications, including messaging apps, social media, and collaboration tools, not to mention O365, and other enterprise-grade cloud systems, makes it imperative that you speak with the tech experts within an organization early and engage external experts if internal resources cannot paint a complete picture.

There is no one right answer here, but places to look include company supplied computers, tablets, and mobile devices, third-party applications and/or cloud backups, company shared drives and backups, company managed cloud and backup, legacy backup devices, and more.

## Challenges and considerations with eDiscovery

One of the biggest challenges with eDiscovery is the sheer volume of data – mountains of digital information that legal professionals must sift through. It's like trying to find a needle in a haystack, except the haystack is the size of a football stadium.

Let's also not forget about the technology itself. It's constantly evolving and changing, which means legal professionals must be constantly adapting and learning new skills. It's like trying to keep up with a treadmill that's on full speed – one misstep and you could go flying off the back.

But it's not just the technology that's a challenge – there are also ethical considerations to think about. Privacy concerns, data protection laws, and the potential for abuse of digital information all must be carefully considered. It's like walking a tightrope, trying to balance the need for evidence with the rights of the people whose data is being searched.

There's also the cost. eDiscovery can be expensive, both in terms of the software and tools needed, and the time and manpower required to search through all that data. It's like trying to balance a checkbook that just keeps getting bigger and bigger.

With all that said, eDiscovery is a critical part of the legal process. It helps legal professionals uncover evidence that would have been impossible to find in the old days of paper documents. While it may be a rollercoaster ride, it's one that legal professionals are willing to take to get to the truth.

## Technology tools for eDiscovery

### Basics of eDiscovery tools

Loosely speaking, the software and legal technology tools available for eDiscovery mirror the eDiscovery Reference Model steps of the eDiscovery process.

- *Collection tools*. Collection tools are used to collect data from various sources, such as laptops, servers, mobile devices, social media platforms, and cloud storage. Some collection tools can automatically identify relevant data and collect only that data, which can reduce the amount of irrelevant data that needs to be processed and reviewed. AI and machine learning algorithms can be incorporated into collection tools to help identify relevant data automatically.
- *Processing tools*. These tools are used to process and organize the collected data so that it can be searched and reviewed more efficiently. Processing tools can perform tasks such as indexing, filtering, deduplicating, and data normalization. Some processing tools incorporate AI and machine learning algorithms to identify and group similar documents, classify data, and perform other tasks.
- *Review tools*. Review tools (or platforms) are used to review the processed data and identify relevant information, privileged information, and other types of information that may be relevant to the case. Review tools often have advanced features such as concept clustering, predictive coding, and machine learning to make the review process faster and more accurate. AI and machine learning algorithms can be used to help reviewers prioritize documents that are more likely to be relevant and to suggest tags or labels that can be used to classify documents.
- *Analysis tools*. These tools are used to analyze the processed data to

gain insights and make decisions. Analysis tools can perform tasks such as entity extraction, topic modeling, and sentiment analysis. AI and machine learning algorithms can be used to analyze large amounts of data and identify patterns and relationships that may be difficult or impossible for humans to detect.

- *Presentation tools.* Presentation tools are used to present the reviewed and analyzed data in a way that is easy to understand and use. Presentation tools can create charts, graphs, and other visualizations to help users understand the data. AI and machine learning algorithms can be used to generate summaries or highlights of the most important information in the data.

## All-in-one Discovery AI

Legal AI is woven throughout the various types of tools available for eDiscovery, with a prevalence in the Early Case Assessment, Review, and analysis phases of eDiscovery. Flavors of AI for eDiscovery today include the following.

### Email threading

One of the most basic flavors of eDiscovery analytics – email threading – identifies and organizes all the emails or comments in a single conversation to review them in order. Grouping the conversation into a single unit improves review speed and consistency across a data set. This allows the human reviewing the data to more quickly connect the dots on long conversation stings.

### Conceptual clustering

A data visualization that uses unsupervised machine learning (algorithms developed without human input), concept clustering presents groups of similar topics to a human reviewer who can then decide how to proceed. While the visualization is generated automatically using unsupervised learning, the human is in the driver's seat in terms of interpreting the data and determining what to do from a workflow standpoint.

Legal teams can use the concept clustering visualization to better understand the key issues on a case, to prioritize what topics get reviewed first or to validate the accuracy of proposed search terms. It can be used on its own or in concert with other AI tools or visualization as part of ECA, the Review or QC process of a document review.

### Social network analysis

Another data visualization that uses unsupervised machine learning, Social Network Analysis presents who is communicating to whom with what frequency. Case teams can use this visualization to prioritize which custodians are reviewed, determine if any key people are missing from a data collection, and/or exclude custodians who are not communicating with the relevant custodians of a matter.

Social Network Analysis can be used on its own or in concert with other AI tools or visualization as part of ECA, the Review or QC process of a document review. It can prioritize custodians for large-scale reviews, outright eliminate custodians from scope who were not in communication with the key people of interest, or uncover a previously unknown subject that ought to be included in scope.

### Technology Assisted Review

Technology Assisted Review (TAR) is a type of supervised machine learning where human input refines an algorithm based on coding decisions. This type of human-centered AI relies on a human to both build the algorithm and determine what to do with the output. The algorithm then promotes similar documents for review based on the human feedback. Legal professionals can use this to prioritize and accelerate a review or upon reaching a level of statistical certainty can end a review without placing eyeballs on every document.

### AI models

AI models in eDiscovery document review are built out of a combination of algorithms that are supervised and unsupervised to identify things like specified issues, behaviors or even privilege. The model is trained using data sets and coding decisions and then learns throughout the new case based on the input from the case team.

Like TAR, these human-centric AI models are built with human guidance and subject to human determination on what is done with the output. The models can be based on linguistic structure, emotional signals, behavioral intelligence, and case team insights from active learning.

- *Portable AI models*. Some AI models can be taken from one case to future cases to take the insights previously learned to accelerate time to insight.
- *AI Model library*. Some models are prebuilt using data scientists and data sets and the case team can apply it to their case to get a jump start.

- *Bespoke AI models.* These build AI models to identify specific issues as part of a complete AI driven solution. They then retain and reuse these models applying what you've learned (your decision IP) to other similar types of cases, increasing your speed to valuable insights.
- *Model layering.* Multiple AI models can be turned on at a time with the system leaning on them all in concert.

### Entity recognition/extraction

This is another supervised learning process whereby the system learns to identify things like names of people, places, or companies, dollar amounts, job titles, account numbers, case/matter numbers, etc. Entity recognition is based on numerical patterns, linguistic patterns, and other AI models, which enable practitioners to refine the documents they review and prioritize information relevant to a case. It can be especially helpful in dealing with personally identifiable information subject to a DSAR or post cyber breach notification.

### Computer vision

Much in the way that AI aimed to teach a computer to think like a human, computer vision aims to make a computer see like one. Used in image recognition and search, legal teams can use this function to identify specific potentially relevant images or types of images that could be relevant. The human-centered AI surfaces likely visual content and specific types of images to empower the human reviewer to make more informed decisions quickly.

### Conceptual search

Concept search is another human-centered analytic process that allows legal practitioners to search by an idea, theme, or example material. Concept search differs from concept clustering in that it is guided by an image, document, or string of text that a legal practitioner uses to search for other conceptually similar material.

Like concept clustering, this analytic tool can help practitioners better understand what is going on in a data set, uncover key facts of a case, and prioritize or exclude material based on the search results. Concept searching is also extremely helpful if you are early on in a matter and not exactly certain about the specific language the organization or people of interest used but have a general idea of the type of concept you want to search.

### Sentiment analysis

A type of Natural Language Processing (NLP), sentiment analysis uses signals in the language to uncover the feeling behind a document. The AI identifies signals of anger, excitement, optimism, or pressure. “I hate this company” vs “the pasta is lovely”. This tool is especially helpful if you are looking for hostile behavior, harassment, etc.

Emotionally charged language can be highly impactful in a variety of litigation and investigation contexts. From identifying language that involves pressure or coercion for a fraud case to emotional language indicating compliance or employment issues, this context building analysis helps surface potentially impactful communication quickly. The sentiment analysis empowers human reviewers to prioritize specific types of communication based on the type of matter they are handling.

### Machine translation and language detection

Many eDiscovery tools now have AI powered language identification and translation built in. Automated detection of language can help identify foreign language(s) within a document so you can shift to fluent members of the case team. Machine translation can be used to get an idea of the subjects covered in a document. This is great for prioritizing or eliminating documents, but I would still advise having a human reviewer as a final pass for more potentially relevant documents because machine learning is not yet perfect.

## The artificial intelligence spectrum

Artificial intelligence helps streamline and accelerate all aspects of eDiscovery document review and can be applied to cases large or small. Human-centered AI for eDiscovery workflows can help law firms and in-house counsel gain insights from day one of a document review. New technology with AI capabilities is entering the market at lightning speed. The legal industry is increasingly adopting AI workflows to address the need to do more with less.

While some AI-powered legal tech is more advanced, there is a spectrum of AI solutions that can be incorporated into the review process. One or multiple AI-powered legal tech solutions can be used to make eDiscovery document review less time-consuming.

At the end of the day, legal professionals have a wide variety of human-centered AI solutions for eDiscovery to make legal work easier and to find key insights faster.

## Legal issues and ethics in eDiscovery

When it comes to eDiscovery, the law can be a bit of a stickler every step of the way.

### Preservation obligation

One of the key considerations is preservation – which means that you better not lose those emails, text messages, or other electronic documents that could be relevant to the case. If you do, you could be in a world of legal hurt. Parties have a duty to preserve relevant ESI when they reasonably anticipate litigation. The scope of the preservation duty is defined by the specific facts and circumstances of the case. Relevant case law includes:

- *Zubulake v. UBS Warburg* (2004).[24] This established the concept of proportionality in eDiscovery, meaning that the scope of discovery should be proportional to the needs of the case.
- *Pension Committee of the University of Montreal Pension Plan v. Banc of America Securities* (2010).[25] This established that parties must issue a litigation hold to preserve relevant ESI and failing to do so may result in severe sanctions.

### Relevance

Another consideration is relevance – just because you have a mountain of data doesn't mean you get to dump it all on the other side. You need to be able to justify why each piece of evidence is relevant to the case, or else you could be facing objections, sanctions, or even a grumpy judge. Parties must produce only relevant ESI and may not engage in "fishing expeditions" or overbroad requests. Relevant case law includes:

- *Bell Atlantic Corp. v. Twombly* (2007).[26] This established the requirement that a complaint must contain "plausible" allegations to survive a motion to dismiss, and a party must have a "reasonable basis" for requesting discovery.
- *In re Gen. Motors LLC Ignition Switch Litigation* (2017).[27] This illustrates that parties may not simply dump large amounts of data on the opposing party but must justify the relevance of the data.

### Proportionality

The scope of eDiscovery must be proportional to the needs of the case. eDiscovery can be expensive, and parties are expected to cooperate to keep the costs reasonable. If you try to take advantage of the other side or go on a wild goose chase for irrelevant data, you might find yourself on the receiving end of a hefty bill.

Relevant case law includes:

- *Zubulake v. UBS Warburg* (2004).[28] As previously mentioned, this case established the concept of proportionality in eDiscovery.
- *Oppenheimer Fund, Inc. v. Sanders* (1978).[29] This established the concept of "discovery costs", which can be shifted to the requesting party if the burden of discovery outweighs its potential benefit.

### Privilege

Parties must identify and withhold privileged ESI from production. Relevant case law includes:

- *In re Columbia/HCA Healthcare Corp. Billing Practices Litigation* (2000).[30] This established the standard for determining whether ESI is subject to attorney-client privilege.
- *In re Genentech Herceptin Antitrust Litigation* (2017).[31] This demonstrates the importance of timely asserting privilege and adequately describing the privilege assertion.

### Production format

ESI must be produced in a reasonable format, and parties may request production in a specific format if necessary. Relevant case law includes:

- *Aguilar v. Immigration & Customs Enforcement Div. of US Department of Homeland Security* (S.D.N.Y. (2017).[32] This illustrates the importance of producing ESI in its original format to ensure authenticity and completeness.
- *In re State Farm Lloyds* (Tex. 2016).[33] This case allowed the requesting party to receive ESI in its requested format because it was necessary for the requesting party to effectively use the ESI.

### Defensibility

Defensibility in eDiscovery refers to the ability to justify and defend the processes and methods used to collect, preserve, and produce electronically stored information (ESI) during the litigation process. The concept of defensibility is critical in eDiscovery as it ensures that the data produced is legally admissible and can withstand legal challenges.

There are several issues around defensibility in eDiscovery that can arise during the discovery process. These issues include:

- *Preservation*. One of the key issues in eDiscovery is the preservation of ESI. This involves taking steps to ensure that all relevant data is retained and not destroyed or altered in any way. Failure to preserve ESI can result in sanctions and spoliation charges.
- *Collection*. Collection must be done in a defensible manner, with clear and documented procedures to ensure the integrity of the data. This includes ensuring that the collection process does not alter or corrupt the data in any way.
- *Processing*. This process can also raise defensibility issues, particularly around the methods used to extract and process the data. The processing must be transparent, with clear documentation of the processes used.
- *Review*. Defensibility issues can arise if the review process is not conducted using appropriate methods or if the reviewer is not qualified to make determinations about the data.
- *Production*. The data must be produced in a defensible manner, with clear documentation of the processes used. This includes ensuring that the produced data is complete and unaltered.

Defensibility in eDiscovery is critical to ensuring that the data produced is legally admissible and can withstand legal challenges. Failure to ensure defensibility can result in sanctions, spoliation charges, and other legal consequences. As such, it is essential that parties to litigation take steps to ensure that their eDiscovery processes are defensible and well-documented.

## The future of eDiscovery

New technological innovation in how we live, work, and play has never been at a higher velocity than we are seeing today. There is a whole new world of electronically stored information (ESI) springing up around us, and the impact on electronic discovery and data privacy is being felt in law firms and corporations across the globe.

The legal industry is no stranger to emerging types of electronic data. It seems like just a minute ago that the Federal Rule of Civil Procedure had to pivot to encompass ESI within discovery requests, spawning eDiscovery in the first place. But the sheer volume of new data sources facing legal teams today is staggering. Legal technology is helping to bridge the gap, but the practice of law is truly in uncharted territory.

Many of the new kids on the ESI block were squarely in the personal use domain, but the pandemic and mass shift to a virtualized workforce accelerated adoption of many new applications in a business context.

In the last few years there has been a mass adoption of ephemeral messaging apps like WhatsApp to facilitate communications in global teams. Video conferencing platforms that once operated on the fringes, like Zoom, Skype and Teams, saw daily active user numbers explode into the hundreds of millions as everyone from corporate professionals to students from elementary to grad school turned to this technology to stay connected in socially distanced times. Both information technology groups and legal professionals found themselves struggling to keep up with this dramatic and shockingly rapid shift.

### AI everywhere!

When it comes to artificial intelligence and the law, many legal professionals find themselves having questions that seem so rudimentary they are too afraid to ask. The result is many brilliant attorneys and case teams shy away from the AI-powered legal technology reshaping the practice of law altogether.

The legal industry is undergoing a technology-driven renaissance today, whilst AI and machine learning-powered technology is reshaping the scope and delivery of legal services. To understand the impact AI technology is having on the practice of law, let's start simply by defining what AI is and then frame it in the context of the legal services industry.

First coined by John McCarthy over half a century ago, the concept of AI is a simple one – the "science and engineering of making intelligent machines". The goal of all AI is a simple one – to make machines that can replicate human thought or intelligence. More recent articles have built on this basic idea of intelligent machines to a more modern conception of AI focused on a system's ability to "correctly interpret external data, to learn from such data, and to use those learnings to achieve specific goals and tasks through flexible adaptation". In plain English – can a system learn from human or data inputs and perform a job or provide insight as a result?

### What is an AI model?

AI models are the building blocks of AI technology. At the most basic level, an AI model is a program or algorithm that learns how to recognize patterns from a set of data. In AI, these mathematical algorithms (AI models) are "trained" using data and/or human expert input to replicate a decision an expert would make when provided that same information. AI-powered legal technology solutions may be comprised of a single model or multiple models grouped together.

Some types of models used in AI include Computer Vision[34] models that are taught to see like a human, Natural Language Processing (NLP) Models[35] that learn to interpret speech the way a human would, and a variety of machine learning models.

## eDiscovery AI Case law

The *da Silva Moore* case is a well-known case in the eDiscovery community and is often cited as a landmark case regarding the use of predictive coding in eDiscovery.

In the case of *da Silva Moore v. Publicis Groupe*, the plaintiff requested that the defendant use predictive coding to identify relevant documents. The defendant objected to this request and argued that keyword searching was a more appropriate method of document review.

The court ultimately allowed the use of predictive coding and noted that it was a more efficient and accurate method of document review. The court also emphasized the importance of transparency and cooperation between the parties in the use of predictive coding.

While there have been some challenges and criticisms of the use of predictive coding, the *da Silva Moore* case and subsequent cases have generally upheld the use of predictive coding as a valid and effective method of document review in eDiscovery.

Other cases involving eDiscovery AI include:

- *Rio Tinto PLC v. Vale S.A.* (S.D.N.Y. 2015).[36] The plaintiff used predictive coding to identify potentially responsive documents. The court upheld the use of predictive coding and noted that it is an appropriate and cost-effective method of document review.
- *Hyles v. New York City* (S.D.N.Y. 2016).[37] The defendant argued that the plaintiff's use of predictive coding was unreliable and sought to force the plaintiff to use keyword searching instead. The court rejected this argument and upheld the use of predictive coding, stating that it was an acceptable and even superior method of document review.
- *United States v. Vasquez-Santana* (D.N.M. 2019).[38] The government

used a machine learning algorithm to analyze text messages and identify potentially incriminating messages. The court allowed the use of the algorithm and found that it was reliable and relevant.

- *In re Broiler Chicken Antitrust Litigation* (N.D. Ill. 2018).[39] The parties used clustering and predictive coding to identify relevant documents. The court noted that these methods were appropriate and efficient and resulted in significant cost savings.
- *Biomet Orthopedics LLC v. Bonutti Research, Inc.* (S.D. Ind. 2018).[40] In this patent infringement case, the defendant used TAR (technology-assisted review) to identify responsive documents. The court upheld the use of TAR and noted that it was a reasonable and effective method of document review.

These cases illustrate that the use of AI in eDiscovery is becoming more common and accepted by the courts. Of course, AI is still subject to potential challenges and scrutiny, but it's clear that the benefits of using AI in eDiscovery cannot be ignored.

## Conclusion

With the exponential growth of electronic data, eDiscovery is no longer an optional add-on to legal practice, but a necessity for managing and exchanging digital information in legal disputes.

The benefits of legal technology in eDiscovery are numerous, including increased efficiency, cost savings, and improved accuracy in identifying relevant evidence. As we've seen, the use of artificial intelligence and machine learning has opened exciting new possibilities for eDiscovery, such as predictive coding and advanced data analytics.

eDiscovery is not without its challenges, particularly when it comes to balancing the need for access to information with concerns around data privacy and security. Legal professionals must be mindful of the ethical and professional obligations that come with eDiscovery, such as the duty to preserve evidence and maintain client confidentiality.

As technology continues to evolve, so too will the practice of eDiscovery, creating new opportunities for legal professionals to streamline their work and improve access to justice for their clients.

*References*

1 Market.us, Mobile App Download and Usage Statistics, https://market.us/statistics/internet/mobile-app-download-and-usage/.

2 Derek Miller, *Streaming and Digital Media: Understanding the Business and Technology* (Routledge, 2021).

3 Federal Rules of Civil Procedure, 82 F.R.D. 65 (1979) (amended to 3 January 2022), www.govinfo.gov/content/pkg/USCODE-2021-title28/html/USCODE-2021-title28-partIV.htm.

4 Fed. R. Civ. P. 16, as amended 1 December 2006, in Federal Rules of Civil Procedure: With Selected Statutes and Cases (Stephen C. Yeazell ed., Wolters Kluwer 2021).

5 Fed. R. Civ. P. 26.

6 Fed. R. Civ. P. 33.

7 Fed. R. Civ. P. 34.

8 Fed. R. Civ. P. 37.

9 Fed. R. Civ. P. 45.

10 Fed. R. Civ. P. 1.

11 Fed. R. Civ. P. 4.

12 Fed. R. Civ. P. 16.

13 Fed. R. Civ. P. 26.

14 Fed. R. Civ. P. 30.

15 Fed. R. Civ. P. 31.

16 Fed. R. Civ. P. 33.

17 Fed. R. Civ. P. 34.

18 Fed. R. Civ. P. 37.

19 Fed. R. Civ. P. 55.

20 Fed. R. Civ. P. 23 (2018) (amending 28 U.S.C. app. foll. Rule 23).

21 Copyright 2023, EDRM. www.edrm.net/frameworks-and-standards/edrm-model/.

22 "Elon Musk's Neuralink brain chip demo explained," YouTube, www.youtube.com/watch?v=KsX-7hS94Yo.

23 Cat Casey, "What Does the Zoom Boom Mean for E-Discovery," Corporate Counsel (31 August 2020), www.law.com/corpcounsel/2020/08/31/what-does-the-zoom-boom-mean-for-e-discovery/.

24 *Zubulake v. UBS Warburg LLC*, 229 F.R.D. 422 (S.D.N.Y. 2004).

25 *Pension Comm. of the Univ. of Montreal Pension Plan v. Banc of Am. Sec.*, LLC, 685 F. Supp. 2d 456 (S.D.N.Y. 2010).

26 *Bell Atl. Corp. v. Twombly*, 550 U.S. 544 (2007).

27 *In re Gen. Motors LLC Ignition Switch Litig.*, 137 F. Supp. 3d 853 (S.D.N.Y. 2015), aff'd sub nom. *Conroy v. Gen. Motors LLC*, 824 F.3d 616 (2d Cir. 2016), cert. denied sub nom. Gen. Motors LLC v. Pfeiffer, 137 S. Ct. 38 (2016).

28 *Zubulake v. UBS Warburg LLC*, 229 F.R.D. 422 (S.D.N.Y. 2004).

29 *Oppenheimer Fund, Inc. v. Sanders*, 437 U.S. 340 (1978).

30 *In re Columbia/HCA Healthcare Corp. Billing Practices Litig.*, 293 F.3d 289 (6th Cir. 2002).

31 *In re Genentech Herceptin Antitrust Litig.*, 855 F.3d 481 (3d Cir. 2017).
32 *Aguilar v. Immigration & Customs Enforcement Div. of U.S. Dep't of Homeland Sec.*, 228 F. Supp. 3d 439 (S.D.N.Y. 2017).
33 *In re State Farm Lloyds*, 490 S.W.3d 455 (Tex. 2016).
34 www.law.com/legaltechnews/2021/08/09/ai-powered-e-discovery-is-turning-computer-vision-into-an-art-form/?slreturn=20230224131824.
35 https://resource.revealdata.com/en/blog/ai-in-legal-sector-obvious-choice.
36 *Rio Tinto PLC v. Vale S.A.*, 143 F. Supp. 3d 352 (S.D.N.Y. 2015).
37 *Hyles v. New York City*, 2016 WL 4077114 (S.D.N.Y. Aug. 1, 2016).
38 *United States v. Vasquez-Santana*, 393 F. Supp. 3d 1289 (D.N.M. 2019).
39 *In re Broiler Chicken Antitrust Litig.*, 290 F. Supp. 3d 772 (N.D. Ill. 2018).
40 *Biomet Orthopedics LLC v. Bonutti Research, Inc.*, 305 F. Supp. 3d 1071 (S.D. Ind. 2018).

Chapter 4:
# Legal data, legal research, and legal analytics – the business of law meets tech

*By Josh Blandi, CEO and co-founder, UniCourt*

We begin this chapter with the overarching question: Why should you care about legal data, legal research, and legal analytics?

The tl;dr answer to this expansive question is that it is in your business' best interest to care, though not always for the reasons you think. The real reason you should care goes beyond the idea that only lawyers should care about legal data, legal research, and legal analytics. It gets to the business of law – the dollars and cents, the hard numbers behind why you should care about something so amorphous as legal data, so esoteric as legal research, and so cutting edge as legal analytics.

The answer to the question "why" always gets down to business. Businesses live and die by the sword of legal data, research, and analytics. They gain the ability to avoid major risks and proactively pivot their business' direction on the basis of new legal data, research, and analytics tools. Businesses can also find themselves in the midst of a publicly embarrassing bankruptcy because they did not have the modern tools needed to avoid collision with an iceberg visible to all outside observers, but hidden by the fog of messy, unstructured, bad internal data.

The tools needed to protect your business are abundantly available, more affordable and cost effective than ever, and even more powerful than before. But it is not just about adding a new singular tool to the mix. In order to fully protect your business interests and truly seize the opportunities sitting on the table, you need tools for legal data, legal research, and legal analytics that work in conjunction with one another.

The legal technology ecosystem is vibrant and growing, and the law firms and legal departments who lean into what the ecosystem and the surrounding legal tech community have to offer will be better positioned to turn their respective headwinds into tailwinds.

In this chapter, we will lay out a common set of definitions for legal data, legal research, and legal analytics. Then, we will list out some of the most prominent and prudent use cases for legal data, legal research, and legal analytics in the law firm and legal department world. Finally, we will end on the importance of businesses leveraging the whole legal ecosystem to gain the insights and intelligence needed to remain competitive.

## Defining terms of art – legal data, legal research, and legal analytics

Before we dive into the core use cases for legal data, legal research, and legal analytics, let's first establish some baseline definitions of what they are and their underlying components.

### What is legal data?

Legal data is a broad and amorphous concept that reaches across all practice areas of law and all facets of running a law firm, legal department, legal support company, or legal tech company. Put succinctly, legal data generally refers to any data connected to the provision of legal services.

For a more detailed sense of what is included, let's list some common types of legal data:

- *Court data.* This refers to data connected to a court case, regardless of the jurisdiction, area of law, or parties involved. This includes data such as court dockets, court filings, and case metadata on the parties, attorneys, law firms, and judges involved in litigation.
- *Legislative data.* This refers to data connected to the constitutions, statutes, rules, and regulations promulgated by a legislative body.
- *Regulatory data.* This refers to data involving administrative codes, agency actions, and policy-making decisions made by administrative agencies, who are often considered quasi legislative bodies.
- *Public records data.* This refers to other data that by its nature is published by a governmental body or relates to the internal communications and documents of a public body that are subject to public disclosure or review. Common examples of public records data are business records from Secretaries of State offices, and associations governing the licensure of lawyers, doctors, financial advisors, and other professional service providers. A key point to note here is that public records data varies widely from one jurisdiction to the next – even within the United States, each state has its own procedures and laws relating to accessing different types of public records data.
- *Transactional data.* This refers to data connected to deals, contracts, and all of the communications related to drafting, negotiating, and

signing agreements. This is a very expansive category of data and represents one of the largest corpuses of non-public (or often non-public) data developed in the legal industry.

- *Legal business data.* This refers to one of the broader categories of data – the data generated by law firms and legal departments during the normal course of their business, including financial data and operational data.

When talking about legal data, an important distinction that is often made in categorizing types of data is internal versus external data. For example, internal data for a law firm would be its transactional data, billing and invoicing data, and knowledge management data. Conversely, external data would be public court data, legislative data, and other public records data.

## What is legal research?

Much like legal data, legal research covers a wide array of different types of research. That said, for the purposes of this chapter, we will review these three main types of legal research – case research, legislative research, and contracts research.

Before breaking down these three types of legal research, it is important to determine what exactly legal research is at its essence. Legal research is the act of searching for "authorities" that will provide an answer or solution to a legal problem.

It is also important to note that there are two main types of authorities:

- Primary authorities, such as statutes generated by legislatures, regulations issued by administrative agencies, and court orders and decisions handed down by courts.
- Secondary authorities, such as treatises, law reviews, and legal periodicals.

Now that we have a general sense of what legal research is, let's get into the three types of research we alluded to earlier:

- *Legislative research.* This refers to any type of research connected to constitutions, statutes, regulations, policy-making decisions, administrative agency actions, and all of the documents and deliberations surrounding these topics. One of the core functions of legislative research from a business standpoint is ensuring compliance with the law, proper positioning before legislative changes take effect, and capitalizing on business opportunities tied to grants, loans, subsidies, and other public governmental programs.

- *Case research.* This refers to the broad category of research connected to court cases and the orders and decisions rendered by judges and other non-judicial entities such as arbitration tribunals. Case research is about applying the facts of a given scenario to both the law, gathered from legislative research, and case precedents, to find the best arguments for or against a particular position or action. A key distinction here is that most traditional case research focuses largely on appellate court decisions, which in most common law jurisdictions are considered binding law, as opposed to rulings from trial courts, which are often not considered binding precedent.
- *Contracts research.* This refers to the wide range of research connected to reviewing contracts against case law, legislation, regulations, your own internal corpus of contracts, and contracts from counterparties and outside repositories. This allows you to ensure that your contracts are valid and enforceable, and also that applicable protective provisions are included to safeguard your interests. Internal contracts research is often geared toward finding potential issues, vulnerabilities, and liabilities within your existing contracts to better gauge transactional risks. It also helps you find potential opportunities for recovery and affirmative litigation claims that your business can make against non-performing counterparties. However, external contracts research largely focuses on searching the outside universe of contract libraries and public sources to build the best agreements possible and leverage what has already been researched, debated internally, and developed by competitors and mainstream corporations.

When defining legal research in the context of law meeting tech, it is also important to note the maturity of the legal tech space as it relates to the research sector. Legal research tools brought forward some of the original technology innovations in the legal industry.

There has been consistent growth of more modern case research tools and contracts research tools within the legal technology ecosystem. In recent years, these tools have been enhanced by the widespread adoption of natural language processing (NLP) and machine learning (ML) to cut down on overall research time and illuminate hidden insights. More recently, Generative AI has introduced new and exciting uses of AI for in the legal research space and across the legal industry.

## What is legal analytics?

The term legal analytics has been defined in a multitude of different ways across the legal industry. In this chapter, legal analytics is defined as deriving insights from data for the business and practice of law.

Legal analytics can also be broken down into three overarching types: descriptive, predictive, and prescriptive.

- *Descriptive analytics* tell the story of what happened in the past by sifting through historical legal data to identify trends and patterns.
- *Predictive analytics* seek to forecast what will happen given a specific set of facts and circumstances for a scenario.
- *Prescriptive analytics* take predictive analytics a step further to suggest specific, best paths to follow based on historical data and likely outcomes.

In the legal industry, both descriptive and predictive analytics are widely used. In contrast, prescriptive analytics are still emerging and have not gained as much traction with legal professionals.

Now that we have discussed the three main types of the broader categories of legal analytics, there are also three major categories of analytics worth noting – litigation analytics, contracts analytics, and business analytics.

- *Litigation analytics*. This refers to analytics connected to all aspects of a court system, including analytics on the entities involved in litigation – attorneys, law firms, parties, and judges, analytics on specific types of cases, and analytics on particular courts and jurisdictions. Litigation analytics can also be used to reveal historical snapshots of what has happened in litigation, predict outcomes of certain scenarios, and provide insights on larger trends within the courtroom. Litigation analytics have an incredibly expansive set of use cases, ranging from litigation strategy to business development, competitive intelligence, due diligence, investigations, underwriting, news reporting, recruiting, and much more.
- *Contracts analytics*. This refers to transforming contracts data and documents into meaningful business intelligence. This most commonly involves using artificial intelligence (AI) to comb through contracts to identify, structure, and develop metadata on clauses and items of interest, such as expiry and renewal dates, payment terms,

arbitration and governing law clauses, irregular language, and missing provisions. Contracts analytics are widely used in the legal industry to slash the time needed for attorneys to manually review contracts and to uncover hidden risks in historical contracts that could expose businesses to outsized liabilities and reputational harm. They can also be used to develop negotiation playbooks for certain contracts, and certain counterparties, in connection with key sticking points, opportunities for compromise, and proactive posturing.

- *Business analytics.* This refers to a far reaching type of legal analytics developed by combining legal data with financial and operational data generated by law firms and legal departments, such as legal spend data, matter management data, billings data, and marketing data. A hallmark of business analytics is the combination of internal operational and financial data with external data sets, including court data, corporate data, and industry-specific data. Through blending internal and external data sources together, law firms and legal departments can develop business analytics custom-tailored to their specific use cases or problems at hand and gain valuable insights leading to a competitive edge in the marketplace.

When referring to legal analytics, most people are alluding to litigation analytics. Due to the increased availability of court data, it is no surprise that litigation analytics attract most of the attention in the legal tech ecosystem when it comes to legal analytics. Yet with the explosion of growth in the contract lifecycle management (CLM) space in recent years, contracts analytics are becoming much more commonplace and vying for greater recognition within legal analytics.

It is also well worth noting that legal data is a foundational element of legal analytics. Without good legal data that has been structured, classified, and normalized, it is next to impossible to build trustworthy legal analytics. As the adage goes, "Bad data in, bad data out", so it goes with legal analytics – bad data in, bad data analytics out. In order to develop the data needed to build meaningful, useful analytics, law firms and legal departments must actively invest in sourcing the right human capital, implementing the right data infrastructure and technology tools, such as data lakes and legal data APIs, and developing the right culture and change management processes.

Legal data, legal research, and legal analytics are inherently interrelated, but also function as distinct tools in the same toolbox. Understanding the correct terminology and underlying technology for these three pillars of the legal industry will help you better determine which tool to pull out of the toolbox and how to best use it for your business needs.

Using the definitions we have outlined, let's now walk through some of the core business use cases for legal data, legal research, and legal analytics, and get back to our original question: why should you care?

### Leveraging legal data in the insurance industry

The insurance industry is leading the charge in using legal data to its fullest extent to develop litigation strategies and manage litigation risk.

With the growing rise of "nuclear verdicts", defined commonly as verdicts where non-economic damages are considerably out of proportion with economic damages, and awards are typically $10 million or more, insurers are looking to legal data for insights and predictions on what to expect for all new cases coming through the courts.

Many insurance firms are taking advantage of legal data by using it to answer several pivotal questions any time a new case is filed against them or one of their insureds that they are defending in court.

Here are some of the core questions that legal data can provide answers to for insurance firms, which also apply to a much broader range of industries:

- How plaintiff- or defendant-friendly is the jurisdiction where the case was filed? Have there been any nuclear verdicts in this jurisdiction, and any for the type of case at hand?
- Who is the judge assigned to this case? Are they plaintiff- or defendant-friendly? How do they typically handle critical motions within a case, such as a motion to dismiss or motion for summary judgment? More importantly, in the realm of nuclear verdicts, has the judge ruled on any prior motions for remittitur or additur and do they typically reduce or increase jury awards when presented with these motions after trial?
- Who is the party who filed the lawsuit? Are they a vexatious litigant, seeking to cause reputational harm or embarrassment by filing multiple frivolous lawsuits? Do they typically settle or seek to take a case all the way to trial?
- Who are the attorneys representing the plaintiff? Do they have experience in this area of law and specific type of case? Have they ever appeared in front of the judge assigned to the case, and if so, how

did they fare? Did they fail to surpass motions to dismiss or summary judgment motions or have they successfully gone the distance to reach a verdict in similar cases?

- What law firm do the plaintiff's attorneys work at? What type of experience overall does this firm have in this specific jurisdiction and practice area? Is this a well-resourced law firm with hundreds or thousands of attorneys and support staff, or a small law firm seeking to punch above its weight?
- Further, does the insurance firm have any outside counsel with experience in front of the assigned judge, who can provide added insights? Have any outside counsel ever squared up against the plaintiff lawyer or law firm on a similar type of case, and if so, how did they fare? Even if none of the insurance firms' outside counsel have experience with the judge or plaintiff counsel, are there other off panel firms that have performed well in front of the judge and opposing this particular plaintiff lawyer and law firm?

With legal data at their fingertips, insurance firms are asking and answering these questions to get closer and closer to a more informed decision on the one critical question that they must address at the start of every case – should we settle or move promptly forward toward trial?

Legal data also empowers insurance firms to automate and streamline process workflows that support data-driven decision-making. In many respects, legal data acts as a springboard for key questions and lines of inquiry that may illuminate the best path forward for in-house counsel at insurance firms.

For instance, take our final series of questions on whether an insurance firm has outside counsel who have experience facing the assigned judge and opposing counsel. If the legal data shows that a particular panel firm does have that requisite experience, it then presents the opportunity for in-house counsel to call and gather more insights and data points for the all-important question: should we settle or proceed?

For insurance firms, the question of why to care about using legal data is starkly clear. Leveraging legal data means reducing litigation risk that has real-world dollars tied to it. It is also about lowering their overall litigation risk at scale for thousands of cases, resulting in millions and even billions of dollars in savings when nuclear judgments are accounted for.

While there are myriad business use cases connected to legal data, this example strikes at the core of why you should care about using legal data as a law firm or a legal department serving or operating in any industry – providing the best legal services possible and protecting your bottom line.

## Legal research impacting online businesses

When most people think of legal research, they likely think of someone poring over stacks of books in a law library, exercising esoteric knowledge to interpret what the law means. Most people are not constantly thinking about legal research and how the law intersects in countless ways with their daily lives and businesses.

A good example of how legal research is critical for all businesses to invest in, whether through developing internal research capacities or working with outside counsel to stay up-to-date, are the evolving laws surrounding clickwraps and browsewraps across different jurisdictions. Legal research connected to clickwraps and browsewraps covers each of the three types of research we defined earlier this chapter.

### Legislative research

As we noted earlier, legislative research relates to any type of research connected to statutes, regulations, agency actions, and other types of written laws. In the context of proper clickwraps and browsewraps, businesses need to research the statutes and laws in the states and countries they operate in, as well as regulations developed by governing bodies, such as consumer protection agencies like the Federal Trade Commission in the United States.

These laws and regulations govern the ways that businesses must provide certain notices online. They also require certain affirmative acts from customers and website visitors to agree to things like terms of service and privacy policies when signing up for an account or just using a business' website. To ensure proper compliance with these laws and regulations, law firms and legal departments must constantly be looking for new updates in this space and positioning themselves before any changes take effect.

### Case research

In addition to legislative research, in order to stay ahead of the curve when it comes to clickwraps and browsewraps, law firms and legal departments also need to conduct case research to understand where the law is heading and what pitfalls to avoid.

Through leveraging case research tools, law firms and legal departments can see how courts have interpreted laws and whether the clickwraps and browsewraps they have in place are enforceable or not in certain jurisdictions. They can also see what novel arguments plaintiff lawyers are making to invalidate online agreements, terms of service, and privacy policies, then adjust the language they are using online to limit their potential exposure to these types of arguments.

While there are no magic bullets for avoiding lawsuits, conducting thorough case research by comparing the outcomes of cases with similarly situated companies using similar online language can give law firms and legal departments a good sense of what immediate remedial steps to take to improve their own online posture.

### Contracts research

Clickwraps and browsewraps are themselves online contracts that businesses seek to enter into with online customers and website visitors to establish basic responsibilities and rights between parties. So when conducting any contracts research, the first place to go is a business' current clickwraps and browsewraps and any historical versioning.

By looking at the business' current and historical contracts, law firms and legal departments can better understand the contours of the types of agreements they are seeking to put into place. Maybe what the business really needs is not a browsewrap or a clickwrap, but a scrollwrap or a sign-in-wrap. Without looking intentionally at what is in place, how it was developed, and why it is needed, law firms and legal departments may incorrectly focus on putting out the wrong type of agreement, which may in turn also throw off their legislative research and case research.

Together with researching their own internal clickwraps and browsewraps, law firms and legal departments should conduct outside contracts research on the language and agreement workflows in use by leading companies in their industry to enhance the enforceability of their own agreements. Further, they should also look at what is in use by companies selling similar products and services to make sure they are comparing apples to apples. What a Software-as-a-Service (SaaS) company needs in a clickwrap may differ widely from what a food services, pharmaceutical, or real-estate company needs.

But why should you care about the enforceability of a browsewrap or a clickwrap?

Look no further than recent court cases invalidating binding arbitration clauses that businesses sought to enforce via browsewraps and clickwraps, which could open those companies to increased risks of class action lawsuits.

Though the inclusion of a checkbox or the magic words "I agree" may seem trivial to the untrained eye, small edits to the language and process of seeking an online assent to a business' terms of service or privacy policy can mean the difference between a binding, enforceable contract and a nuclear judgment spawned by creative arguments put forth by plaintiff law firms.

As with the use case we explored for leveraging legal data in the insurance industry, it is not always about protecting against just one bad case outcome. For any business with a large online presence, it is about avoiding the scenario where a key protective clause in your browsewrap or clickwrap is unenforceable for all your customers and preventing the exposure that presents.

## Using legal analytics for market share analysis and risk management

Ushering the "why" (why law firms and legal departments should care about legal analytics) forward cuts directly down to one throughline – improving the bottom line of their legal business.

There are countless use cases for legal analytics in the business world. In the context of the legal business of law firms, legal analytics provide an empowering business development tool for winning more business from clients, reducing client churn, and pivoting to new practice areas, new clients, and new cross-selling opportunities when they present themselves.

An important running question for law firms is: What is their market share with important clients? Moreover, how do they know whether their relationship is expanding or contracting, whether it has been profitable, and ultimately, whether they should expend more business development resources to nurture the relationship or walk away as fast as they can?

Here are some of the other pivotal market share-related questions law firms can develop insights and intelligence on when conducting white space analyses for key clients:

- What percentage of overall litigation work is a client sending to the firm?
- What percentage of litigation work is the firm receiving from specific practice areas?
- What are the trends over time? Is the firm receiving more or less work, and is it losing work in more profitable practice areas?
- What are the broader trends in the practice areas the client has litigation work?
- Are the overall trends forecasting a decreasing or increasing volume of cases?
- Are there cross-selling opportunities available that align with the firm's practice areas and business strategy goals?

In addition to answering these questions, law firms can also develop insightful business analytics by merging financial data and operational data with litigation analytics to see a more holistic picture of their relationship with a client. Instead of just seeing whether an opportunity exists and forecasting the likelihood of the opportunity existing in the future, which are both important descriptive and predictive analytics for business development professionals, firms can also determine whether or not they should continue to pursue a relationship.

Through merging billables data, matter management data, realization rates, and other firm-generated data sets, along with litigation analytics, law firms can develop prescriptive market share analytics identifying which clients have work that the firm should pursue. They can also develop analytics prioritizing what clients, and what specific case types with a certain client, law firms should spend additional business development dollars on for a better return on investment.

From the legal department perspective, legal analytics are fast becoming a mainstay in managing legal risk at scale. Although litigation analytics often garner a lion's share of attention in the legal analytics space, one of the best examples of how in-house teams are leveraging analytics is the use of contracts analytics to uncover hidden risks in old, legacy contracts.

Many of the modern contract lifecycle management tools with analytics capabilities provide legal departments with the ability to easily upload their entire corpus of corporate contracts onto a legal technology platform and run AI and ML on those contracts to then identify potential exposure and suggest remedial actions to take. These modern AI contract analytics tools are incredibly powerful and perform gargantuan reviews of years' worth of contracts in a fraction of the time and for a fraction of the cost it would take for outside counsel to conduct the same review.

More than anything, contracts analytics tools allow legal departments to practice preventative law and avoid risks that never need to come pass, further reducing strains on budgets and personnel by eliminating future legal issues. However, the use of contract analytics is not only for uncovering risk, but also for discovering affirmative recovery opportunities, otherwise described as meritorious plaintiff-side litigation brought by the corporation.

With the increasing availability and maturity of litigation finance options, legal departments are more actively looking for these types of affirmative recovery opportunities within their agreements and relationships to reduce their overall legal spend. Providing their business teams with options for affirmative recovery opportunities also transitions legal departments from being seen purely as a cost center to a revenue generator.

Going a step further, legal departments leveraging contract analytics to find affirmative recovery opportunities can take advantage of litigation analytics to understand the viability of their claims. Most claims may go unpursued to maintain business relationships with suppliers and to avoid possible counterclaims. However, if legal departments and their business teams do decide to go to the mat, they can use litigation analytics to develop the best litigation strategies possible. They will also be able to use litigation analytics to determine the best outside counsel to face off against the law firms that specific company will likely hire to represent them for the type of claims being brought.

While legal analytics still represent the cutting edge of legal technology for some in the legal industry, for many businesses – especially those in finance, insurance, and information technology – legal analytics are integral to their core processes and critical to safeguarding their company's future growth.

There may appear to be an unending number of use cases for leveraging legal analytics, stretching from underwriters building predictive analytics to identify future coverage risks in certain jurisdictions, to litigation finance firms building predictive models to find cases to invest in, and even to SaaS companies using analytics to surface inadequate contract provisions that could impact their long-term profitability. However, they all come back to the same primary purpose – better managing the legal business to improve profitability, risk management, and decision-making.

## The legal ecosystem is your oyster

Law firms and legal departments should constantly be looking to the broader legal ecosystem for new ways to apply advances in technology and implement new, prevailing process workflows.

Returning to the question of why you should care, it is not because the authors of this book say so, but because your clients and the greater business community does. They expect you to be using the legal ecosystem to your own benefit and theirs. They expect you to have a modern tech stack and the processes and people in place to run it effectively. They expect you to be looking to the future of law to remain relevant, competitive, and capable of providing strategic, data-driven legal services.

Those who invest in building their data infrastructure, and take the plunge to implement their own data lake architecture and integrate their internal data resources with external data sources via APIs will be better positioned to capitalize on the next generation of intelligence, strategy, and business development.

In the context of turning to the legal ecosystem for legal data, legal research, and legal analytics, law firms and legal departments should note that there is no one provider or solution that will solve all of your problems or that has complete coverage of all the data, research, or analytics you will ever need. Rather, the promise the legal ecosystem holds for law firms and legal departments is that they have options, and a vibrant, knowledgeable, and welcoming surrounding community to help them make informed choices.

The legal ecosystem is your oyster. Firms and in-house teams are no longer dependent on a small stable of legacy providers. The ecosystem is teeming with legal tech options, but this also presents its own unique challenges. The sheer number of solutions in the legal technology market can make it seem intimidating for law firms and legal departments needing to vet and differentiate between solutions.

Do not underestimate the complexity of legal tech buying decisions or the difficulty of implementing them, and do not go it alone. Start by identifying a valuable problem to solve. Make sure to loop in key stakeholders from critical teams, such as IT, finance, engineering, and your core business teams to get the buy in you need early on. If you are unsure of what direction to take, seek guidance from the legal tech community and find leaders from other firms and in-house teams who have been in your shoes.

Even if you are not able to acquire and implement your ideal tech stack and data infrastructure in the near future to solve your needs for legal data, legal research, and legal analytics, at least become aware of what options are on the table. Use checklists to find the right vendors. Build out your roadmap. Develop your strategy. Break down silos. Pursue integrations where possible. Keep your eyes on the road and remember your why.

# Chapter 5: A skeptic's guide to contract lifecycle management

*By Tony Thai, CEO and chief engineer, HyperDraft*

I apologize ahead of time. This chapter is intended to be both entertaining and informative, but let's be real, the bar for entertainment in any contract lifecycle management discussion is low or non-existent. I'll introduce some concepts in organizational systems theory to help frame a greater discussion on contract lifecycle management. My goal is not to extoll the benefits of contract lifecycle management systems and how they will "change your life". There are salespeople at many legal tech companies that can do that for you. Rather, I'll dive into what it is, how to assess need, and how to navigate design and implementation, and attempt to bring a new perspective to a typically lackluster topic.

## Why all the fuss about contract lifecycle management?

Contract lifecycle management (CLM) has been around for a while, but the noise surrounding it over the last few years has surged to unprecedented levels. If you are a legal professional, you've likely encountered some email, social media post, or ad about how a CLM solution will change your life. For those legal professionals working in-house, we'd like to apologize for our peers for the spam you've been forced to endure.[1]

Although there is a lot of noise about CLM, it is an area that most legal professionals are confused by due to unclear marketing or unsuccessful implementation. How do I know? Because as the CEO and chief engineer of a legal tech company that recently launched a CLM product after countless customer requests, I field weird questions and complaints from legal professionals every day.

Here are a few anonymous variations of common questions and complaints that arrive in my inbox:

> *"So, I thought I knew what CLM was, but I realized in describing it to others in my organization that I don't really know. What does a CLM solution do?"*
> *"It's so expensive, all the websites look the same, and at the end of the day I can't figure out what I'd be buying."*

*"I didn't realize that I needed to be more involved with design and implementation until we were onboarded. Now I fear I've used all my organizational goodwill and budget and am stuck with this solution when I want another one. What do I do?"*

Typically, this confusion is quelled or converted to anxiety by my mention of the root of these inquiries – there is no one-size-fits-all or off-the-shelf CLM solution. Yes, vendors can present feature lists and use cases, but each solution needs to be designed and implemented by both the vendor and the client for that specific client's organization. Because CLM is not redesigning an organization's existing contract workflows, there are a lot of other factors beyond features and use cases that contribute to what a CLM solution will look like. This makes the needs-based analysis, design, and implementation phases the hardest and most vital parts of every CLM selection process.

The reality is, you probably don't need a CLM solution. In fact, you probably don't even need a formal document management system (DMS),[2] since for most purposes a shared cloud drive would probably do just fine. Most businesses operate on the premise of organic needs-based growth and only implement solutions and systems as wants become needs. If that's the case, why aren't we still using filing cabinets and paper records management? You want me to say it's because of efficiency, but there's more to that story, because pure efficiency has seldom been a good reason to do anything. It's largely a weighing of the net cost and ease of implementation.

That's a long-winded way of saying businesses will only realize what they need as those needs arise. So then, what warrants a need versus just a want? Wants for a CLM solution become needs when you have started to build a formalized process for some legal or operational process within an organization. If you're looking for a platform to provide you with a structure and process handling certain items, then it's probably too early for you to implement a tech solution. That's a hard truth that many folks can't accept, which is one of the many drivers for the plethora of CLM solutions that have emerged in recent years.

Understanding the need for CLM can be studied any number of ways, and often we see sales anecdotes about how CLM has changed the entirety of an organization's makeup and performance. While that might make sense from the perspective of companies building and selling you the technology, it feels like the wrong approach to determine whether a CLM system is a solution that is actually wanted and needed. It's similar to selling paint brushes by only describing how one artist uses them. There are different styles that can and should be used. As a result, a more generalized theory is warranted for analyzing organizations and the need for CLM. Lucky for us, there's already a field of study that focuses on the study of such things, aptly named organizational systems theory.

Organizational systems theory is a field of study focused on the premise that organizations are comprised of many subsystems that must not only co-exist but also operate in harmony. This theory is helpful for understanding organizational behavior and the likelihood of behavior change including the assessment, design, and implementation of a CLM solution.

The goal is that through this discussion you will understand what CLM is and, more importantly, come away with some basic tools for assessing the need, design, and implementation of a CLM platform for any organization. It's far from perfect, but it's a generalized approach that provides the bumper rails for analysis rather than force-feeding you a solution.

So, here's how we're going to breakdown our discussion:

- Basics of CLM – what is it?
- Needs analysis – how do I know if I need it?
- Design exercise – how do I design a solution users will use?
- Implementation – how do I make the most of implementation?
- The future – what's ahead for CLM?

## The basics of CLM

Back to CLM itself, what is it? A generally accepted meaning of a CLM solution is "a digital platform for managing the creation, negotiation, and execution of legal agreements".

At its core, the best way to think of CLM is the combination of:

- A document/file management system (DMS) (e.g., Google Drive, Microsoft OneDrive/SharePoint);
- A calendar system; and
- A spreadsheet.

To explain that comparison in painfully obvious terms, the DMS system is just a place to store your files and documents. The calendar system is the driver for the notifications and action items that result from the data in the DMS. Finally, the spreadsheet is used to describe the content within the files in the DMS system, often referred to as metadata. Examples of metadata may include data fields such as "Effective Date", "Expiration Date", etc.

More recently, CLM solutions have evolved to include various ancillary features, including automated workflows, electronic signatures, contract analytics, collaboration features, and other bells and whistles that add to its underlying techstack.

A CLM solution is typically used by in-house legal, operations, compliance, and finance professionals during the lifecycle of a contract to streamline the contract process. A typical process involves:

- *Stage 1: Contract request.* A business stakeholder requests for or initiates a contracting process.
- *Stage 2: Contract creation.* A contract is created, based on existing forms or templates.
- *Stage 3: Contract negotiation.* A contract is negotiated by relevant parties, including potentially multiple rounds of redlining and review.
- *Stage 4: Contract approval.* A contract that is prepared and negotiated in the previous stages is submitted to internal or external approvers.
- *Stage 5: Contract execution.* The approved contract is then sent out for execution by signing parties.
- *Stage 6: Contract storage.* The executed contract is saved and stored on the company's DMS.
- *Stage 7: Contract performance.* The contract is reviewed periodically to confirm that the obligations within are being performed or what recourse exists for lack of performance.
- *Stage 8: Search and retrieval.* Legal and business owners quickly search, apply filters, and retrieve relevant information from contracts in the normal course of business, when negotiating other contracts, or conducting audits or reports.
- *Stage 9: Renewal and amendment.* Once the contract reaches its end date, the contract and effect of the performance of obligations are reviewed to determine if the contract will be renewed. If renewed, another contract lifecycle consisting of the same stages will begin. An amendment to an existing contract due to changes in deal conditions will similarly trigger another contract lifecycle.

Is CLM new? No, not at all. CLM has slowly been evolving for the past 30 years. CLM software solutions came about because certain parts of the contracting process started to become digitized – first the adoption of computers, then more formalized DMS, then e-signatures – and as people found value in these digital processes and mediums, interest sparked in automating the entirety of the process.

Like most software categories in the legal technology vertical, it took a while for CLM to take off. Digital contracting processes started gaining ground in the late 1990s as the use of digital files became more widespread and acceptable, and again in the early 2010s, piggybacking on the takeoff of customer relationship management software (CRM).[3] This demand continued to grow in parallel with the growth of digital transformation and investment in organizations of all sizes and industry until 2020 when its growth exploded. Suddenly, the pandemic's shift to remote-first workforces drove digital processes from "nice to haves" to mission-critical. Unprecedented times put extra pressure on legal departments to help internal stakeholders make informed decisions quickly and the selling point was that CLM solutions made that easier.[4]

## Do you need CLM?

Let's get back to the elephant in the room. How do you know you need a CLM solution?

Do you need a faster car? There are instances where having a faster car means you can outrun a dangerous object on the road. Does that potential need justify the cost of purchasing a vehicle for its 0-60mph time? Unlikely. The same needs-based analysis applies to any technology you adopt for your organization.

For decades, enterprises have operated without a formal CLM system. What justifies the need for one now? If we approach these systems skeptically, we may find that they are nothing more than repackaged cloud-based file and document management systems with some added visual appeal. While there is much discussion about their crucial role in organizational development, in practical terms, we are either repurposing existing technology or reinventing the wheel at best.

If we're managing business units, then we have to be careful what we propose in terms of new processes and procedures, since educating teams is a heavy lift. There is inertia built into the current process, which results in a large cost associated with introducing anything new to an existing process.

If we are managing business units, we must practice caution in suggesting new processes and procedures as it requires significant effort to educate existing teams on new processes. Introducing anything new to an established process incurs significant costs due to existing inertia built into an organization.

Therefore, there are going to be preliminary questions that a manager of the contracting process should ask – see Figure 1.

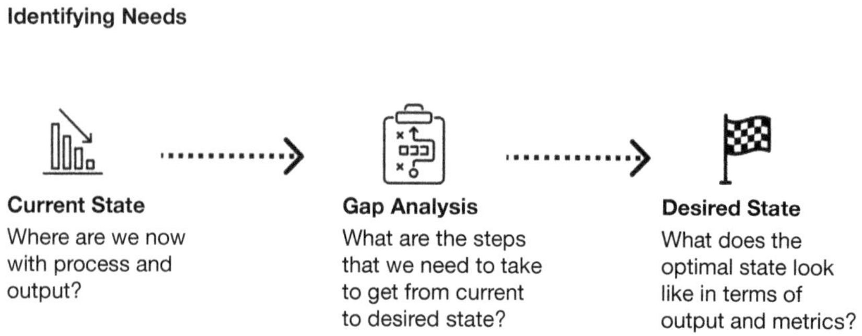


*Figure 1: CLM needs analysis.*

- *Feel.* Do we have any processes that feel clunky and inefficient? Do you have to remind people to perform tasks and are any of those tasks manual processes that could impact the data that the organization relies on?
- *Desire.* What is the organization's appetite for change? For projects of similar size and complexity, how long has it taken? Is there expected pushback from any groups? If so, what groups are likely going to create the most blockers?
- *Effect.* Does efficiency contribute to the bottom line of the organization? Are there metrics that you can or have tracked that you can correlate with a more efficient process?
- *Legacy.* Have you developed any documentation that you use to guide a particular process? Who are the stakeholders for the existing process?

If the answers to any of these questions are no, or the desired metrics unclear, then the need for a CLM solution may not be established just yet. That does not mean that implementation of a CLM solution would not benefit the organization, it only means that the needs are not readily evident yet, so you should proceed with low expectations around success for any such system.

## How to design a CLM solution

So, you've determined that you've crossed the threshold for needing some sort of formalized CLM solution. Now it's onto the next threshold – designing.

One of the biggest misconceptions we see when it comes to designing CLM systems is this – although a provider will give you the tools and technology, you still need to play an active role in designing that tool's application to your organization.

It's good for us that there are some organizational theory concepts that will help us with the design process. Organizational theory is used to both analyze and design teams/processes in a way that, among other things, 1) maximizes efficiency, 2) reduces cost, and/or 3) increases productivity.

I'll leave you to your own devices when it comes to doing a deep dive on organizational systems theory,[5] but here are a few tools we can use for the purposes of designing an approach to adopting a formal CLM (see Figure 2):

- *Systems thinking.* This involves considering the CLM solution as a whole, rather than just its individual components. This involves understanding how each part of the system affects the others and how changes in one part of the system can impact the entire system.
- *Process mapping.* This involves visualizing the steps involved in the CLM process (for example, "How does a user generate a sales quote? How does a user generate an NDA?"), including the roles and responsibilities of each team member. This allows for the identification of areas of inefficiency or redundancy that can be eliminated.
- *Standardization.* To implement a solution, we need standard procedures that we can express in the CLM solution to ensure consistency and efficiency across all teams and departments. Standardization reduces the likelihood of errors or delays and makes it easier to train new team members.
- *Automation analysis.* This is an obvious reason for adopting CLM in the first place, but what's probably not extremely clear here is performing the analysis on what could be automated versus what should be automated. There are many cases where automation could work, but the gains are so small that manual process might be fine (or even better in some cases where judgment is required).

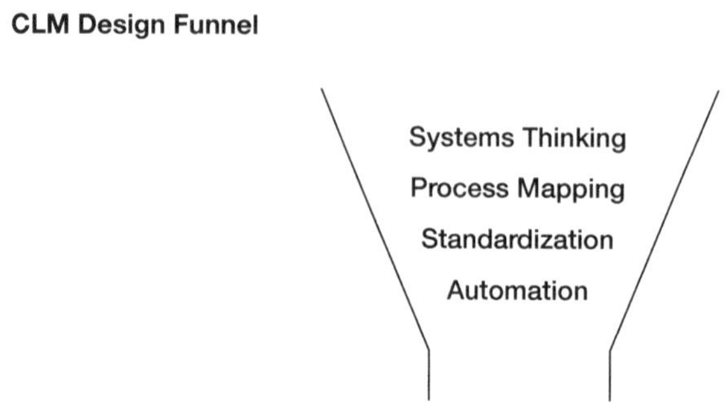


*Figure 2: CLM design funnel.*

## Systems thinking

First, we'll take a systems thinking approach and identify the various user groups. Based on my experience at multiple organizations running legal departments, this is how I would break down the typical user groups for a CLM solution:

- *Human Resources.* Core use case would be documenting incoming and exiting employees as well as everything in between. At this point, they most likely have their own Enterprise Resource Planning (ERP) system in place, so the ability to integrate would be key.
- *Finance.* They need to track the financial progress of the business. I view them as compliance but for money inflow/outflow. They need to ensure that spend is within budget, so their use case for a CLM solution would involve visibility around cash amounts.
- *Compliance.* There are so many different types of compliance teams and it would largely depend on the business type, but assuming the business is large enough, then they would definitely be in the decision/approval flow for contracting.
- *Marketing.* They are largely considered the cowboys of a business (at least to legal) because they usually want to operate unrestricted to help sell the business/service/product for the organization. Marketing will have legal review requests and contracts for vendors, events, and partnerships, etc.
- *Engineering.* Often overlooked as a decision-maker and more as a service arm. They make a lot of buying decisions and have increasingly become more critical to businesses in the decisions over third parties.

- *Sales Teams.* They sell products and services of the business, so need non-disclosure agreements and many form agreements to go out and get signed. They are often commission/bonus focused.
- *Legal.* This includes your in-house team and any outside counsel.

## Process mapping

Now that we've painted a big picture view of the organization's user groups for a CLM solution, let's use process mapping to break down the processes within those groups. The purpose of process mapping is to visually communicate how business processes work within an organization so that you can analyze, compare, and streamline processes.

The following steps can be used to create a process map:

- *Step 1:* Identify users and their processes.
- *Step 2:* List all the major and minor activities involved.
- *Step 3:* Write out the sequence of steps, who is responsible for each step, and quantify each step (i.e., the number of days, templates, processes, and other resources associated with each step).
- *Step 4:* Create a flow chart, spreadsheet, or other visual way to map the process in an organized, concise way.
- *Step 5:* Analyze the map to find areas of improvement.

When process mapping for a CLM solution, it is best to start with processes that have caused confusion or delays in the past. Also, it is important to get input from those who are the frontlines of the process, and not just those in legal. It's important to understand all points of view and how the process happens from the ground up as opposed to just at a managerial or review level.

## Standardization

Once you have mapped the processes that make your organization run, it's time to assess and develop standardized procedures.

Different teams often develop their own ways of doing things. A single process such as billing, accounting, or contracting can be executed in many different ways in the same organization. Standardization refers to the process of establishing a set system of dealing with tasks. This way, all details are available in a standard format, making it easy for all in the organization to understand.

What should you standardize? Processes that are repetitive or used in parallel or otherwise by multiple groups within one organization. Not all tasks can be standardized, especially those requiring individual discretion or those with no consistent process, but you can standardize the framework around these variables to help maximize efficiency.

The following steps can be taken to undergo a standardization process:

- *Step 1:* Review process maps and compare them across teams.
- *Step 2:* Identify processes that are parallel, routine, repeatable in multiple departments/functions, or routine processes that touch multiple departments.
- *Step 3:* Prepare document standards, preferred workflows, and contract templates in a manner that is simple, clear, but robust enough to withstand when key employees transition out of the organization.
- *Step 4:* Get buy-in from all the stakeholders (make the process collaborative!).
- *Step 5:* Slowly weave standardization into the company and create a maintenance/check-in schedule to ensure that buy-in remains (and strengthens!) within your organization.

Now you may read that list and think "How do I prepare document standards, preferred workflows, and templates? Won't that take FOREVER?" No, you are probably already standardizing and just need to take a closer look.

Most legal departments already have formal or informal playbooks and templates. A contract playbook is a document that contains an explanation of the terms and conditions of a contract as well as clear guidance on how to negotiate the provisions of the contract. Templates are contract templates that are pre-approved by legal for use for common processes or deal types within an organization. In a standardization process, both playbooks and templates are updated with information gleaned from process mapping and are also used as a point of reference as standard procedures are created. Process mapping also creates a great outline of what other types of playbooks and templates would be helpful to your organization and the questions/information that users will likely need as they are assessing the relevant documents of those deals.

Standard procedures are complementary to playbooks and templates as they are documented guides that can include process maps, additional annotations, and general descriptions of best practices including templates, playbooks, and other guidelines that should be used to execute processes in the most beneficial manner for the organization. These provide the basic structure for any CLM solution.

### Automation analysis

Lastly, we need to think *honestly* about automation. Although most processes *should* work towards standardization, not all processes should be automated. In fact, choosing to automate ill-suited tasks and processes can hinder organizational momentum towards change. An organization should do a serious analysis of whether standardized processes should be automated or whether those processes could merely benefit from advanced notifications and/or analytics.

Understanding what *should* be automated can be challenging, but not impossible. So how do you select the right processes to automate?

First, the key is understanding the skills that humans and computers specialize in. Humans are great at dealing with uncertainty, ambiguity, and qualitative analysis. They are also very adaptable and can effectively handle quickly changing variables or new scenarios. On the other hand, computers are rules-based machines. They thrive on routine and repetition and are great at time-consuming and time-critical tasks.

These differences define the factors that should be considered when selecting which process is ripe for automation.

It's also important to ascertain the level of difficulty of the desired automation by focusing on the nature of the process, the frequency/timing, the input and output, and the likelihood of internal support.

- *Nature*. Is the process well-defined and standardized? What is easily capable of being automated? Is the process so simple that automation would not make an impact? Is the process scalable?
- *Volume*. How frequently is the process being done? Is it repetitive? Is it so infrequent that it is cheaper to do manually? Are there time-consuming or time-critical attributes?
- *Input and output*. Is the required data digital or analog? Does the process include any unstructured data? What is the form of the desired output?
- *Support*. Will the cost of automation outweigh revenue gains? Will automating the process help the bottom line? Will automating the process help management or stakeholders make progress on initiatives or goals? Are there processes, technologies, or structures that bookend the process that would be supportive or frictional?

To build internal momentum and a favorable outlook on automation, it's best to start with processes with low levels of difficulty and where internal support at some level is likely.

## CLM implementation 101

Now that you've designed the system and found an appropriate platform to build out your design, how do we go about implementing it successfully? Your first reaction might be for the lawyers/in-house team to take the first swing at it. This is often the wrong approach.

It may be tempting to assign the implementation task to the legal or in-house team, but this approach is flawed at best. The implementation process should involve legal and the lowest lift/highest impact user groups identified in the design phase to ensure that the system is user-friendly and meets their specific needs.

Think about it: people rarely listen to lawyers first, so why would CLM implementation be any different? You need to form an alliance with the group who will find the most value out of the solution and then work with that internal validation to get what you need.

The common error is trying to do what in software development terms is referred to as "waterfall" development.[6] This is a term used to describe a project management approach that takes a linear progression from beginning to end of a project where one step has to be completed to go to the next. For many organizations, this is the standard approach that has been used for applications like CRM, human resource management systems, and supply chain management systems.

Taking this approach with CLM typically ends poorly because CLM's success is based upon how much value is delivered to the organization via customization and iteration on the solution's original design. That's why an approach commonly referred to as "agile" development[7] leads to more success because it advocates for multiple parallel development cycles to run at the same time to allow for more accurate customization based on user feedback. Most agile development methods break development work into small increments so that feedback can be collected and iterated at each stage of the process. Agile development processes contain the same steps as waterfall development but typically all steps are done a couple of times in small sprints to make sure that user feedback is used to highly customize the solution. See Figure 3.

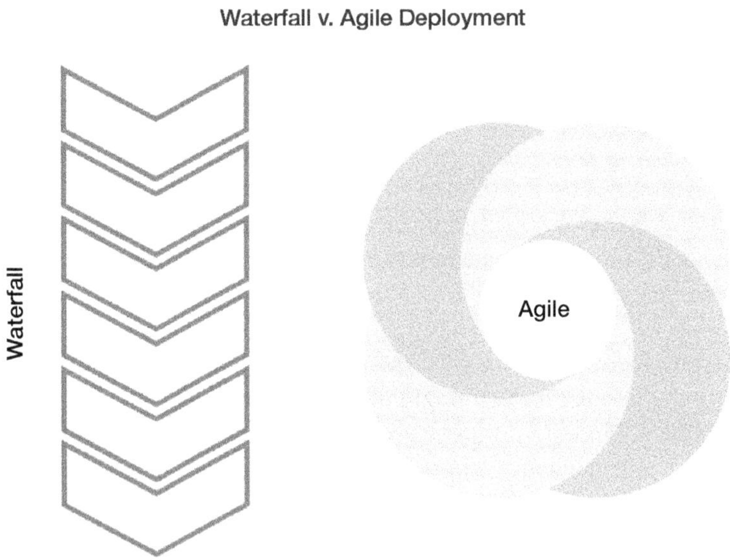


*Figure 3: Waterfall v. Agile deployment.*

An effective implementation plan should include the following steps:

- *Training.* Proper training should be provided to all the user groups to ensure that they understand how to use the CLM system. Training sessions can be conducted either in-person or online, depending on the user group's location.
- *Testing.* A pilot test should be conducted with a small group of users to identify any potential issues or inefficiencies in the system before rolling it out to the larger user groups.
- *Data migration.* Existing contract data should be migrated to the new CLM system to ensure that all data is stored in one central location. Redundant stores are fine, but don't let the users get away with not having a single source of truth and storing data in too many places. There should be a unique identifier that maintains the fingerprint of data across multiple data stores.
- *Customization.* The CLM system should be customized to meet the specific needs of each user group. Customization can include adding or removing fields, creating custom workflows, or setting up automated notifications.
- *Integration.* The CLM system should be integrated with other systems, such as ERP or accounting software, to ensure seamless data flow between systems.

- *Support*. Ongoing support and usability check-ins should be provided to all user groups to ensure that any issues or concerns are addressed in a timely manner.

By involving all the user groups in the implementation process, providing proper training and support, and customizing the system to meet their specific needs, organizations can ensure a successful implementation and adoption of the CLM system.

## Predictions for the future of CLM

Following this discussion you might ask, "Well then, why did you build a CLM product?" Because our clients asked for it, and we'd be remiss if we didn't listen to our clients. That said, we still very frequently insist that CLM solutions aren't for everybody.

CLM, like any other tech, can amplify success but it can't fix what's not working inside of an organization. That's why we focus on an organizational approach that can guide those who are looking to assess whether CLM is for them.

Is CLM the magic silver bullet tech that every legal organization needs? If they are just starting out with legal technology, probably not. It requires an entire organization to be on board. In reality, sometimes it's easier to implement solutions that only require a small user group for success (i.e., document automation, AI-powered insights, reporting, and research, etc.) and use that success to build up the technological framework of an organization.

Can CLM make meaningful change within an organization? Absolutely! We'll leave it to the many CLM vendors out there (including us) to sell you on the many CLM success stories, but by completing a needs analysis, designing a solution, and undergoing implementation, any organization will learn a lot about how to make meaningful technological and organizational change to increase the bottom line and reach company goals faster.

AI is all the rage right now.[8] Its actual viability is still up in the air. Thanks to OpenAI and the hype surrounding ChatGPT, the entire world, not just the legal industry, is having a large-scale conversation about what types of legal work can be automated. There is no doubt that the chatter about generative AI and ChatGPT is likely to fuel monumental interest in CLM from organizations that otherwise would not have sought such a solution. As a result, it's likely that solutions that do not already have AI features or integrations will quickly adapt to adopt them to stay competitive in the space. It'll be interesting to see how the role of AI shapes the CLM landscape in the next few years.

Another recent trend in CLM that is likely to continue is the expansion and adoption of CLM into new user groups within an organization. As lawyers have unsuccessfully tried to tell their stakeholders and clients for years, *contracts run business*. With CLM success stories and chatter about AI, non-lawyers are finally starting to absorb the message. As discussed here, typically the best way to launch a CLM solution is to involve high-use, low-risk user groups such as legal, compliance, or sales. Once value is communicated and shown within an organization through the early adopters, expansion to new user groups will continue. With more and more vendors providing collaboration and self-service features, more and more user groups will be using CLM with greater authority in years to come.

Integrations will continue to be a buzzy topic in CLM. CLM vendors talk a big game about integrations, but typically the results can be underwhelming. Whether it's usability, speed, or other factors, typically integrations leave users wanting more. Over the last ten or so years, some vendors have tried to create a potential solve for this by developing their own competitive solutions. This weird dynamic has continued to make integrations awkward and sometimes antagonistic between vendors and can halt adoption of solutions in certain user groups. As CLM adoption continues to rise, users will want more integrations than ever so that they can connect all their favorite tech tools to their CLM solution. Vendors will have to figure out how to work better together in a more seamless way.

Where do we think CLM will be in the next ten years? It'll be old news. CLM is buzzy right now because people are into the benefits of the tech but haven't found a way to maximize value. Once that is cracked, it will be table stakes for every organization. CLM will be the gateway to other forms of meaningful legal technology that will make the legal profession more enjoyable and allow businesses to run more efficiently. Once organizations feel the value, it's only a matter of time until they are addicted to the rest of the legal tech spectrum and require outside counsel to be too.

### *References*

1 Ready, Frank. "'Aggressive' and 'Demeaning': Some In-House Departments Aren't Happy with Recent Tech Sales Pitches" (*Legaltech News*, 20 August 2021), www.law.com/legaltechnews/2021/08/20/aggressive-and-demeaning-some-in-house-departments-arent-happy-with-recent-tech-sales-pitches/.

2 Document management systems are how many organizations store, manage, and track electronic documents. It involves the use of a shared server and specialized software to store, manage, and track documents and files (AIIM. "What Is Document Management (DMS)?", www.aiim.org/what-is-document-imaging).

3 Customer Relationship Management software manages and supports customer relationships. CRM technology helps companies build and grow customer relationships across the entire customer lifecycle. It is typically used by sales and marketing teams in an organization ("Customer Relationship Management" (Bain, 29 April 2020), www.bain.com/insights/management-tools-customer-relationship-management.).

4 Since we're not taking an economic analysis approach to the justification of CLM systems, I'll avoid the macroeconomic effects of record low interest rates and the free flow of investment capital that was being deployed with little to no prejudice.

5 von Bertalanffy, Ludwig. 1968. *"General System Theory: Foundations, Development, Applications"* New York: George Braziller, Systems Theory Applied to Organizations, https://bear.warrington.ufl.edu/centers/purc/docs/papers/0018_Corlett_Systems_Theory_Applied.pdf), and *"Introduction to Systems Theory"*. (n.d.). www.igi-global.com/pdf.aspx?tid%3D94651%26ptid%3D85858%26ctid%3D17%26t%3Dintroduction+to+systems+theory.

6 "Comparing Traditional Systems Analysis and Design with Agile Methodologies" (*The Traditional Waterfall Approach*), www.umsl.edu/~hugheyd/is6840/waterfall.html.

7 "Agile methodology and system analysis", www.umsl.edu/~hugheyd/is6840/agile.html

8 Patrice, Joe, "The Legal Industry Has a Long Way to Go before GPT Matches the Talk" (*Above the Law* 30 March 2023), https://abovethelaw.com/2023/03/the-legal-industry-has-a-long-way-to-go-before-gpt-matches-the-talk/ and Perlman, Andrew, "The Implications of CHATGPT for Legal Services and Society" (*Harvard Law School Center on the Legal Profession*, 24 March 2023), https://clp.law.harvard.edu/knowledge-hub/magazine/issues/generative-ai-in-the-legal-profession/the-implications-of-chatgpt-for-legal-services-and-society.

Chapter 6:
# How document automation is transforming the way legal services are delivered

*By Dorna Moini, CEO and founder, Gavel*

Document automation originated in the 1980s with floppy disks, and then CD-ROM software companies. It's the process of creating documents from a set of rules, and was originally called "electronic document management", a term that is now a broad category of its own.

The most common areas document automation was and still is used in include estate planning, family law, transactional matters, and court forms (e.g., family law forms or other government forms). For example, when drafting a deed or affidavit based on a known data set, bespoke work is one option. You have to take all the data you've gathered from a client and transfer it into the document based on legal rules that you've stored in your own head or as bracketed language in the template. But if you have rules that you can apply to the situation, document automation saves you time. This in turn allows you to generate and customize a document template to a specific situation, rather than having to fill in the blanks and adjust grammar every time a document is used. Answer a few questions, and a new document is generated with the language that fits the situation.

This is where *internal* document automation has historically been used. That is, document automation that a firm uses internally to more quickly, accurately, and effectively create documents. In this original way of using automation, only law firm team members use the technology. The client never touches the software.

## Benefits of document automation

So what are the practical benefits? Time saved, error-proofing, data storage, and the ability to spend your time on higher-level work. Document automation reduces the time necessary to draft the documents, and then to regenerate, organize, and manage them based on new or updated data.

In fact, a survey carried out by the document automation software platform Gavel shows that users save up to 90 percent of the time they spend drafting documents.[1] The main benefits are:

- *Time and cost savings.* With document automation, organizations can save time and money by reducing the time spent on manual document creation, editing, and management.
- *Increased efficiency.* Automated document creation and management can help reduce errors and increase accuracy, improving overall efficiency and productivity.
- *Improved compliance.* Document automation can help ensure that documents are created and managed in compliance with regulatory requirements, reducing the risk of legal issues.
- *Consistency and standardization.* Document automation can help ensure that documents are consistent and standardized, reducing the risk of errors and improving overall quality.
- *Enhanced collaboration.* Document automation can make it easier for teams to collaborate on document creation and management, reducing the need for manual processes and improving communication.
- *Improved client experience.* Document automation can help organizations provide faster and more accurate responses to client requests, improving the overall client experience.

With the invention of cloud computing and the growth of technology, document automation tools have become more accessible, affordable, and easy to use.

## Evolution of document automation

In the last few decades, document automation has evolved from a ready-built software with mandated and immutable forms to software that you can use to build and customize your own rules and logic into a system.

As a "builder" or author on a document automation platform, you can create and edit your own templates and forms, customize fields, and add logic. The ability to add complex logic and formatting is critical, because it means that each firm can customize their documents to their own rules or jurisdiction's rules, and those rules can be updated at any time.

This shift also expands the areas of law where document automation can apply. Whereas previously, document automation was available for only the most popular areas, democratizing the use of software for anyone to build their expertise means that more niche areas of law can also be automated.

## The rise of no-code systems

No-code software is a type of software that enables users or "builders" to create applications and software without writing any code. Instead, these builders can use visual interfaces, drag-and-drop tools, and pre-built modules to design and build applications. Figure 1 on the next page gives an example of how the no-code legal automation platform Gavel allows users to set up and launch workflows through a drag-and-drop interface.

The idea behind no-code software is to empower individuals and teams with little or no technical programming skills to create software solutions that are customized to their specific needs. This can include anything from simple web forms and landing pages to complex enterprise applications.

No-code software is often used by businesses to speed up the development process and reduce costs. It can also help to democratize software development, as it enables people from a range of backgrounds to create custom software solutions.

The last decade has seen an explosion in no-code software, both in document automation and in other areas like website building. Historically, automating your documents in a law firm meant that you had to hire an expensive developer to set it up for you. With the rise of no-code software, anyone can build automation into their firm by using drag and drop prompts in collaborative cloud software.

## Internal and third-party collaboration

Collaboration has also had a transformative effect on the use of document automation, both within a law firm and with external users. Within law firms, multiple legal professionals are increasingly collaborating on building the best systems and documents for the firm in a centralized and standardized fashion. With external clients, the collaboration typically takes the form of client intake.

This increased collaboration also means that multiple users within a firm have a central source of truth for their data and can integrate their documents with the rest of their technology tools. For example, 2020 alone saw a 35 percent increase in the use of cloud technology by lawyers.

The shift to external collaboration has had a dramatic impact on the way legal services are delivered. This external collaboration is both with other legal professionals and also with the client, but the latter has been the source of expanding business models.

Over the last few decades, document automation has transformed from a critical internal law firm technology to a way to build client-facing intake tools that transform both the practice of law and the scalability of each lawyer's services.

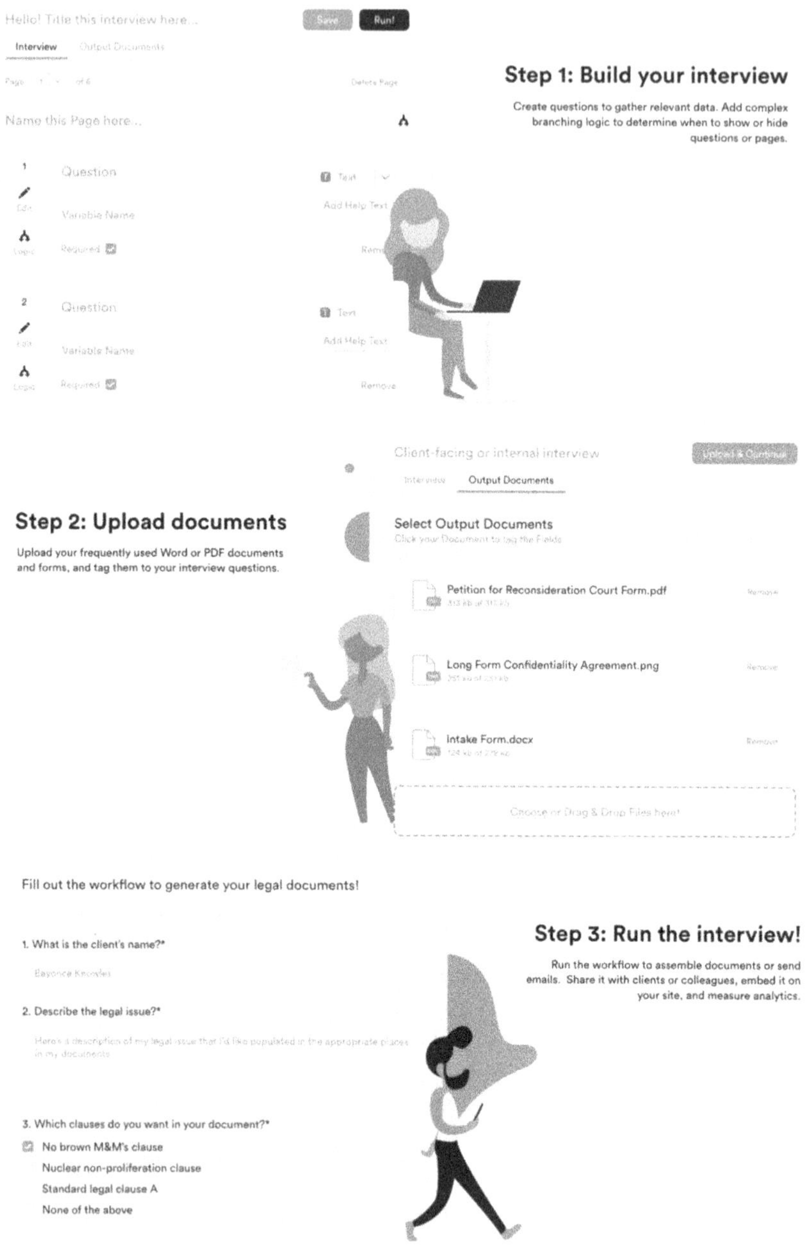


*Figure 1: Setting up and launching workflows through Gavel's drag-and-drop interface.*

As discussed later in this chapter, clients are now participating in the document creation process by entering their own data into document automation software systems as part of the intake process. Taking this approach a step further, many attorneys are building full-fledged legal technology products with these document automation tools (often called "legal apps" or "legal products") that are changing the legal business model altogether.

### Why are document automation and legal productization on the rise?

Document automation and the use of cloud software are on the rise in law firms of all sizes, and they're transforming the legal business model.

The result is legal productization. Legal productization refers to the process of creating and selling a legal product or service as a standardized, packaged offering. This can involve taking a legal service that is traditionally offered on a bespoke basis and turning it into a repeatable, scalable product that can be marketed to a wider audience.

Legal productization can take many forms, but some examples include creating standardized legal documents, offering online legal courses or workshops, or creating software or other tools that automate legal processes. The goal is to make legal services more accessible and affordable for consumers while also creating new revenue streams for the legal professional.

As an example of legal productization, the team behind Landlord Legal[2] is a law firm that realized it could provide a scalable solution for Illinois landlords who needed assistance with legal matters on their properties. As of this writing, they charge $250/year on a subscription basis to offer a set of forms that they are constantly updating with the latest law, on-demand learning, answers to frequently asked questions, a community, and attorney help upon request.

Landlord Legal is not alone. Forces on both the supply and demand side of the market are expanding the creation of legal products, and it's estimated that 90 percent of legal services will be delivered online in the next ten years.

### The supply side of legal productization

On the supply side, some lawyers have historically shied away from implementing technology because of the difficulty of use. Yet the rise of both no-code software and increased resources in online marketing have propelled many attorneys into implementing software and document automation as a critical part of their practice.

Cloud security is another force on the supply side. Now that cloud-based solutions are industry standard and can be just as secure as on-premises servers, lawyers are flocking toward a wider variety of software tools that can be easily implemented in a firm without IT support.

And finally, pricing. Lawyers have historically had a very narrow view of pricing – the billable hour. While the billable hour will never go away, new pricing models like flat fees, pay-per-use, and subscription fees are taking off. Document automation is the enabler for these new business models.

### The demand side of legal productization

On the demand side, consumers are looking for both affordability and convenience. Law firm competition and price transparency has led to savvier consumers who are pushing back on pricing for certain consumer-focused areas of law. Regardless of affordability, the billable hour has always been confusing for consumers of legal services (this includes both individual consumers and corporate consumers), so pricing that is more certain and calculable is attractive and leads to a rise in adoption and use of attorney services.

Along with pricing, consumers want a digitally convenient experience that is akin to the seamless experience they have with consumer apps and software they use daily.

The statistics support the move. Better organization and more efficiency leads to client savings, increased productivity, and overall better results. For example, the average law firm spends 20 percent of available hours on routine drafting, but about half of firms see *significant* results from efficiency efforts, like document automation, according to the Altman Weil 2020 study of Law Firms in Transition.[3]

This transformation of document automation from internal law firm technology into client-facing delivery of products and information is a critical path to delivering legal services to more consumers, many of whom have disposable income to spend on legal services but simply can't afford the hourly rates that are based on bespoke work. Legal service providers can use document automation tools to provide legal services to consumers in an efficient and accessible manner.

For example, law firms can create questionnaires (like Intuit's TurboTax[4]) to walk users through a legal matter and generate documents for them. Those documents can either be reviewed by the attorney and finalized or provided in a do-it-yourself (DIY) manner.

MyProbateDocs[5] is another great example of a law firm that has productized its work to create a booming legal technology company, in this case selling to an attorney audience. Attorney John Fritz of Fritz Law, LLC[6] launched the company to automate the creation of legal documents for estate planning and probate cases. The platform is used by other attorneys to populate their case files, sometimes in minutes, depending on the type of case.

The client-facing features of a legal product that make the end-to-end online legal experience possible are:

- Client intake;
- Document automation;
- Electronic signatures;
- Online billing;
- A full client portal; and
- Real-time collaboration with the attorney through the platform.

While there are several features that make legal products possible, document automation takes on the bulk of the heavy lifting, as it's the piece that creates the legal work product and needs to be robust enough to handle all the rules embedded in the system.

## Getting tactical – what are the components?

Let's get into the nitty gritty of how you set up document automation systems for your firm. There are two steps and four tools as part of your toolkit that can help you automate just about anything.

The two overarching steps to set up document automation are:

1. *Data collection.* This is the data you're collecting about the unique facts of the case of matter.
2. *Setting up output documents.* What documents will be generated at the end of the process?

Starting with step one, data collection about the case or matter can be answered internally or externally. That is, you or other members of your organization might enter the data directly into the system, or you can have this step operate as a client intake that you send to clients to input their own data. Alternatively, you can do both – fill out some of the data that requires legal knowledge for the client, and then have the client fill out any data that is personal.

Step two is to connect all of the data that you've collected in the data collection process to your set of documents. The most common document types to automate are .docx documents (typically Microsoft Word or Google Docs) and PDF documents.

This second step will allow you to correlate all the data you've collected with outputs on the document. This is everything from grammatical and formatting changes (e.g., subject/verb agreement based on the data entered) to complex logic and calculations. The data will be inserted and will modify your document according to the rules that you create. The data will also be stored in a database for later use.

For example, in a real estate matter, the intake or questionnaire data may indicate that the leased location is in Florida. This extracted data will be transformed so that the documents will recognize and identify the information correctly, labeling the jurisdiction as Florida. This means that the address of the property, insurance coverage requirements, jurisdiction, and other clauses in the document will automatically populate according to Florida-specific language. Finally, required language, such as Florida's radon gas disclosure, will automatically be inserted into the lease language, because the document automation has loaded as a rule that this language is mandatory in a Florida lease.

By identifying just one fact, that the lease is in Florida, document automation can automatically insert the correct language in the correct place in a lease in multiple different places. A properly prepared intake system will collect all the relevant information and generate multiple documents as part of a document set.

## The four arrows in your document automation quiver

A builder who is automating their expertise will use four main tools as part of their toolkit to automate any rules-based or process-oriented area. These tools are:

1. Simple variables.
2. Conditional logic.
3. Calculations (numerical and date).
4. Repeating items (i.e. lists).

Below, we dive deeper into each of these.

### Simple variables

Simple variables are the basic components of document automation. Think of them as old-fashioned mail-merge – you have a piece of data, and you want to plug it into specific locations in the document, potentially with special formatting.

In some cases, several variables may make up one piece of information. For example, an address is a piece of information composed of several variables. One variable is the numerical address (1234), then the related variable for the street name (Main), then the street suffix (Drive), then the city, the state, and the zip code.

Within a document, a user may want to populate only the city and state and not the entire address in some places. The address might be formatted differently (such as **in bold** or ALL CAPS) in different locations in the document or in different documents as part of the document set. The builder of the automated system will set up rules to make sure that the different variables of the address show up in the right place and in the right format.

### Conditional logic

Conditional logic refers to the ability to create documents that change based on certain conditions or criteria. This means that the content, format, or structure of a document can be automatically adjusted based on certain rules or conditions. Usually, you'll set conditional logic rules up as a set of "if this…then that" statements.

For example, if you know your client is married rather than single, you may want to ask additional questions about their spouse. Then, you may want to populate additional clauses or paragraphs of text into the documents. Finally, you may want to generate additional documents that you never would have created if the individual was single.

Conditional logic can be complex and/or nested. Complex conditional logic refers to multiple sets of if/then statements separated by and/or statements. For example, *If the client is married and they have children and they are in California, then populate this section of text in the document.*

Nested conditional logic is logic embedded in other logic. For example, you may have a paragraph in a document that applies to married individuals, but then within that paragraph, you may have California-specific language.

### Calculations

Calculations are a critical part of your automation toolkit, and there are two types – numerical and date calculations.

Numerical calculations are equations. For example, after gathering all the assets and debts that a client has, you may want to add all the assets, subtract all the debts, and then compare that total to a separate number to determine whether the client is eligible for a fee waiver.

Date calculations allow you to calculate the amount of time between two dates, or to add or subtract time from a date. For example, if you have a user's date of birth, you may automatically want to insert their age. Or, if you have the date of a car accident, you may want to add the statute of limitations period to that date so that you can calculate whether the user is still able to file a claim.

Rules can be set up to consider holidays, weekends, and court closures, or to perform additional conditional logic to set up more rules based on these calculations.

### Repeating items

The final tool in your document automation toolkit is repeating items or lists of information. While simple variables collect one piece of information, repeating items can collect a list of information with potentially infinite entries. There can be none, one, or many in a list.

Two common examples are *children* and *shareholders*. In the example of children, you don't know upfront whether your client will have zero or many children. For each of those children, you may want to gather multiple attributes of information, like their names, dates of birth, states of residence, and more.

The user can then customize how the repeating item attributes will be inserted into the document. For example, you may want the list of children displayed as a table or as a list with commas and an oxford comma before the last item. Alternatively, you may want a separate document created for each of the children. To go a step further, you may even want to ask about how many children each of those children have.

The structure of lists or repeating items are the final tool allowing you to turn your expertise into an automated and systematized software tool.

## The access to justice gap and how technology can help

The access to justice gap is the discrepancy between the legal needs of individuals and their ability to access legal services and remedies. Many individuals in the US and beyond cannot access the justice system or get legal assistance, either because they cannot afford it, they are not aware of their legal rights, or they face systemic barriers that prevent them from obtaining legal representation or accessing the courts.

While the criminal system provides legal representation to everyone, regardless of income, the civil system does not. There are some resources for individuals who qualify as low-income, which is typically between 125 and 400 percent of the federal poverty level, but even where those resources exist, there are geographic, temporal, and other barriers preventing qualified individuals from accessing those resources. It's difficult to assess if these resources are effective for this group of low-income Americans, because records indicate many low-income Americans are turned away due to a lack of qualified available workers and a lack of available resources, not just because of their income bracket.

Additionally, there is a huge middle class that does not qualify for legal aid, but that also cannot afford the average hourly rate of an attorney for bespoke legal services. In both of these groups, unmet civil legal needs mean that these individuals either attempt to solve their own legal dilemmas without any assistance or they do not avail themselves of legal rights at all.

### The justice gap continues to rise

The Legal Services Corporation's "The Justice Gap: The Unmet Civil Legal Needs of Low-income Americans"[7] survey states that 92 percent of low-income Americans do not receive any help, or enough help, with their substantial civil legal problems.

The pandemic exacerbated the challenges these Americans face in obtaining needed civil legal assistance – 33 percent of low-income Americans experienced at least one civil legal problem linked to the COVID-19 pandemic. Almost three-quarters of low-income households (about 50 million Americans) experienced at least one civil legal problem in 2021. Not unsurprisingly, the people who have these civil legal problems state that these legal issues have a substantial impact on their lives, with 55 percent experiencing consequences that affect their finances, mental health, physical health and safety, and relationships.

### The most common problems of low-income Americans

The most common problems low-income populations face are consumer issues, health care, housing, and income maintenance. These needs are often related to securing and protecting basic needs, such as education, health care, utilities, and safety. More than 15 million children and nearly eight million seniors are within this low-income bracket, and they, along with veterans, people living in rural areas, and survivors of domestic violence, disproportionately suffer due to a lack of affordable and accessible legal resources. Lower incomes directly correlate to lower numbers of people seeking assistance, going without help (or enough help), and fore-going legal assistance due to the anticipated cost.

"Just the Facts: Trends in Pro Se Civil Litigation from 2000 to 2019",[8] published on 11 February 2021 by the Administrative Office of the US Courts on behalf of the Federal Judiciary based on data collected by the Judiciary Data and Analysis Office, cites an ongoing survey of the more than 15,000 US civil case courtrooms. Each year, an estimated 46 million people attempt to resolve cases involving civil legal cases such as custody issues, divorce, housing, child support, and consumer disputes, and this survey consistently finds a self-represented litigant in three in every four cases. As a result of statistics like these, low-income Americans lose 96 percent of their cases. These cases aren't decided on the merits, but often turn on procedural issues or technicalities such as a missed filing deadline or an incorrect document.

### Document automation and legal technology can help close the justice gap

This is where legal technology comes in. While solving the access to justice gap requires a multi-pronged approach, technology can help make a dent in the gap by allowing both nonprofit and for-profit legal professionals to provide scalable legal solutions that are both more affordable and more accessible to these groups.

Document automation can assist in closing the justice gap by making it easier for people working in the legal field to educate and assist low-income Americans. Legal professionals and other workers who have the education and experience to assist this population can better deploy tools and resources made available by technology.

When legal service providers can access and use technology tools, such as document automation systems and workflows, they can produce more work, and better work, faster. This means that more people can be helped in less time, and less time means less cost to low-income Americans, as well as to other users of legal services. When all members of the legal team are more productive, the resources allotted can go farther and help more people.

We are still in the beginning of this transition. The future of legal services is in its construction phase, and automated software built by subject matter experts is leading the way to a more equal and scalable legal system.

*References*


1 "Study: Legal Document Automation Saves 90 percent of Drafting Time", Gavel www.gavel.io/resources/study-legal-automation-saves-90-percent-drafting-time.
2 www.landlordlegalteam.com.
3 www.altmanweil.com/law-firms-in-transition-2020-an-executive-summary.
4 www.turbotax.com.
5 www.myprobatedocs.com.
6 www.fritzlawstl.com.
7 https://justicegap.lsc.gov/the-report/.
8 www.uscourts.gov/news/2021/02/11/just-facts-trends-pro-se-civil-litigation-2000-2019.

# Chapter 7: Technology considerations in alternative dispute resolution

*By Rich Lee, CEO and co-founder, New Era ADR*

One of the most dynamic but underdeveloped areas in legal technology is the world of alternative dispute resolution, or ADR for short. As a much-needed alternative to our overburdened court systems, there are substantial opportunities to improve the process and technology behind ADR as it exists today. Doing so can bring about wide-ranging positive change that saves people and organizations massive amounts of time, money, and acrimony while bringing many positive societal benefits – from greater accessibility to our justice system to significantly fewer acrimonious disputes.

## Background

While there are a number of sub-categories, ADR generally refers to one of several processes by which parties in conflict seek out neutral arbitrators or mediators who help them resolve their issues in the hope of not spending the extraordinary amounts of time and money required to resolve a case in overflowing and backed up court systems.

### Mediations

In mediations, one of two main categories of ADR, the process consists of a neutral mediator hearing each side's perspective of a case, offering what they think of each side's positions, sharing what the most likely outcome might be in court or arbitration if they don't reach a mutually agreed upon resolution, and then shuttling between the sides to help bridge differences, negotiate compromises, and occasionally tell each side the hard truths they may or may not want to hear, all in an effort to motivate the parties to reach an agreement on their own.

### Arbitrations

In arbitrations, the other main category of ADR, an arbitrator or a panel of arbitrators hears a case in a similar manner to a case in court and, unlike mediations where the objective is to help the two sides reach an agreement, the arbitrator(s) rule in favor of one side based on the law and the facts. Often, the arbitrator(s) also include a monetary award for one side as part of their ruling. The benefits for parties in arbitration include certainty (generally, arbitrations cannot be appealed), speed (arbitrators can control their caseload, leading to reduced wait times, especially when backlogged court systems must prioritize criminal matters over civil (aka non-criminal) matters), and lower costs. The time and cost savings are particularly helpful to lower-income parties, giving them greater access to the justice system.

### Confidentiality

A hallmark of mediations and arbitrations is the confidentiality of ADR proceedings. While that confidentiality has (rightfully) been cast in a poor light in recent years due to the "Me Too" movement, confidentiality in ADR is in fact an important element to maintaining individual and business relationships. For example, a sports team will have a roster of sponsors and partners – each of them valuable business relationships. Disagreements will happen, at times one party may feel like the other isn't holding up their end of the bargain, and a means of dispute resolution will be needed to resolve these differences. But the sports team will not want to publicize its fights with its partners and sponsors, or even the fact that it litigates against its partners and sponsors, so the confidentiality in arbitration and mediation plays an important role in relationship dynamics.

### The role of technology

Where does technology fit in ADR? First, the advent and wide acceptance of videoconferencing spurred by the COVID-19 pandemic has made scheduling hearings easier, as parties and attorneys no longer need to factor in transit time or even out of state travel arrangements. Although courts conducted remote aspects of trials during the worst of the pandemic, and many status conferences and hearings still take place remotely, trials in federal and state courts still likely take place in person.

More importantly, because ADR is private, the parties can mold the process however they want, and they can test and use new technologies to improve the system. Here lies the opportunity for technology in dispute resolution – to create highly accessible, fair, and efficient means for parties to resolve their differences and maintain a good relationship during and after a dispute.

In addition to that, there's an opportunity for technology to enhance a party's understanding.

## Why ADR?

The real dynamics of traditional litigation, and the impact it has on individual and business relationships, is on display daily in businesses all across the US and the world. Yet, these practical dynamics are often never discussed. Consider that as soon as individuals or a business find themselves at an impasse when seeking an amicable resolution to a conflict they're dealing with, the only next step available to them was traditionally a lawsuit in court. Each side knows that litigating in court will consume their time and attention over the next several years while also costing them outrageous amounts of money. At this point, and especially if a lawsuit is actually filed, both sides stop trying to air their grievances to resolve the matter amicably. Instead, they turn their efforts to focus on positioning themselves for a legal fight, start to pull procedural levers, and hope to ultimately win a war of attrition. In the worst case of all, one side engages in serious gamesmanship to inflict significant financial pain against the other to bend them into submission (usually in the form of a massive money settlement). While we know that most disputes in the United States settle without a trial, here lies the ugly truth: far too often, parties settle purely to avoid the pain, expense, and distraction of going through the litigation process and not because they actually did anything wrong. As a result of settlement, neither side actually gets to have their story heard – a cathartic moment for most individuals and organizations. Resentment, animosity, and acrimony between the two sides escalates, and many relationships become irreparable as a result. In the worst case of all, those without the expertise (or means to hire someone with the expertise) to navigate our court systems can be pressured or bullied into taking far less than should be owed to them simply because they have fewer resources than their opposing party.

However, these same dynamics are increasingly common in ADR, especially as arbitrations start to resemble court proceedings by allowing endless motion practice and unnecessarily long discovery periods. Just as in court, parties often settle cases simply to stem the costs and distraction of litigation. Just as in court, unnecessary process resulting in arbitration endurance contests over run-of-the mill disputes rarely, if ever, bring about the catharsis that occurs when parties get to the point and tell their sides of the story. As a result, due to its increasing inaccessibility and difficulty to navigate, ADR's critically important confidentiality has received recent criticism for being a mechanism to shield bad actors from negative publicity.

So, the question is, what parts of litigation are truly necessary for the vast majority of disputes that individuals and organizations face? Our traditional systems are good for large scale, highly complex types of litigation – for example, trade secret misappropriation cases, patent infringement claims, or mass tort claims such as those about to take place in East Palestine, Ohio as a result of the recent toxic train derailment – but people and organizations don't regularly deal with this type of litigation. Far more often, it's employment disputes, standard commercial disputes, and consumer disputes that dominate company litigation portfolios and court and traditional arbitration dockets. Does it actually make sense to have these types of disputes go through the same burdensome process as complex cases stemming from a train derailment that introduced vast amounts of toxic chemicals into the environment? Real alternatives are needed.

Technology and business innovations in the ADR space can create such an alternative. Given the accessibility of computing power and all the tools available to build upon, centering a true alternative to courts and traditional arbitration should start there. But in dispute resolution, technology without accompanying business and procedural innovation likely won't achieve the faster, less painful, less acrimonious, less expensive alternative that individuals and organizations universally crave.

## How can we improve existing dispute resolution systems?

There is an opportunity to create an improved dispute resolution process for the majority of disputes, but it has to ensure due process and fundamental fairness, or else that alternative process introduces new problems.

At its bedrock, due process starts with knowing consent. The parties coming to any dispute resolution forum have to do so voluntarily, typically by agreeing in their contracts to take any disputes to a named forum for resolution. Beyond consent, the other element of due process is the opportunity for each side to be heard by a neutral and informed third party. Fortunately, there is an abundance of smart, impartial, and experienced attorneys, non-attorneys, and retired attorneys and judges who can serve as neutral arbitrators and mediators. But to empower and incentivize them to conduct efficient and cost-effective dispute resolution proceedings, they ought to be given the authority to keep the parties focused on the relevant allegations and defenses, rather than let the process devolve into excessive motion practice and fishing expeditions involving largely unnecessary requests such as a decade of emails and documents for a straightforward claim – the kind of discovery that leads to years of delay and distraction.

### Procedural alternatives

In a simplified system, issues raised in preliminary motions (e.g., motion in limine, motion to dismiss, etc.) need not call for a separate and formal briefing and hearing process. These issues can be effectively addressed more informally during the course of standard arbitration proceedings and certainly during the hearing portion of the process. Similarly, in many ways discovery rules in the United States can be revised to resemble discovery procedures in European courts and other parts of the world, under which judges are empowered to assert more control over the collection of evidence and expert testimony than in the United States. Together, motions and discovery account for the overwhelming majority of time and money spent on litigation in courts and traditional arbitration. So, as one can imagine, improving and reimagining these processes can lead to a far more efficient and cost-effective dispute resolution experience.

Another area of seemingly obvious and simple innovation that is enabled by a simplification of typically-onerous procedural elements in arbitration is fee structure. In traditional arbitration forums today, litigants encounter a complex and extensive schedule of fees that include procedural fees, administrative fees, technology fees, and hourly fees for one or more arbitrators and mediators. All these fees add complexity and difficulty to litigation budgeting for both parties to litigation and their attorneys. Moreover, flat fees provide psychological benefits and lessen the pressure that leads to the state of pure animosity that can exist in litigation, where each side presumes any action by their opponents is done to drive up cost and pain.

Overall, for the majority of disputes, simpler, more efficient, more cost-effective resolutions to litigation leave room for healing in the relationship between the opposing parties, and, perhaps, new chances to extend the relationship.

## Technology opportunities and the technology balancing act

Beyond procedural innovations, there is a large opportunity for technology to inject substantial improvements to the arbitration and mediation process. In the age of exciting boundary-pushing new technologies such as generative artificial intelligence (AI) and blockchain applications that can (and should) fundamentally improve the legal industry, the technology opportunity in the ADR industry starts with the core user experience throughout the entire arbitration and mediation case lifecycle. Much like litigation in our courts, the core arbitration and mediation experience today is still largely analogue, and if portions are digital they take place on disparate systems that typically were not built for the ADR use case.

As for the use and inclusion of advanced technologies in the ADR experience, there are certainly countless applications and opportunities, but if the core experience isn't done right, then the layering on of fancy and exciting new features is like adding features to a car with three tires and a half-built steering wheel. Not to mention the risks and rewards of adding incremental features to an experience with such profound legal and business implications ought to be considered carefully. After all, individual livelihoods, business relationships, and large sums of money are at stake, and the accessibility, integrity, and reliability of the technology is paramount. A platform too advanced for less tech-savvy users (of which there will be many) or with too little effort dedicated to ensuring that everything "just works" will simply not gain the user trust needed for widespread adoption, or if it does, it will quickly cease to be used as people question its reliability. Ultimately, a tool, no matter how great or useful, is only as good as its adoption.

Generally, in my experience as a former general counsel and early executive of two technology companies – one a pioneer in data science and another that pushed boundaries in financial technology – and now as a co-founder of a legal technology company building for the litigation and ADR industry, I've found that companies have to balance the risks and rewards and carefully think through the implementation of advanced tools and techniques, as well-intentioned as the tools may be. For example, some years ago a major tech company had to scrap an AI-based employee recruiting program. As reported at the time,[1] the system inadvertently discriminated against women because it based its search on patterns in resumes submitted to the company over a ten-year period, when men dominated the industry even more than they do today. In another example, AI-powered healthcare patient care systems reduced the amount of care recommended for black patients as it did for white patients due to bias introduced in the training of that algorithm (an implementation error). As I write this, critics of large language models express concern that training algorithms based on historical content inherently runs the risk that such models could suffer the same problems.[2] In each of these cases, trust in these algorithms could be forever lost, so even if its biases are fixed it may never see the scale of usage that's needed to fuel the innovation and positive change that its creators intended.

In another example, one idea often floated in the ADR space is around the idea of an algorithmic dispute resolution engine in which automated decisions are made on existing arbitration claims using a dispute resolution model that trained on previous cases. In addition to potential problems around sample size and relevance of certain historical cases, it's hard to see lawyers or litigants trusting this kind of AI arbiter. While lawyers could benefit from a historical view of similar cases, their human experience is trusted more than an algorithm. The "black box" decision-maker also eliminates the human element of litigation that most people and organizations consider essential – the catharsis parties get from sharing their side of a dispute with a wise, trusted jurist who then weighs the law and facts in rendering a decision.

For now, given the vast technology opportunity in ADR, the industry would be better served by technological efforts centered on improving and perfecting the experience of seemingly rote elements like online remote hearings, scheduling, document sharing, payments, etc. Beyond the core experience, however, exciting possibilities exist to upgrade the ADR and overall litigation experience. Large language models like Open AI's GPT-4 and Google's Bard show much promise to expedite the claim filing process and the drafting and summarizing of arbitration complaints and mediation statements. Although more training and human quality control are needed before these tools can be used with regularity to draft legal documents of such consequence, they can already save litigants large amounts of time in drafting and document generation. On top of LLMs, the amount of data in litigation can be harnessed not just to facilitate faster arbitration and mediation processes, but also to encourage pragmatism – perhaps before a lawsuit is even filed. Empirical evidence can help parties better focus on the core issues at hand and arrive more quickly at mutually agreeable resolutions. Lastly, data and generative AI coupled with ever more sophisticated transcription and translation tools promise to significantly improve efficiency and productivity in ADR and litigation, but more importantly, they promise to greatly improve accessibility. In the United States, there are numerous individuals for whom English is their second or third language, and the prospect of getting involved in a dispute in court or arbitration where language is so critical to a successful experience is daunting. Building tools that allow for inputs in their native language would be game-changing.

## ADR, tech, and access to justice

Any person interested in advancing and improving legal technology should always maintain the advancement of accessibility of our legal system as a north star in anything they build. Dispute resolution is no exception.

Nowhere is the inaccessibility of our justice system more apparent than in dispute resolution. Our court system is already difficult enough to navigate for attorneys who don't spend their time on litigation matters. Now imagine how much more difficult it is for an individual or small business that cannot afford to hire a lawyer to help them resolve their legal disputes. Current arbitration systems are no better. This is largely a result of the overly complex processes, onerous procedures, and the lack of technology that collectively define litigation in courts and traditional arbitration and mediation today. The procedural and technology opportunity before us for innovation is not only a chance at making the dispute resolution experience better for all involved, but more broadly, an opportunity to make a societal impact that can truly lift everyone up.

After all, the protection of the rule of law is the entire foundation of the United States and most other countries, and it's this confidence in this protection that allows us to live our lives, take care of our families, and pursue our dreams. But, if access to that protection is beyond reach and confidence that the law will protect us is shaken, the ability to live our lives is profoundly disrupted. Yet, this is what so many people experience today.

For example, imagine the very common scenario of being an apartment renter dealing with an abusive or combative landlord. For many of us who are blessed with a sound knowledge of our justice system or the means to hire an attorney, the straightforward answer is to initiate legal proceedings against that landlord. However, for so many others, this straightforward answer is not so straightforward at all when they cannot navigate existing dispute resolution systems, when they cannot hire a lawyer to do it for them, and when they also have logistical considerations to account for that may prevent them for attending a legal proceeding in the first place (for example, finding child care, workplaces that are not accommodating, or living rural areas with no convenient access to physical dispute resolution forums).

Organizations like the Legal Services Corporation – a US Senate-funded 501(c)(3) organization – and countless legal aid organizations across the United States are doing admirable and much-needed work to increase access to our justice system, but it will take significant improvements in the justice system landscape to truly propel these efforts forward. Innovations in process and technology can address all these problems and make it far more possible for countless more individuals to assert their legal rights and gain that access to the protections of the rule of law that's a fundamental right for everyone in the United States.

## Making ADR make sense

ADR is a much-needed alternative to litigating in courts. However, as it exists today, there is an opportunity to do so much more to more pragmatically resolve the vast majority of legal disputes, to make our justice system more accessible for all involved, and to improve the lives of so many as a result. I look forward to ADR's evolution and the many positives changes that come from it.

*References*

1 www.reuters.com/article/us-amazon-com-jobs-automation-insight/amazon-scraps-secret-ai-recruiting-tool-that-showed-bias-against-women-idUSKCN1MK08G.

2 www.insider.com/chatgpt-is-like-many-other-ai-models-rife-with-bias-2023-1.

Chapter 8:

# Lessons from a legal tech start-up

*By Daniel Farris, founder and CEO, NMBL Technologies*

Few things have the power to disrupt an industry like technology, and there aren't many industries more susceptible to radical change and rapid disruption than the legal industry. Legal publications tout the potential of artificial intelligence or warn lawyers that the robots are coming. An increasing number of Am Law 100 firms have dedicated innovation teams. Investors have poured billions of dollars into legal tech providers over the last few years. And yet, despite significant investment and no shortage of companies or products, legal technology has had only minimal impact on the way in which most legal services are delivered and consumed, legal outcomes, or the cost of legal services.

According to a 2022 Ernst & Young market trends report,[1] two of the three technology products most adopted by corporate legal departments are eSignature and document management solutions. Law firms have similar adoption statistics, with knowledge management and research tools also at the top of their list. In other words, providers like DocuSign, Thomson Reuters, Dropbox, LexisNexis, and Wolters Kluwer dominate the market share of corporate legal department and law firm spending. Arguably, none of these are legal tech providers primarily offering legal tech solutions. Outside of perhaps Clio – which licenses firm management solutions to small-to-medium sized law firms – there aren't many legal enterprise solutions. The most successful legal point solutions are still eDiscovery and contract management systems.

How can this be? Why haven't legal technology products had the transformative effect that tech products have in other industries? Does it all come down to protectionism and the monopoly power exercised by lawyers and state bars? Is the legal industry just that far behind others? Will there be a breakthrough and what might that look like? Or is legal tech all hype?

There is no simple or right answer. The problem is complex and undoubtedly combines elements of many of these considerations. An examination of the current legal technology landscape suggests that, despite some unique barriers to entry and sales challenges, the problem may actually be how legal technology is built and sold. Solve that, and the opportunity for success is significant. Find the right product-market fit and deliver a good client experience and you can dominate the legal tech market.

This chapter is a case study in how one early-stage legal technology company, NMBL Technologies, built and brought its legal workflow management and collaboration product, Proxy, to market. We will examine how NMBL identified the problem it is addressing, the design thinking concepts it used to develop Proxy, and we will share some of the lessons NMBL learned along the way.

## First, some history

Prior to 2008, many corporate legal departments – perhaps the majority – were lands of misfit toys. Legal departments were smaller, misunderstood by much of the business, and often left to their own devices in some far away corner of corporate headquarters. The job of in-house counsel was commonly intake (i.e. to receive requests for legal support from various internal stakeholders and departments), issue-spotting (i.e. identifying the substantive legal issues), retaining and managing outside counsel, and coordinating the performance and delivery of the relevant legal services. Of course, that is not to say that this was a universal truth, or that all corporate legal departments prior to 2008 can or should be viewed this simplistically, but many in the profession consider the time before the last recession as being the "golden age" of in-house practice. Burnt out firm lawyers, or those starting a family, went in-house to "slow down" and work a normal "nine to five".

Like so many other things, the "Great Recession" changed all that. Besieged companies looked for ways to cut expenses. Legal departments, historically viewed as overly conservative costs centers, were an easy target. In-house lawyers lost their jobs and spending on outside counsel was slashed. Law firms felt the pinch and experienced associates and partners who saw hours decline or were unlucky enough to specialize in an area disproportionately impacted by the economic downturn found themselves unemployed.

Eventually, the tumult of 2008 and 2009 began to subside, the economy stabilized, and companies began returning to a "new normal". Facing a more highly regulated business climate, corporations realized the need to reinvest in the legal function, but the process of re-examining business practice to find costs savings and improve efficiency remained. For many companies a simple truth emerged – a senior associate or junior partner at a law firm likely cost over a million dollars a year if engaged full-time at hourly rates, but the same person cost a fraction if employed directly. And it just so happened that there were a good number of well-trained and experienced firm lawyers looking for work. What happened next was the catalyst for a sea change in the legal industry, accelerating and/or giving rise to legal ops, alternative legal services, and drastically increasing the uptake of legal technology by corporate legal departments.

## Changing tides

As corporations began to hire more in-house counsel, the role of lawyers working in corporate legal departments began to change. In-house attorneys were asked to do more substantive work. They became more engrained in the business. Rank and file lawyers handled more day-to-day operational matters and general counsel became important members of executive teams, expected to participate in strategic enterprise decision-making. As legal departments grew, so too did the need for general departmental controls, legal KPIs, and better data and metrics to demonstrate legal department ROI. General counsel, no longer managing small groups of somewhat autonomous lawyers, recognized the need for policies to promote consistency, predictability, align advice and outcomes with business goals, and manage budgets.

Lawyers who fled firms for in-house roles were all too familiar with the inefficiency inherent in the billable hour. A new generation of lawyers who had grown up with technology entered the workforce with a skeptical eye for the tedious manual and analog ways of old. Companies investing in digitization to gain efficiency and scale were less tolerant of the archaic and unpredictable nature of legal services. General counsel were pushed to do more with less, and to justify their budgets. These trends created the perfect environment for three important shifts in the way companies performed and consumed legal services.

First, unlike many law firms, corporate legal departments were more willing to engage alternative legal service providers (ALSPs) for high frequency low risk and routine tasks that were not yet or could not be digitized. For many ALSPs, this began with a simple staffing model providing contract and temporary attorneys to companies at rates substantially lower than law firms could provide. In some instances, ALSPs took on an outsourced services model, providing certain functions utilizing human capital "as a service".

Second, companies began adopting legal operations principles within their own corporate legal departments and hiring legal operations directors to manage the process. For perhaps the first time, the lawyers themselves were not completely in control of the way they practiced. Legal ops directors adopted new policies focused less on the "quality" of the legal services, which had become table stakes by that point, but instead aimed to create consistency and predictability, improve efficiency, better align legal services with business goals, and better manage risk. These legal ops professionals introduced business management principles into the legal function and, in so doing, changed the expectations of corporate legal departments in ways that many law firms are still struggling to satisfy today. They pushed legal departments to provide a "customer experience" to their internal business stakeholders that was more similar to the way other departments already worked.

Third, and most relevantly here, corporate legal departments began looking to technology providers to digitize and automate more of the legal function. By that time, eDiscovery had already begun to take hold in the legal industry. Companies adopted electronic billing solutions and sought to apply new standards and better analytics to their outside legal spend. Document management software helped many corporate legal departments create repositories for historical and existing legal documents and aided in standardization through use of templates and centralization of key materials. Many corporate legal departments saw their contracting function as another easy target for digitization. After all, contracts tend to have standard categories of terms, they are rule-based documents, they tend to be handled manually, and most corporate legal departments view contracting as their highest volume of work. A new wave of contract management solutions began to emerge in the market and many companies were all too happy to give them a try.

Between the use of ALSPs, the adoption of legal ops principles, and the use of new legal tech products, corporate legal departments started to digitize and transform the way they did business in significant ways. And yet, change did not always come easy.

## New practices, new problems

While legal ops principles, the use of ALSPs, and new legal tech products held tremendous potential for change, many in-house lawyers struggled in this new environment. After all, most lawyers are trained in law, not business. The business operations and management principles they were being asked to implement were foreign. Attorneys could understand them conceptually but putting them into practice was a different story altogether.

Progressive and innovative thinking was, in some respects, antithetical to their legal training, which placed a premium on historical precedent, analytical thinking on the uniqueness of each situation, patience, and small incremental changes. For some, this new world order was disorienting.

For others, the promise of legal technology did not deliver. Convinced (sometimes by sales literature) that legal technology products alone could solve many or all the problems they faced, some in-house lawyers found themselves frustrated and less efficient than ever. At NMBL, we often heard from lawyers confused as to how and why the technology products they had purchased weren't doing more to improve their operations. As we listened and heard from more people, a few fairly consistent trends emerged.

Perhaps most prominent was the lack of adequate planning before legal technology solutions were implemented. Technology products tend to amplify process. Applying automation to an inefficient process will only serve to magnify the inefficiencies. Not enough companies were focusing on people and process before selecting and implementing technology products. All too often, corporate legal departments desperate to do more with less saw legal tech products as some sort of cure-all silver bullet. By 2018, when we founded NMBL, many corporate legal departments were learning the fallacy of this sort of thinking, but few knew how to address the problem.

Similarly, corporate legal departments were misusing point solutions as enterprise solutions. We often heard from lawyers frustrated that their CMS was ineffective at handling matters outside of the contracting space, despite the fact that those CMS products were never designed or intended to handle other types of matters. Some legal tech providers, ranging from CMS and DMS to matter management, case management, and e-billing solutions, attempted to recast their products as being capable of managing other types of legal workflows. This only tended to exacerbate the problem.

Without good productivity tools, in-house lawyers felt overwhelmed. Unlike their colleagues in other areas of the business, who might have had enterprise tools like Salesforce, SAP, or Oracle, lawyers in corporate legal departments were trying to manage their entire function via email and the Office Suite. Few had access to products that allowed them to manage, organize, delegate, track, or report on the myriad legal requests they received every day. Some had tried business productivity tools such as Monday.com, Asana, or Smartsheet, but without proper training or experience, and without sufficient support to configure and administer these products, many in-house lawyers found these business tools were simply adding new administrative burdens that had the opposite effect of what was intended.

At NMBL, as we engaged in market research, interacted with focus groups, sought feedback from in-house counsel, and began our requirements gathering, some consistent trends emerged. There was (and still is) unmet need for subject matter agnostic, intuitive, secure, and modern end-to-end workflow tools that help lawyers minimize or control their administrative overhead and manage their day-to-day workload. Many legal tech tools offered solutions in search of a problem, created significant technical and administrative overhead, and far too many placed a premium on features rather than user experience. We embarked on a plan to address these issues using design thinking and emphasizing people and process. Here is how we did it, and a bit about what we have learned along the way.

## Workflow reimagined

Before jumping into the lessons we have learned, a bit about legal workflow management and how we have attempted to reimagine it with Proxy. Typically, workflow tools allow users to create, automate, manage, and monitor a defined set of tasks arranged in a sequence (e.g. the workflow). Many systems assume (1) the user is aware of, and can identify and order, most or all tasks in advance; (2) the tasks, workflows, and projects (if they exist) are hierarchical; and (3) things tend to flow in a structured manner based on time or interdependencies. For example, in the typical model, a company might set up a process for entering into non-disclosure agreements with third party vendors. The process might include receipt of the request, confirmation of the third party's contact information, selection of the correct company NDA template, drafting/modification of any special terms, review and approval by appropriate personnel, and execution. In this case, the process is standardized, known, easily repeatable, structured, and easily automated.

In theory, the above makes sense. In (legal) practice, it does not. Any lawyer will tell you that most legal matters are somewhat messy. In-house lawyers in particular tend to be juggling many different legal projects, workflows, and tasks all at once. A good number of those tasks are *ad hoc*, meaning they don't relate to some larger or more formalized workflow or project. Once the attorney completes the task, there is no follow up. The task still needs to be tracked and data about it may be important, but it isn't part of some larger formalized flow. Even when there are more easily defined workflows, they rarely move in an orderly and hierarchical fashion.

With Proxy, we attempted to address these issues by turning the traditional workflow management process on its head. Tasks are our most basic data elements, and what a task is can vary. For some users, a task is the deliverable – a contract, policy, or brief, for example. For others, the task is a more discrete unit of work related to the deliverable – e.g. drafting, reviewing, researching, or approving the ultimate deliverable. We set out to build a tool that was flexible enough to all attorneys to work however they choose. Tasks are easy to enter into the system with minimal input, though a user may add substantial additional metadata. Tasks can have start and end dates, they can be assigned to one or more individuals, a group or team, they can be dependent on other tasks, etc., and they can relate to or involve zero, one, or many documents.

With tasks being Proxy's foundational data elements, we allow users to group those together into workflows, predefined or otherwise, because again some legal requests will lend themselves to known or anticipated process, consistency, and automation, while others will arise and evolve organically throughout the life of the project or workflow. In essence, a workflow is a container that holds a number of tasks necessary to complete the necessary legal request or work. Projects, in turn, are essentially containers holding multiple workflows. With this framework, we intend for Proxy to facilitate key legal ops concepts and principles, most importantly starting with people and process. The tool is fluid and flexible, allowing for each company or law firm that uses it to implement its own processes while gaining the power of automation, consistency, and greater transparency. The tool also allows users (primarily attorneys) to work the way they already do, allowing adoption more easily without the added difficulty of change management as well. This is key, as we discuss below, because understanding user behavior is essential for product success.

## Understand user behavior

One of the most common mistakes in any type of software development is failing to adequately identify or understand user needs and behavior. In the legal tech world, there is perhaps no more commonly used phrase – or clearer warning sign – than "built by lawyers for lawyers". Many well-intentioned legal tech companies use the phrase to signal to perspective customers (i.e. other lawyers) that their product was built with some understanding of what lawyers need and how lawyers work. But when was the last time a group of lawyers created any process that is easy, intuitive, or efficient? How often do you remark on how enjoyable a legal process is? Think about buying a house, closing a transaction, or any judicial proceeding. Easy and fun, right? Just like the tax code.

Legal process and legal systems are more commonly archaic, rigid, inefficient, slow, difficult to understand, expensive, and they often lead to inconsistent outcomes. For software to be useful, it must essentially be the opposite – intuitive, efficient, reliable, consistent, flexible, and fast. Balancing these competing interests is the key to success in legal tech. Automate existing process and you're likely to amplify its inefficiency. Stray too far from how things are done today and your product will seem foreign to the lawyers you're courting as users. Flexibility makes a product robust, but also complex. Complexity often requires more user input, which undermines ease and speed.

If you are a lawyer, think about the software development process much as you might think about writing a good legal brief. The best and most persuasive legal writing is that which can distill complex legal concepts into simple and plain language that even the most uninitiated can understand, and then addressing the key issue(s) at the core of those concepts. When it comes to legal technology, products that can distill complex process into the fewest and most intuitive steps are generally the most successful.

### Do one or a few things well

When it comes to creating better user experience, do less. This may be the single most common mistake we see. The desire to be a "one stop shop" or to solve all of the user's problems is overwhelming. It is also wrong, and I can prove it.

Take out your smartphone and see how many music, mapping, delivery, entertainment, or social media apps you have. If you are an "average" consumer, you have two to four music apps (e.g. Apple Music, Spotify, and Pandora), two to four mapping apps (e.g. Apple Maps, Google Maps, and Waze), three to five delivery apps (e.g. DoorDash, Uber Eats, Grubhub, Instacart, and PostMates), three to six entertainment apps (e.g. Netflix, Hulu, Amazon Prime Video, YouTube, Apple TV, and Disney+), and three to five social media apps (e.g. Facebook, Instagram, Twitter, LinkedIn, and TikTok). All the applications in each of the categories mentioned do essentially the same thing. And yet you, like all consumers, use each of these applications for discrete and different purposes. That is likely true in any category, whether it be travel, banking/finance, news, or any of the categories mentioned above.

I can already hear the protestations – but those are consumer apps, and we're talking about business software. The same is not true for enterprise applications, right? Well, how many tools do you use to communicate daily? Email? Slack? Text? Phone calls? Have you used Teams lately? Zoom?

WebEx? Let's take Teams for a moment. How often do you use Teams for more than videoconferencing and chat? It has far more features, but do you utilize them meaningfully?

Still not convinced? DocuSign is worth roughly $9.5bn, and it allows users to digitally sign documents. Twitter allows users to send 280-character messages – its functionality is far less robust than email – and Elon Musk recently acquired the company for $44bn. When it comes to software, doing one or a few things really well beats doing lots of things every day of the week.

A well-known and generally accepted software development principle is to start with a minimally viable product, or MVP. The emphasis here is on *minimal*. MVP is a version of your product that contains just enough features to allow early adopters to use the product and provide feedback. Essentially, MVP allows you to test an idea or a concept for a product before fully committing. It allows a company to "fail fast" – that is to learn quickly and without significant investment what works and what does not. If you start with MVP, you can add features while keeping an eye out to be sure you aren't overbuilding. Feature creep is real, and you should avoid it. Stay true to your application's main purpose and one to three killer features.

As we will address below, the line between consumer and business applications is blurring. Legal tech user experience increasingly has to mirror consumer user experience. Lesson one, therefore, is do less. Keep it simple and let others fill in the blanks.

## Lawyers want it both ways

Perhaps the most difficult lesson we have learned, and the hardest to put into practice, is that lawyers want both flexibility and simplicity. Whether this trend is, in fact, limited to lawyers is unclear, but it definitely exists in the legal industry. Here is how it manifests.

Lawyers like autonomy. If, for example, you tell a group of lawyers that you have reviewed, analyzed, and processed hundreds of thousands of, say, non-disclosure agreements, analyzed the case law from all 50 states, and that you have ultimately developed the most perfect NDA possible, the majority of lawyers will reject it. We lawyers love choice, we are confident that our way is the "right" or "best" way, and we want software that gives us flexibility to handle legal matters the way we see fit. This is one reason that AI has had mixed results at best, as we discuss further below.

On the other hand, if you give that same group of lawyers a system that is highly flexible and allows users to build their own process, lawyers will complain that the system is too complex and requires too much input. This was the most common refrain we heard from lawyers who had tried highly customizable business and legal solutions ranging from Monday and Asana to HighQ and Thomson Reuter's Panoramic. Those tools required too much work to be useful. They create additional administrative burdens that exacerbate the problem we were seeking to solve when we founded NMBL. General counsel often complained that they needed full-time staff just to manage the software. Given their resource constraints this wasn't an option, and the software therefore served to make matters worse, not better.

If you sell a product that seeks to automate legal process, you will have the same issue. How do you make something simple but powerful? How much flexibility is enough without creating too much? There is no silver bullet, but our research suggests that good UX tends to involve building standardized and simple flows that are easily approachable and useful for the majority of use cases. Those flows and use cases should be built on a highly flexible and customizable foundation, the controls for which can be separated out into administrative tools for power users to control. Research and testing can help you separate the primary "lanes" from the edge cases. In other words, think of the use cases like a bell curve and build the fastest and easiest UX for those scenarios within one standard deviation. Push all other cases to the edge and enable them through flexible feature controls and customization in administrator tools.

Steve Jobs is credited with believing that if a user needed a manual then the product's design was flawed. "Simple is harder than complex", he said. "You can't ask customers what they want and then give it to them. By the time you get it built, they'll want something new." If you can master this balance between simplicity and flexibility you will be well on your way towards building a successful product.

## Last best experience

Along similar lines, know your competitors and build a user interface that addresses current user behavior and expectations. In this regard, the concept of "last best experience" is key. Last best experience is a term that refers to a user's most recent best experience interacting with a technology product. The typical user will measure your (or any) product against his or her last best experience. This means that, when it comes to customer experience, you're competing against far more products than you think.

Many legal technology products compare themselves to other products in their own category or to a manual process. For example, Ironclad might compare its CMS tool to products sold by Malbek, SpringCM, Cobblestone, Conga, or Onit. Ironclad's sales reps might demonstrate to customer leads how Ironclad's tools improve upon the often analog process of drafting, negotiating, and managing contracts. There is nothing wrong with these comparisons, but they are incomplete because they ignore a user's "last best experience".

If the average user of your product is ordering groceries to be delivered to her house on Instacart while using Lyft to get a ride into the office just before launching your app, those other CMS products are irrelevant. The user doesn't have any experience with them. Instead, the user will subconsciously compare how your application operates to Instacart and Lyft – consumer apps with a very different purpose. Throughout the day, that user might spend her day switching back and forth from Microsoft or Google productivity tools on her laptop and communicating or using other apps on her iPhone. All of these activities impact and inform her view of how a technology product should operate. If your product deviates significantly, users will notice.

Traditionally, enterprise products were sold top-down. If the CIO – or in the case of legal tech, the GC – approved, that tool was implemented. This resulted in a degree of forced user adoption, but companies often found user engagement (e.g. the quality and frequency of user interactions with the product, and their satisfaction with it) was awful. Companies like Slack have popularized a bottom-up approach known as "product-led growth" that focuses on simplicity, low barriers to adoption/use, and interfaces that feel far more like consumer applications than business software. This is what you're competing with and your UX better address it if you want good user engagement metrics.

To quote Steve Jobs once more, good design must "start with the customer experience and work backwards to the technology". Customers gauge their experience relative to their last best interactions, and that will include consumer products. Ignore that at your own risk.

## Play nice with others

As the legal tech ecosystem continues to grow, the need for products to easily integrate with other common tools only intensifies. A decent number of technology products – legal and otherwise – hold themselves out as a "one stop shop", purporting to be the only tool a user needs. Aside from being essentially impossible, this thinking also ignores many key user behaviors already discussed (e.g. most apps are used for one or a few key features). Suggesting to a user that he or she use only your tool is actually asking the user to fundamentally change the way he or she currently operates on a daily basis. This is a monumental change management challenge that will undoubtedly create significant impediments to adoption, as well as sizeable technical overhead.

On the other hand, if your product can seamlessly integrate with other third party tools, this creates minimal resistance to adoption, allows the user to continue to benefit from third party features the user might love, and requires the least change in existing behavior. Essentially, integrations allow your application to deliver both desired output and convenience with the minimal input required. This is why Amazon, Instacart, and Netflix have been successful. Why get dressed, leave the house, and travel to a grocery, restaurant, or video store when you can get the groceries, meal, or movie delivered to you from the comfort of your own couch?

The same concepts apply here. Can a user access key features of your app without logging in and/or being in the tool itself (e.g. much as you can schedule a Teams or Zoom call from within email clients like Outlook or Gmail)? Can other products interact with yours (such as a restaurant application may actually rely on DoorDash for delivery fulfilment)? Are you able to pull useful features of other tools into yours? Can you easily share data with others?

When we set out to build Proxy, we knew that certain features commonly associated with document management systems, contract management systems, docketing systems, and many other well-used tools would be expected or useful in a workflow management system. But recreating the relevant functionality already in DMS, CMS, docketing, and other products was not only difficult, time consuming, and expensive, but it was also a losing proposition. We couldn't deliver ancillary feature sets that performed as well as those same feature sets in tools where they were central. In other words, we couldn't build DMS features that worked better than those of DMS products. And why create that competition or ask a lawyer to stop using a product he or she might already enjoy? In some cases, the tool selected may not even be a choice made by the corporate legal department, but rather others in the enterprise.

This early acknowledgement of the need to maximize integrations was important, as it allowed us to build our product using a microservices architecture. In a microservices architecture, small code sets are developed to accommodate a single application feature and handle discrete tasks. Each microservice then communicates with other services through simple interfaces to solve the relevant business problems. In other words, the architecture allows you to make discrete features available to third party products with minimal work, as compared to other more traditional models that would require integrations with many or all features within the application in order to access any part of it. Understanding and implementing this sort of framework early in your software development process can save a tremendous amount of time and money down the road, and make your product more flexible and scalable.

**Be careful with "artificial intelligence"**

"AI" is perhaps the most in vogue, and most misused, acronym in legal tech. In reality, artificial intelligence is an entire field of computer and data science that has tested numerous approaches over the last 60 years, includes concepts ranging from machine learning to neural networks, and calls upon disciplines such as computer science, advanced mathematics, philosophy, linguistics, psychology, and others. As most commonly used in legal tech, the term is intended to imply that the algorithmic logic used by the applicable software can learn and "train" itself through use, ultimately improving its performance over time. Very few products actually deliver on the hype.

This isn't an issue unique to legal tech. It highlights just how difficult real "AI" is to develop. Take self-driving cars, for example. Google founded a company now known as Waymo in 2009 to focus on the development of AI to control autonomous vehicles. Google is one of the wealthiest and most technologically sophisticated companies in the world. It has access to the greatest talent available. By and large, the "rules of the road" are well known. Certainly, AI systems controlling a vehicle must draw inferences from their surroundings, but the basic logical controls are built into traffic laws. Cars nowadays generate thousands of data points a second, and there are many millions of cars on the road. This leads to an absolute mountain of data from which an AI system could likely test any scenario imaginable. And yet, despite incredible technical and scientific brain power, significant financial resources, and nearly unlimited amounts of data, Google still hasn't been able to sufficiently solve the challenge of self-driving cars, even after more than a dozen years.

Bringing this back to legal tech, if one of the wealthiest companies in the world with some of the greatest technical talent in the world and a veritable mountain of available data can't solve this AI problem, I'm not entirely sure how a legal tech start-up expects to use AI in an industry that is fundamentally contextual. In other words, programmatically, an autonomous driving system might need only know if the light is red, yellow, or green, but a legal AI system may have to consider the meaning of the term "use" (e.g. does "use" in a contract mean put into action, access, consume, or something else?).

Even if I am wrong on this, and a good number of relatively small legal tech companies, relying on tiny datasets, have somehow developed mind-blowing artificial intelligence systems, do their buyers actually want it? Few of the lawyers we spoke with wanted machines to do the thinking for them. In fact, lawyers tend to be deeply distrustful of anything that purports to replace or circumvent their professional judgment. So, even if you can overcome the quite significant technical challenges, you're potentially delivering something your customers don't really want.

What most lawyers want, in our experience, is automation. Tools that eliminate tedious manual tasks and make the user more efficient are well-received. And given the archaic and outdated nature of so many parts of legal practice, there is plenty of low-hanging fruit. Our advice – do away with the AI talk and simply focus on automation, efficiency, and user experience.

## Selling legal tech is difficult and slow

Last, but certainly not least, be sure to develop and commit significant resources to a go-to market and multichannel sales strategy. Even the best apps don't necessarily sell and selling to lawyers is not for the faint of heart. Of all potential buyers, lawyers might be the most skeptical and most resistant to change. It will do you no good at all to invest resources into building a fantastic product if you cannot sell it, so do not under-value or underestimate the resources necessary to acquire customers and generate revenue.

Entire books are written on this subject. Courses are taught on it. People dedicate their careers to knowing how to sell. We cannot do the subject justice in what little space we have available in this chapter. Instead, we will lead with one piece of advice – consider whether Product Led Growth (PLG) might be a good strategy for your product.

PLG is essentially a framework that allows buyers to self-select. To illustrate, consider traditional enterprise applications like SAP or Oracle versus tools like Slack. SAP and Oracle are sold using more traditional sales channels – often sales reps engaged in direct sales. They quote the products to internal buyers, and then have to deploy the technology, train users, onboard, provide support, and offer customer success personnel to their customers. Slack, on the other hand, allows anyone to sig up for a Slack workspace for free in seconds. The barrier to getting customers or users on the platform is very low. Once a PLG platform has a captive user, the tools tend to require users to pay for certain features, for more users, after the passage of a certain amount of time, or when use hits certain levels. In other words, a product using PLG can make a sale without all of the infrastructure Oracle or SAP needs – without the sales reps and trainers, without the SOWs and vendor questionnaires, and without much human capital at all.

PLG is still a relatively new concept that has not yet been widely adopted in legal tech. This creates an opportunity for those products that deploy PLG and lower the barriers to a purchase or sale. Whatever methods you choose, however, be sure to invest time, effort, and financial resources into your sales force. No matter how incredible your product is, it likely will not sell itself.

*References*

1 Legal Tech Market Overview, EYCA Technology Group, November 2022.

# Chapter 9:
# Legal operations

*By Tom Stephenson, vice president, Legal.io*

Corporate legal operations is defined as managing and optimizing a legal department's day-to-day resources with a strategic, data-driven approach to drive better outcomes, reduce costs, and increase efficiency. Legal operations is often viewed as corporate architects tasked with running legal like a business through designing, implementing, and managing the systems, processes, and procedures that enable a company to achieve its goals. Critical in navigating our complex legal landscape, legal operations partners with various stakeholders to protect the company's interests while supporting its success.

To understand the critical elements of a functional corporate legal operations department, let's break down the duties and responsibilities into six core components:

1. People operations and strategic planning.
2. Knowledge and risk management.
3. Outside counsel and external initiatives.
4. Financial planning and spend analysis.
5. Technology and data analytics.
6. Project management and practice operations.

Effective corporate legal operations teams require a holistic approach that considers all of these core elements and aligns with the company's overall business goals. By focusing on these key components, corporate legal departments can ensure that they deliver value to the company and support its success.

## Corporate legal operations' functional competencies

### People operations and strategic planning

The corporate legal operations' function supports an organization's business objectives. As such, it is essential to have a strong, effective, and balanced legal team in place. Optimizing the performance of a corporate legal department requires a strategic plan that focuses on talent acquisition, culture, career framework, employee success, and diversity, equity, and inclusion (DEI) programs.

### Knowledge and risk management

A robust knowledge management program within a legal team focuses on developing a systematic approach to creating, sharing, using, and managing informational assets. Corporate legal operations should pay attention to the importance of compliance, privacy, and governance initiatives and partner with various stakeholders to identify potential risks and ensure that the company's operations are conducted according to all relevant laws and regulations.

### Outside counsel and external initiatives

A corporate legal department often requires the support of outside counsel, vendors, and other external partners to fulfill its responsibilities. To effectively manage these relationships, it is essential to have transparent processes in place for selecting and managing outside counsel, negotiating contracts and fees, and tracking performance and results. Internship and secondment programs can be valuable tools and provide opportunities for legal professionals who have never worked in a corporate setting to gain practical experience and develop their business acumen to complement their legal skills.

### Financial planning and spend analysis

Financial planning, forecasting, and budgeting are critical elements for the success of a corporate legal department. A legal operations function drives strategic fiscal initiatives to optimize the allocation of resources, manage legal spending, and provide visibility and real-time reporting of the department's budget and variance. This will help the legal team provide the best possible legal advice to the organization while managing its finances responsibly and sustainably.

### Technology and data analytics

A corporate legal department must automate routine tasks and streamline operations by leveraging technology and data analytics to provide a clear picture of the team's activities and achievements. This can free up valuable time for your team to focus on higher-value tasks, such as providing strategic legal advice to the organization. Technology and data analytics can also help identify areas for improvement, enabling corporate legal operations to drive continuous improvement initiatives and improve overall efficiency and competitiveness.

### Project management and practice operations

Project management is vital to ensure that corporate initiatives and tasks are executed efficiently and effectively. A robust practice operations strategy can also help the legal team to improve its data management and governance, enabling it to make informed decisions based on data-driven insights. As the business landscape evolves, corporate legal teams must embrace project management and practice operations to remain competitive and provide value to an enterprise organization.

## Growth and innovation within the corporate legal operations profession

Legal operations and technology have evolved significantly over the past few decades, leading to significant changes in the function of a corporate legal team. Various factors, including technological advances and the increasing importance of data and analytics in decision-making, have driven these changes. One of the primary drivers of the evolution of legal operations has been the expanding use of technology. Legal technology can help teams work more efficiently and effectively and improve their ability to manage and analyze data. Some examples of widely used legal technology in organizations include eDiscovery tools, contract lifecycle management systems, and workflow automation platforms.

Another factor contributing to the evolution of legal operations is the changing nature of the legal industry. In recent years, there has been a trend towards alternative legal service providers, such as legal process outsourcing and using artificial intelligence to automate specific legal tasks. These changes have led to a shift in the role of corporate legal teams, with an increasing focus on strategic thinking and data analytics to inform decision-making. Legal teams are now expected to be able to use technology, dashboards, and metrics to inform their decisions and to track the performance of their operations. This has led to new roles within legal teams, such as data analysts, technical program managers, and solution engineers.

As a result, legal teams are better equipped to meet the challenges of a rapidly changing legal landscape and provide more effective and efficient legal services. Those successful within the legal operations profession have a strong understanding of the legal industry, knowledge of business operations, and the ability to think strategically. Legal operations professionals must be highly organized and able to manage multiple priorities and deadlines. They must also have excellent communication and interpersonal skills, as they will often be working with various stakeholders, including corporate legal teams, outside counsel, and business units.

Legal departments are now seen as integral parts of a corporation's overall strategy, providing legal advice and support in risk management, compliance, and intellectual property management. The rise of technology has also significantly impacted corporate legal operations, with many companies using artificial intelligence, machine learning, and other advanced technologies to streamline their processes and improve efficiency. The history of corporate legal operations reflects the changing needs of businesses in an ever-evolving legal landscape. From their early origins as compliance-focused legal operations departments, the industry has expanded to become a trusted, strategic partner to leaders through meeting the needs of the modern corporation.

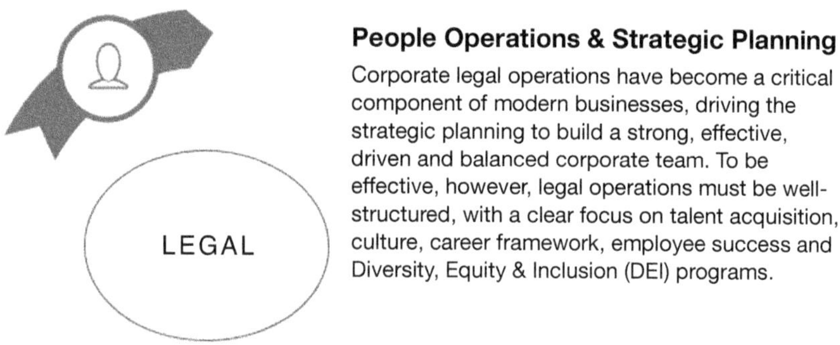


*Figure 1: People operations and strategic planning.*

A critical component of modern businesses, it is important for corporate legal operations to partner with the chief legal officer or general counsel to build a strong, effective, driven, and balanced legal team. Legal teams must be well-structured and focused on talent acquisition, culture, career framework, employee success, and diversity, equity and inclusion (DEI) programs.

A vital aspect of any successful legal operations role is talent acquisition. This involves identifying and attracting the best professionals for the corporation, focusing on hiring individuals who not only possess strong technical skills but also align with the company's culture and values. In conjunction with your legal leadership and human resource business partners, a strategic talent acquisition plan should focus on identifying the skills and experience needed to support the organization's business objectives and creating a recruitment process that attracts and hires top-performing candidates. In the age of remote and hybrid work environments, you must account for the unique needs and challenges – such as the geographic location and maturity – of an organization.

Culture is an essential component of any legal operations strategy, as it sets the tone for the work environment and shapes the behavior of employees. A positive, supportive culture can lead to improved employee satisfaction, greater collaboration and teamwork, and better overall performance. To build a robust legal culture, corporations should focus on creating a workplace environment that values diversity, inclusiveness, and mutual respect where employees feel valued, supported, and empowered.

A well-designed career framework is critical to ensuring the success of your legal team, as it provides employees with clear pathways for growth and development. This framework should include opportunities for professional development, such as training programs and mentorship opportunities, as well as a transparent and fair performance evaluation process. A career framework can ensure that the legal team is aligned with the organization's overall direction and that its work is focused on delivering results that support the broader business strategy.

Companies that invest in a diverse, equitable, and inclusive corporate legal team reap many benefits, including better representation of their customer base, improved problem-solving skills, and more positive company culture. By embracing diversity and inclusiveness, companies can not only meet the needs of their customers but also create a more vibrant and successful workplace. A robust DEI program can help create a workplace culture that values and respects differences while promoting equal opportunities and outcomes for all employees.

People operations and strategic initiatives are critical components of a successful corporate legal department. By prioritizing these areas, companies can ensure that they have a highly skilled and motivated legal team, stay ahead of the curve, and create a positive workplace culture. By investing in talent acquisition, culture, career framework, employee success, and DEI programs, legal operations can create a more vibrant and successful legal department that supports the organization's overall goals.

**Knowledge & Risk Management**

Capture, distribute and effectively use structured and tacit knowledge assets to support an organization's compliance and operational requirements. The goal is to effectively and efficiently manage the vast amounts of information that legal teams are responsible for, improve their decision-making processes, and provide better advice to business stakeholders and regulatory agencies.

*Figure 2: Knowledge and risk management.*

The landscape for corporate legal operations is evolving rapidly, driven by several factors, including increased regulatory requirements, changing technology, and the need for more efficient and effective legal services. One of the critical areas of focus for corporate legal operations today is knowledge management and risk management initiatives. In today's fast-paced business world, corporate legal teams are constantly pressured to provide timely and accurate advice to their organizations. With the increasing amount of information being generated daily, it can be overwhelming for legal teams to keep track of the vast amount of data they manage.

A robust knowledge management program under the guidance of legal operations should involve systematically collecting, organizing, and disseminating information and knowledge within the team. This can include practices such as document management, contract management, and legal research, as well as the use of technology to automate and streamline these processes. Effective knowledge management can improve the accuracy and efficiency of the legal team, reducing the time and effort required to complete tasks and increasing the quality of the work produced. By implementing a knowledge management system, legal teams can access this information quickly and easily, providing better advice to their organizations and supporting their decision-making processes.

Risk management is a critical component of a corporate legal team's responsibilities, and legal operations can play a vital role in supporting these initiatives. By prioritizing risk management initiatives, companies can create a more robust and resilient legal team better equipped to navigate complex legal and regulatory challenges. Legal operations can help to streamline risk management processes to help ensure that the organization can effectively manage risk and protect its interests, such as:

- Monitor and track changes in regulations to ensure that the organization complies with all relevant laws and regulations;
- Partner with compliance, privacy, and other governance practice groups to develop and implement policies and procedures to manage risks, such as data privacy policies, anti-bribery and corruption policies, and conflict of interest policies;
- Conduct regular risk assessments to identify and prioritize risks to the organization and develop strategies to mitigate those risks;
- Utilize technology to automate routine compliance tasks, such as document management and contract analysis, and developing training programs to educate employees on compliance issues; and
- Build crisis management plans to ensure the organization is prepared to respond effectively to potential legal and compliance risks, such as data breaches, product recalls, and fraud.

Corporate legal operations teams must leverage technology and data analytics to manage knowledge and risk to provide valuable insights effectively. This can include using artificial intelligence (AI) and machine learning (ML) tools to automate routine tasks, such as contract analysis and legal research, as well as data analytics to identify and manage risk. Integrating technology and data analytics into the legal operations process can provide a more holistic view of the organization's legal and compliance risks. Practical knowledge and risk management can improve the efficiency and effectiveness of the legal team, protect the organization from potential legal and financial liabilities, and enhance its reputation and competitive position.

*Figure 3: Outside counsel and external initiatives.*

A corporate legal department often requires the support of outside counsel, vendors, and other external partners to fulfil its responsibilities. To effectively manage these relationships, legal operations must document transparent processes for selecting and managing outside counsel, negotiating contracts and fees, and tracking performance and results. Choosing the right outside counsel is critical to the success of any corporate legal team. This requires a clear understanding of the organization's legal needs, as well as an assessment of the qualifications and expertise of the potential outside counsel. To ensure effective management of the relationship, it is important that legal operations establish clear communication channels, set expectations for the scope of work and deliverables, and regularly assess the performance of outside counsel.

Corporate legal operations departments also build relationships with technology providers, consulting firms, and alternative legal service providers (ALSP) to support their business requirements and improve the efficiency and cost-effectiveness of their legal services. When engaging outside counsel or vendors, it is essential to negotiate contracts and fees that are fair and reasonable. This requires a clear understanding of the organization's budget and the services being provided, as well as a negotiation strategy that considers both parties' goals and objectives. Using ALSPs and effective outside counsel management can improve the efficiency and cost-effectiveness of their legal services, access specialized legal expertise, stay ahead of regulatory changes, manage increased workloads, and enhance collaboration with external legal teams.

Internships, externships, and secondment programs can be valuable tools for a corporate legal team to build relationships with outside counsel and other external partners. These programs should also align with your DEI initiatives to create a more inclusive and diverse legal industry. By participating in these programs, corporate legal operations can build stronger relationships with law schools and bar associations, which can help raise their organization's visibility and attract talented legal professionals.

To ensure that the relationship with outside counsel and other vendors meets the organization's needs, it is essential to track performance and results. This can be done through regular assessments, including performance evaluations and invoice audits, and monitoring the effects of legal actions. Practical billing guidelines are essential for managing the costs of outside counsel. They should outline the expectations for billing practices, including the types of expenses that will be reimbursed, the rate structure for legal services, and the process for submitting invoices and accruals.

By implementing these elements, corporate legal operations can effectively manage relationships with outside counsel, vendors, and other external partners. Focus on developing transparent processes for selecting and managing these relationships, negotiating contracts and fees, leveraging internship and secondment programs, and tracking performance and results through billing guidelines. By doing so, the legal team can ensure that it has the support and resources to fulfil its responsibilities and provide the best possible legal advice to the organization.

*Figure 4: Financial planning and spend analysis.*

Financial planning, forecasting, and budgeting initiatives are critical components of today's evolving landscape for corporate legal operations. Legal departments must effectively manage their finances to maintain a competitive edge, starting with a clear understanding of their financial performance and future financial needs. This requires a robust financial planning and forecasting process that helps to identify future expenses, allocate resources, and set achievable financial targets.

One of the key challenges facing corporate legal operations is balancing the demands of delivering high-quality legal services with the need to operate responsibly financially. This requires a deep understanding of the financial implications of the various legal initiatives and programs being pursued and the ability to make informed decisions about how resources should be allocated. Legal operations and financial business partners start by defining the department's budget and financial goals for the upcoming year. Once the plans have been established, legal operations and financial partners work together to develop a detailed budget for the department.

Managing legal spend is a critical component of legal operations' financial planning and budgeting initiatives, requiring a clear understanding of the costs associated with the legal department's operations, including personnel costs, outside counsel fees, and other expenses. Effective spending management also requires a commitment to ongoing cost containment and reduction efforts. To achieve these goals, corporate legal operations must have access to accurate and up-to-date financial data and the tools and processes necessary to analyze that data effectively. Data analytics, e-billing software, and other financial management tools can help legal departments better understand their financial performance, identify areas for improvement, and make informed decisions about allocating resources.

Performance metrics are critical for measuring the effectiveness of the legal department's operations. This includes metrics such as the cost per matter, the average cost per hour of outside counsel, and the ratio of in-house to outside counsel spend. By tracking these metrics, legal operations can make informed decisions about resource allocation and spending and identify opportunities for cost savings. Variance reporting is essential for monitoring and managing the legal department's finances, providing real-time visibility into the actual versus budgeted costs for each expense category to quickly identify and address any discrepancies.

In today's rapidly changing business landscape, it is increasingly important for corporate legal operations to be agile and flexible. Close collaboration between legal operations and internal financial business partners is critical to the success of the legal department and the overall enterprise. This requires a deep understanding of the financial implications of different legal initiatives and the ability to respond quickly to new demands and changing market conditions. By working together to plan and assess the department budget and financial performance, legal operations and financial partners can ensure that the legal department is operating in a manner that supports the enterprise's objectives, is financially responsible, and is sustainable for the long-term.

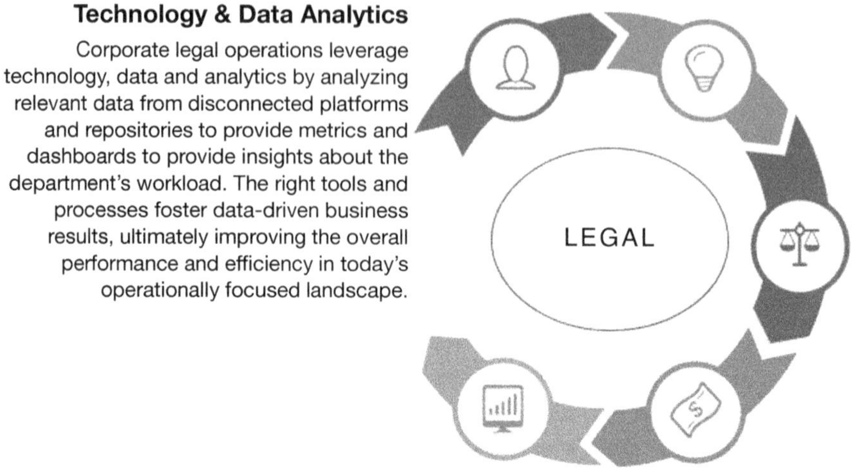


*Figure 5: Technology and data analytics.*

Corporate legal operations must leverage technology to analyze relevant data from disconnected platforms and repositories to provide metrics and dashboards, ultimately providing insights about the department's workload. The right tools and processes foster data-driven business results, ultimately improving overall performance and efficiency in today's operationally focused landscape. As the business landscape continues to evolve, legal operations must embrace technology and data analytics to remain competitive and provide value to the organization.

A corporate legal department's success heavily depends on the tools they use to manage legal operations. This includes legal practice management software, contract lifecycle management solutions, eDiscovery tools, and other operational applications. The selection and implementation of system tools are critical components of using technology to support the work of a corporate legal department. This includes evaluating available technology solutions, conducting a cost-benefit analysis, and working closely with IT to implement the chosen solution. The legal team should also develop a clear implementation plan and work closely with business stakeholders to ensure that the solution is implemented smoothly and efficiently.

Artificial intelligence (AI) is a rapidly growing field that has the potential to revolutionize the way in-house legal teams work. A key area in which AI is making a significant impact in corporate legal operations is contract review and analysis. Traditionally, lawyers have reviewed and analyzed contracts manually, which can be time-consuming and error-prone. With the advent of AI, legal teams can now automate reviewing and analyzing contracts. AI algorithms can quickly scan contracts for key clauses and identify potential risks, allowing lawyers to focus on high-level strategic tasks rather than routine contract analysis. This can lead to faster and more accurate contract analysis, helping to minimize risk and increase efficiency.

Additionally, AI-powered chatbots and virtual assistants are used to answer common legal questions and guide employees. These tools can handle routine questions and provide your corporate workforce with quick and accurate answers, reducing the workload of in-house legal teams and improving the speed of response.

Dashboard analytics is a powerful tool for visualizing and interpreting data generated through the front door of legal operations. Dashboards can provide real-time visibility into the organization's legal performance, including matter volumes, costs, and case outcomes. This information can be used to identify areas for improvement and support data-driven decision-making within the legal team. For example, if the average length of time to negotiate a contract is increasing, it may indicate a need for additional training or a review of negotiation strategies. Similarly, if legal service costs are increasing, consider alternative service providers or negotiate more favorable rates with existing providers.

Technology and data analytics play a critical role in supporting the needs of an in-house legal team, regardless of company size. By implementing the right tools and processes, the legal team can drive data-driven business results, improve its overall efficiency and competitiveness, and provide better legal advice to the organization. As these technologies continue to evolve and mature, we can expect to see even more innovative applications in the legal industry, helping transform the way legal teams work and deliver value to their organizations.

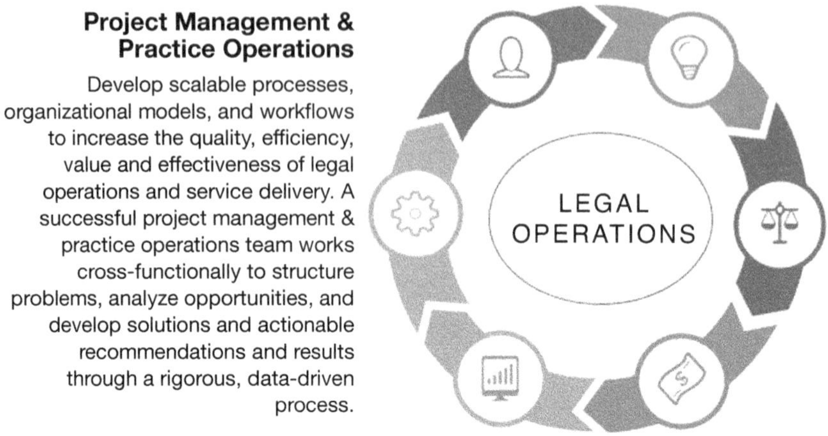


*Figure 6: Project management and practice operations.*

Many legal departments have turned to project management and practice operations initiatives to achieve these goals. The legal team can improve its efficiency and competitiveness by implementing effective processes and systems. The landscape of project management initiatives within a corporate legal operations department has undergone significant change in recent years. As legal teams look to deliver value to their organizations, they have turned to project management as a key tool to achieve these goals. In the past, project management within corporate legal operations was often informal and ad hoc. To support these initiatives, many legal teams have adopted formal methodologies such as Agile, Lean, and Six Sigma to improve their project management practices by reducing costs and minimizing risks.

Along with the adoption of formal project management certifications, technology has also played a significant role in shaping the landscape of project management initiatives within corporate legal operations. Legal teams leverage project management software and tools to help them manage cross-functional programs, prioritize tasks, and allocate resources. Additionally, technology has enabled legal teams to automate many of their processes, reducing the risk of human error and improving the speed and accuracy of their work.

In addition to project management, efficient operational initiatives are critical for an in-house legal team's success. By implementing effective processes and systems, the legal team can streamline its operations, automate routine tasks, and free up valuable time for higher-value tasks, such as providing strategic legal advice to the organization. Another key trend in the evolving landscape of program and practice operation initiatives within corporate legal operations is the development of standard operating procedures (SOPs) and best practices. By establishing SOPs and best practices, legal teams can ensure that their work is consistent, high-quality, and in line with the broader objectives of the enterprise. Efficient operational protocols can also help the legal team to improve its data management and governance, enabling it to make informed decisions based on data-driven insights.

The landscape of project management and practice operations initiatives within corporate legal operations has undergone significant change in recent years. Legal teams are adopting formal project management methodologies, leveraging technology, and emphasizing collaboration and communication to improve their project management practices. As these initiatives continue to evolve and mature, we can expect to see even more innovative solutions emerge, helping legal teams to deliver greater value to their organizations.

## The modern era of corporate legal operations

The corporate legal operations profession has undergone a rapid transformation in recent years, with growth and innovation that has been nothing short of astonishing. Legal operations professionals are now seen as key business partners, bringing a fresh, results-oriented perspective to the legal function. The future of the corporate legal operations profession is bright and full of opportunities. As businesses seek new and innovative ways to optimize their operations, the demand for legal operations professionals with solid business acumen and a deep understanding of technology will only grow. In addition, as the legal landscape becomes increasingly complex, the role of legal operations professionals in risk management and compliance will become even more critical.

One potential area of growth for the corporate legal operations profession is using artificial intelligence (AI) and machine learning (ML) technologies. These technologies have the potential to revolutionize the way legal work is done, from legal research and document review to contract analysis and risk assessment. Legal operations professionals with a deep understanding of these technologies and how to apply them in a business context will be in high demand in the coming years.

We are witnessing the legal operations profession grow and mature – shifting from a big question mark about the profession to hiring legal operations roles that add value and drive a clear strategic vision aligned with legal leadership and business stakeholders. The key to success for a legal operations professional is maintaining a strong relationship with the general counsel and being in tune with the ever-changing business priorities of the organization. Legal operations teams are now shifting priorities from solely tactical administrative duties to strategic areas such as process improvements emphasizing consistency (workflow automation), metrics and data analytics, outside counsel spend and diversity programs, and risk management initiatives.

Now more than ever, legal operations are actively looking to partner with law firms, alternative legal service providers, and legal technology vendors to discuss practical solutions and strategies focused on collaboration, process efficiency, and operational excellence in delivering legal services. With the increasing complexity of the business world and legal landscape, and the rise of technology, legal operations professionals are poised to play a critical role in helping companies navigate these challenges and succeed in the future. The future of this fast-paced, business-oriented industry is bright and full of opportunities for those willing to embrace change and stay ahead of the curve.

# Chapter 10: Artificial Intelligence

*By Joshua Walker, CEO, System.Legal*

## Basic principles

"Failstorming." That's a management philosophy my friend and publisher Ed Walters, CEO of Fastcase, uses for new technology projects (and *all* projects, in fact). "Failstorming" is the opposite of its more optimistic cousin, "brainstorming". According to Walters, an experienced project manager will likely know, ex ante, all the areas where a prospective project is likely to fail. Addressing those "danger points" in advance helps build successful projects and business outcomes. I would suggest that the "failstorming" metaphor is precisely the right place to begin with legal AI projects.

In my book, *On Legal AI (OLAI)*,[1] we cover the doctrinal framework for legal AI. It's a kind of operational and legal "cookbook", building and/or using enterprise legal systems. If you need doctrine and detailed case studies, that's a great place to start. For example, understanding what a "confusion matrix" is may be essential not merely to using and building AI, but to understanding the law. Ditto for real life applications. Here, we have to be a bit more… condensed.

First, we are going to identify some "archetypal failure modes" for legal AI – how people typically mess these things up. (And yes, there are identifiable "Fail Clusters" or FCs.)

Second, we are going to outline three basic flavors of "AI" (to be defined and fleshed out below) – including information extraction, analytics (including something called "predictive modeling"), and generation (or "generative AI").

Third, we are going to briefly address how to achieve collective and individual success in legal AI – kind of the *opposite* of the FCs.

These case studies – successes and failures alike – are, as advertised, based on real life. For the most part, they are things I have personally seen over 25 years in legal AI and legal practice. The entailed (or "synthesized"?) examples range from basic mathematical modeling to deployment in Supreme Courts, and other fora, from solos to giant, international law firms, from start-ups to large enterprise, from US federal and state contexts to other countries, from public to private sector and back again.

When my colleagues and I were initially engaged in the type of work that is the subject of this book, pure academic theory, and most business books, were essentially useless.

What was valuable were stories from people that had actually built things themselves. Experiential narrative outclasses theory because life, and AI, are never as simple, nor as linear, as one might think at "Time Zero" (i.e., the beginning of a project). The reality is ever more complex than the model, and, used wisely, AI *helps us* deal with that entropy. Stories about navigating the entropy of real life provide useful background for entrepreneurs, academic researchers, and yes, even legal professionals.

Doing anything well is hard. Doing anything well automatically is automatically a step function harder than that. (Though, if you succeed, the rewards and, particularly, the social value, may reflect the difficulty.) This book is written by people that have engaged in this precise struggle – creating and successfully deploying legal automata. So, for starters, congratulations on getting it. You can learn from our mistakes as well as the things that have gone well. This will be valuable whether you are an AI user or creator. (We are all both.)

However, if I can impart one basic principle from the get-go, especially in a technology-based book, it's this. You should be agnostic as to technology. Perhaps that's an unpopular opinion amongst my brethren. But I stand by it.

The fundamental question you need to ask yourself is: *How can I realistically help my client?* This can include interstitial clients, like a law firm, but it should ultimately consider the actual client – the end-user of a real product or service.

*How do you calculate Return on Investment (RoI) on a project? Did you include the cost of change?*

One of the most pernicious failures modes I've seen in Silicon Valley is "technarcissism" – people falling in love with their own tech (and, alas, drowning in it, from a business perspective). The Valley is *littered* with all kinds of "cool" tech and product that no one wanted to buy, and that no one *would have* wanted to buy in any realistic variant of the universe. See FC's, below.

What pressing, bleeding, *urgent* problem are you uniquely addressing? If you have a good answer to this question, you are halfway to a sale. If you don't, you may be spending 20 million dollars developing yourself off a cliff. (And yes, the latter thing happens all the time. Maybe *most* of the time.) If you can sell to a small group that is incredibly passionate about your product, so the better. Find that group. Try to sell your product before you build it.

Second basic principle. Essentially, all things on the earth – math, empirical data, automation, and, yes, even that bedevilingly-difficult to qualify and corral, that amorphous, hyperactive morass called "artificial intelligence" – are all useful for solving problems, for helping people. Math doesn't need you to fall in love with it for it to be useful. It just is. So is any well-formed empirical analytica. In fact, you can't legally compete anymore in a quantitative and empirical vacuum. The world changed.

But, again, on the other hand, this isn't a religion, or a tulip festival, or a rave. To build great AI you need to start with a human need. *Who am I helping? Why? What's the RoI over how they are solving this problem now? Is it worth the change? Can I prove that and sell it to them?* (Yes, if you are building for government or non-profit, it's the same calculus, the same questions. In fact, the above questions are more essential because your subsidy and/or monopoly will insulate you from sense if you don't get direct user and beneficiary feedback.)

## Legal AI fail clusters (negative archetypes)

Books. Actual books. With words. Words side by side. Prose even!

There is no more powerful testimonial to the value of books than the flight trajectories of those that hate them. Contemporaneously, for example, Sam Bankman-Fried, Kanye / Ye West, and others in their respective circles, have *gleefully* described how stupid books are, weighing in (inveighing in?) on alternatives. *Make a blog instead! Or a video! Books are useless. What a waste of time to write or read!!*

The net social harm, and contemporaneous career flight trajectories, of these same individuals comprise the best possible testament to *why* books are so essential to avoiding historical pitfalls, crashes, and general apocalyptica (or even personal apocalyptica). These individual "anti-testaments" personify why books (a) are an essential substrate of a functioning society, and (b) entail something that (present) AI cannot provide – common sense, even "wisdom". (As we will discuss below, contemporaneous AI may generate prose beatifically, *but it does not understand what it is saying*. Ergo: Be cautious. See Aesop on AI.)

You can learn from others. Historical patterns reveal "grooves" in the ways to get things done successfully and/or catastrophically. It's true of Silicon Valley companies too. These things may be learned at the speed of prose (but not at the speed of discrete start-ups).

We already have *multiple decades* of data on legal AI projects and related systems. Learn their patterns – whether with respect to the people, the automata, or their chaotic admixture. Learn the "grooves", the signs and signals, of both the upsides and the downsides. Below follow a few.

This is what AI does; it learns patterns. Its progenitors must as well, on a macro level.

Again, the ways in which people screw up legal technology projects generally, and legal AI projects specifically, tend to fall into specific historical "molds". You can read about them at length and your leisure – but since you likely have none of the latter (being "legal"), I'm just going to "brief" them, below. See *OLAI* for detailed examples.

## Examples of legal AI fail clusters

### Innovation theatre

This is certainly a popular way to fail at legal AI. "Innovation theatre" occurs where, under pressure from an external (e.g. law firm) or internal client (e.g. CEO, marketing), a legal group develops some showpiece project that doesn't really move the needle for any actual client. These projects are like fireworks – in spectacle and long-term effect – rather than major firm infrastructure.

To paraphrase a former aerospace CEO of mine, *"There is no more [salient] indicator of likely innovation failure than the inclusion of the word 'innovation' in the title of the entity."*

In other words, overall, there is an inverse relationship between innovation marketing and effect. Pretension is the thief of action.

Lesson: Under-promise and over-deliver. Focus on client RoI, not on how fancy or adept your group is. Who are you helping? Why? How much?

### The engineer's hubris

A second promising, battle-tested, and highly efficient way to fail at legal AI is to keep lawyers out of the entire productization cycle – from client requirements intake, to design, to development, to legal data characterization/collation, to deployment and product iteration.

Just ignore the domain. (Don't even bother to look up what "sui generis" means. We don't have time!) Have engineers run everything (because they get stuff done). Don't bother with quality legal review of the data that is powering your legal AI. Don't bother to understand the special nature, or ethical requirements, of the client–attorney relationship. It's just data!

Ignoring legal nuance helps burn up capital while insuring that nothing you build will be actually useful or marketable in the real world. Great for a capital inferno that warms our egos and placates our implacable ire towards the legal profession.

*Lesson:* Embed lawyers – as contributors and, ideally, leaders – at every single layer of the process and integrate all. (Lawyers must adapt as well. Creating is harder than killing a deal.) Hide them if you must. Camouflage them as engineers. Have them drink beer or claret or tea with the engineering and product requirements teams. But integrate attorneys.

One of the things we learn about AI is that AI is just math + data (operationalized math, yes, but really just math). If your data is garbage, your concomitant AI is also garbage / Ye Childe O' Garbage. Your legal data cannot be non-garbage if you don't have legal experts curating it. Good legal AI requires good legal curation by good legal experts.

## Data-law equivalence fallacy

Law is not data. It may be *reflected* in data, but the "law" is not equivalent to the snowflakes that show up in a data store. Legal data is therefore not the *same* as physical or medical data picked up by an AI's sensor network. (This is one of the reasons why the above is such an efficient way to fail.)

For example, a legally-dumb sensor may imply that the words "claim construction order" or "clause X" mean that it is precisely that.

Not so! It can be mere reference! It may be superseded by an Article III judge, or on appeal, or over-ridden by statute. You need a legal expert to determine the legal state. The data are just "snowflakes" that let legal build the "law graph".

Lesson: Use lawyers / top experts to *extract* legal classification / reality from legal data. The latter is not equivalent to the former.

## Legal narcissism

The opposite world / inverse of the engineer's hubris is the lawyer's narcissism. We, the lawyers, are *incredibly* narcissistic, mayhap ostrich like.

Pretending that law is completely immune to math / empiricism helps consultants and accountants take over the legal profession. The latter are already preferred – vastly – by enterprise for contract review (which *should* be a predominantly legal function) because they are fast, know how to acquire companies, and… are fast. Lawyers need to get their heads out of the sand to compete. It's true that fancy law firms believe that large-scale contract review is beneath them. But they could increase their addressable market ten times if they used AI. More importantly, the legal profession is addressing a tiny fraction of actual human (and enterprise) legal need.

## Technarcissism

Addressed earlier in this chapter, the "Technarcissim" FC is necessarily neither an engineering nor a legal foible. It is when we fall in love with our own technology or product idea – regardless of whether the enthralling beauty is from legal, technical, or some intertwined feature.

To be great at product development, your empathy must exceed your ego. And your calculus of client RoI must be brutally honest, continuously.

The remedy to – or, more accurately, the "preventative" for – the Technarcissism FC is design thinking, client empathy, and proper UX testing (and retesting, and re-retesting, and re-re-retesting). Better yet: If you can sell something *ex ante creatio*, even for a small amount, that's a great signal.

## Business hubris

This is a variant of engineer's hubris. This is where the businesspeople have taken over a formerly successful legal AI. Egos abound in VC, general investment, and MBA land just as much as in JD land; they just smell differently. To the other, the outsider is always more piquant.

*Lesson:* Use business acumen but let the legal craft lead legal AI. Law is a unique domain. Don't pretend we are selling toothpaste or making candy / candy blockchains.

## Flavors of legal AI

*Law* is the art of regulating human behavior, state, and relations.
*Engineering* is the art of getting things done.
*Legal engineering* is the art of getting things done legally, and legal things done.
*Artificial intelligence* is software that does analysis.

## Information extraction

Our base context for AI is, essentially, data mining, or "information extraction". Using IE, we can, after, say:

- Conducting top notch legal review of historical legal events (e.g., litigation events filings / docket events / manifest discovery / doctrinal nodes / opinions / statutes / rules / etc.; ditto for contract; ditto for regulation; etc.),
- Deploy the AI trained on such data corpus to scale that review times *n*, to cover millions of filings / contracts / terms.

We like to say that every (legal) AI is unique, like a child, because the composition, functionality, and classification patterns of any AI depend on the data upon which it was trained, or otherwise constituted. (This is true even for training done without direct human involvement.) This means that if you are running a legal AI system on data classes on which it has never trained (never had reliable and precise legal determinations and classifications to learn from), your model may produce garbage decisions / responses. The data corpus, and the policy decisions / network upon which your AI relies, is determinative to AI functionality and User RoI.

## Analytics

Once we have a base of empirical data, we can use AI – again, essentially operationalized math – to do predictive modeling and other advanced forms of analytics.

But, like alcohol, the word "prediction" should be used abstemiously – at least in work contexts – and *especially* where client interest is involved.

Certain folks may do a great job predicting Supreme Court and other outcomes… for a time, anyway. But, generally speaking, predicting what sophisticated humans will decide in the immediate future – especially given new data and new ground conditions – is a complex enterprise, especially at the trial court or entity level. It gets infinitely (yes, mayhap, literally "infinitely") more complex when the decisors are aware that their decisions are being heavily observed, scrutinized, and "predicted". (No one likes being predictable. They will mess you / your AI *up*…)

As with the Heisenberg Uncertainty Principle, overt outcome prediction itself may skew the outcome. Analogous things may happen with hedge funds and high-speed traders using AI – *the other active players may distort a previously "predictable", human-only environment into something less predictable*. You can see how AI makes AI less predictable. System complexity compounds.

Transparency in general, or "sunlight", historically has strong (positive) effects on legal systems of all varieties. For example, it allows us to cross-correlate legislative intent with economic and legal procedural reality. It shows us anomalies, including where "equivalent" cases / procedures / transactions get wildly different outcomes, depending on things unrelated to the merits. For example, damages or criminal sentencing may vary wildly across jurisdictions.

Making the data truly transparent allows appeals courts (and/or legislatures) to improve critical standards, harmonize systems, improve citizen outcomes. It can also, interstitially, help improve legal procedure itself. One judge we helped learned that holding procedure "X" early in the litigation correlated very strongly to early settlement. Our findings correlated with his judicial instincts (his "hypothesis"), but with hard data he could credibly recommend advancing procedure X to every judge in the nation. This, in turn, may increase business and social utility.

One of my favorite things to do is take hard-core legal data and cross-correlate it to non-legal data corpuses (social benefit / utility, finance, you name it; ideally equally reliable data sets). You can then run prediction models on these things and even (theoretically) tweak legal procedure to improve social or business outcomes.

Like meta-analysis in the medical research world, comparing and cross-correlating completely different data sets with heterogenous data classes is not for the faint of heart. One is often comparing apples to orangutans. So it is important to be able to zero in on the precise data extracted of any and all kinds observed. And, generally, *assume all data are false until proven otherwise*. But we have been able to build myriad useful products by (carefully) synthesizing, and cross-leveraging, legal with business and/or social data. Humility and rigorous empiricism can empower you to create significant benefits from even small interdisciplinary projects.

### Generation

At the time of writing, there is a sea change in the public's perception of AI and law (and just about everything else) because of the 2023 release of new "generative AI" – chatbots that can produce seemingly competent college and high school essays, (bad) poetry, good / grammatical prose, and so on. Even the most techno-jaded law firm partners have to wonder about the potential for these tools to change – in one way or another, for good or ill – the practice of law.

In truth, AI tools have been generating complaints, constraints, and sundry other legal product for years now. It's not super public at present. But this has been happening all over the world. Interface technologies for legal marketing are also relatively commonplace – routing people with legal need (demand) to lawyers with legal answers or skills (supply).

Generative AI will increasingly provide drafting tools and "advisors" (flagging potential anomalies and issues – from judges to negotiation points) for attorneys to cross-check, edit, leverage, and file / transmit. This cross-check element is important for the following reason: *None of the present generative AI tools on the market understand what they are saying.*

They are just doing "predictive mapping" between one set of text (the user's prompt) and another set of text (the AI's answer/output – which is just a probabilistic concatenation of the raw data it has been trained upon against such user prompt text). In other words, the generative AI is "BSing", and doing so masterfully. So well, in fact, that an uninformed user may have no idea that she or he is being advised off a cliff, or filed into oblivion.

It's like giving an AI robotic mandibles, then letting it do brain surgery based on some patterns in past manual surgeries. It may work fine, *most of the time* – but tell that to unlucky Aunt Edna (another kind of *ex ante*).

When faced with an anomaly that is not fully covered in the data corpus with which it has been fed, it may make material errors. In other words, understanding *why* we take certain actions, or not, as attorneys, is often a determinant in the outcomes we can deliver (or avoid) – and *no present AI has any idea as to the why… of anything*.

Understanding how, and under what conditions, a legal AI is likely to fail, is an art. And you, or your group more generally, must now master it. Like it or not, that is now part of the *legal* art.

Again, we should not be like the cynics who pooh pooh every technical AI breakthrough. Well-crafted legal AI has and may continue to provide great and amazing benefits, and the present technicians – especially since they are now *competing* for your business, and all your attention – should be commended for progress of all shapes and sizes. These are powerful tools.

But people shouldn't brain themselves, like Phineas Gage, on iron assumptions about AI. We should start with percipient, and ever-evolving foreknowledge of AI's limitations. We should use our heads, and our professional care, to improve outcomes – not as inertial dampeners.

In short, generative AI may be a great precursor of, and assistant to, legal work. But it is not yet the end – either of the profession, or for the end-user. Generative legal AI works best when paired with highly competent legal IE and analytics (*because* it does not actually know or understand anything). So legal acumen *before* generation is as important – and perhaps more scalable – than legal acumen after the fact.

Lastly, we must, under our legal ethics guidelines, use AI to (a) increase access to legal services (scale, cost reduction per unit of legal work) and (b) improve quality. AI is best served as a catalyst to law. Not an antidote thereto.

## Positive use cases

There are a number of positive use cases covered throughout OLAI, as well as a practical framework for building or using legal AI. See, for example, the discussion of EDEN: Empirical, Design, Evolution, Net. That being noted, there aren't very many successful legal AI use cases yet, in the grand scheme of things. We are careening between arrogances and narcissisms of one kind or another.

Sometimes, we think generic AI products work for legal, when there are plenty of *sui generis* reasons why they don't. Or, at least, trusting something that is textually accurate 80 percent of the time becomes incredibly dangerous for the unlucky 20 percent (the Aunt Ednas).

Sometimes people assume their English legal AI will work anywhere, regardless of jurisdiction or language. But, generally, everything is entropy. There are an almost unlimited number of things that can destroy legal AI's efficacy. You have to systematically root every single one of them out – from basic engineering to basic data quality to advanced computer science and cutting-edge level, world class legal review.

Most people (or most VCs?) don't have the time / money / patience to be sufficiently systematic for legal engineering. Legal is therefore slower to evolve than it should be, given its social and economic importance.

Sometimes the hubris of lawyers, or the opiate-like effect of steadily increasing revenues for purely traditional practices, effectively lobotomizes our evolution. That will send the profession towards another kind of cliff.

Instead of listing positive use cases here, I suggest that we are just beginning. We should make better ones through the artifice and movement of this book, sharing whatever shareable within the legal tech community. *That* would be great social, as well as artificial, intelligence.

### *References*

1 *On Legal AI*, Joshua Walker, Full Court Press, 2019.

Chapter 11:

# Blockchain and blockchain-enabled applications in law – a lawyer's guide

*By Olga V. Mack, vice president and CEO, Parley Pro*

The world is changing. We live in the digital age, with new technologies emerging daily and fundamentally changing our lives. Perhaps one of the most transformative of these new technologies is blockchain. One way or another, it will transform how we live, work, and transact.

Blockchain is a distributed database that allows for secure, transparent, and tamper-proof transactions between two or more parties in a peer-to-peer (P2P) – without an intermediary – manner. Its applications are endless, and it has the potential to revolutionize many industries, including law.

This is a guide for lawyers who want to understand blockchain, how it could be applied in law, and how it can enhance law practice.

## What is blockchain?

Before diving into blockchain's applications in law, it is essential to understand what blockchain is and how it works.

At its core, blockchain is a distributed database. It is a type of distributed ledger technology (DLT). This means that, instead of storing the transaction details on one centralized database (as is the case with most traditional transactions), the data is spread across a network of computers (or "nodes"). Each time a transaction is made, it is recorded on every node in the network. The growing lists of records, called "blocks", are securely linked using cryptography.

Each block contains (1) a cryptographic hash of the previous block, (2) a timestamp, and (3) transaction data. This way, each block contains information about the previous block. This makes blockchain transactions irreversible. That is why blockchains are secure by design.

Blockchains are typically managed by the P2P computer network. Nodes collectively follow a consensus algorithm protocol to add and validate new transaction blocks.

This decentralized structure has several advantages.

First, it makes the data more secure, as there is no single point of failure that can be exploited by hackers. To tamper with the data, one would need to hack into every node in the network, which is virtually impossible.

Second, it makes the data transparent. Because each transaction is recorded on every node, anyone can view the entire history of a particular asset (like a house or a piece of land). This transparency can help to prevent fraud and corruption.

Finally, it makes the data tamper-proof. Once a transaction is recorded on the blockchain, it cannot be changed or deleted. This immutability is one of blockchain's most valuable features.

## How does blockchain work?

When a transaction is made, it is bundled up into a "block" with other recent transactions. Each block contains a unique cryptographic code known as a "hash", which links it to the previous block.

This chain of blocks is stored on every node in the network. So, if someone wanted to tamper with a particular transaction, they would not only have to change that transaction in the block, but they would also have to change the hash of that block and every subsequent block in the chain. This is virtually impossible, which is why blockchain is so secure.

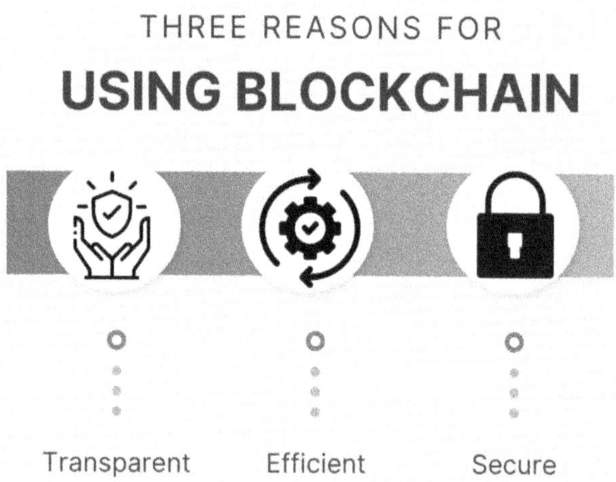


*Figure 1: Reasons to use blockchain.*

## Why use blockchain?

Before we explore the various applications of blockchain, it is first essential to understand why you want to use it.

From what we have covered thus far, it is clear why blockchain is valuable in any industry where there is a need for transparency and trust. For example, blockchain could track the provenance of a piece of art or goods. By recording each transaction on the blockchain, you create a complete history of the artwork that would be impossible to forge.

Another reason to use blockchain is that it is very efficient. With no need for a central authority to verify or approve transactions, they can be processed much faster than traditional transactions. For example, a blockchain-based system could be used to settle stock trades in near real-time instead of the two days it currently takes.

Finally, blockchain is often used for its increased security over traditional databases. As mentioned, blockchain is distributed across a network of computers, meaning there is no single point of failure that can be exploited by hackers, and it is very difficult for data to be corrupted or deleted.

## Blockchain-enabled applications

Now that we've covered blockchain basics, let's look at how it can be used.

### Application 1: Much more intelligent contracts and contract analysis

Blockchain can create smart contracts, a self-executing code based on if-then logic, written in code and stored on the blockchain. They can be executed automatically without the need for human intervention. Thus, they can transform an asset into a programmable asset.

Smart contracts have several advantages. Some of the most important are listed below:

- *They are more efficient.* Smart contracts can be executed automatically and in seconds without human involvement. This can save a lot of time and money. For instance, if you are buying a house, the whole process could be completed in a matter of minutes rather than the months it currently takes. During the 2008 financial crisis, much money was lost due to delays caused by the slow manual processing of paper-based contracts. With smart contracts, this would not have been an issue. An additional benefit is that, while traditional paper contracts can be easily altered, smart contracts are stored on the blockchain, so they cannot be changed or deleted after they are created.
- *They are more secure.* As discussed, the blockchain is a decentralized database spread across a computer network, ensuring no one weakness is exploitable by hackers. Smart contracts on the blockchain are executed automatically, eliminating the need for a third party (such

as a bank or a lawyer) to act as an intermediary. This makes the process more efficient and reduces opportunities for fraud and corruption. Consider, for example, a situation where you want to buy a house. With a traditional contract, you must go through a real estate agent, who contacts the seller. Then, the agent draws up a contract and sends it to both parties for approval. This slow and cumbersome process leaves room for human error and fraud. With a smart contract, the whole process is automated. You simply send the appropriate amount of money to the contract, which executes the sale and transfers ownership of the house to you. This would all happen in seconds, independent of any human involvement.

- *They are more transparent.* Storing these contracts on the blockchain makes them fully transparent. Anyone can view the entire history of a particular contract. This stands in contrast to traditional paper contracts, which are often obscured and inaccessible. This transparency could help to reduce fraud and corruption, as it would be immediately apparent if someone tried to change a contract.
- *They are fairer.* Smart contracts are executed automatically and in seconds, without human intervention. This means they are less likely to be biased or influenced by human emotions because all decisions are automated and self-execute when certain conditions are met. This contrasts traditional paper contracts, often drawn up by lawyers or third parties. These contracts can easily be biased in favor of one party. In addition, smart contracts can be programmed to include certain conditions that must be met before they can be executed. For example, a contract could specify that the payment is automatically remitted when certain goods are delivered in good condition. This would help to ensure that both parties are treated fairly.
- *They have a wide range of applications.* Smart contracts can be used for various applications, including financial transactions, voting, and managing supply chains. For instance, smart contracts could automatically manage a product's supply chain. The contract could specify that the product can only be shipped if it is delivered to the customer within a certain timeframe. This would help to ensure that the product is not damaged or lost during transit. In addition, smart contracts could be used to create a decentralized marketplace, allowing buyers and sellers to connect with each other directly without the need for a third party such as eBay or Amazon.

As you can see, smart contracts have the potential to revolutionize the way we do business. They are more secure, transparent, and fair than traditional paper contracts. Plus, they have a broad and ever-increasing range of uses.

### Application 2: Streamlined payments in legal instruments and litigation/settlement

In the past, making payments in legal instruments and litigation/settlement has been a slow and cumbersome process. This is because the process often requires the involvement of banks or lawyers. With blockchain, payments can be made directly between parties without needing third-party involvement. This would streamline the process and make it much faster and more efficient.

Here's how it would work:

1. Party A and Party B agree to the terms of a legal instrument or settlement.When making payments, they can do so directly without needing a bank or lawyer. The blockchain platform will take care of the rest.
2. The blockchain platform records the terms of the agreement and processes the payment. Even if one of the parties defaults on the agreement, the payment will still be processed and recorded on the blockchain. This provides a degree of security and peace of mind for both parties.

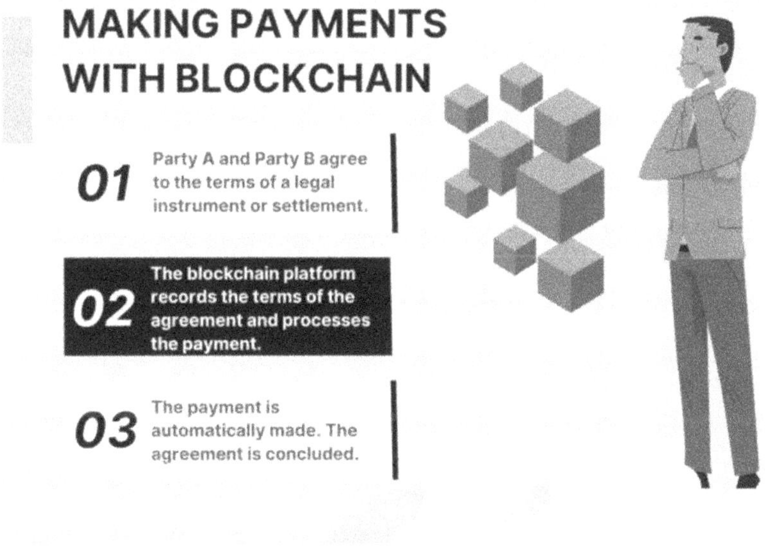


*Figure 2: Making payments with blockchain.*

3. The payment is made, and the agreement is concluded. This process is much faster and more efficient than the traditional way of making payments in legal instruments and litigation/settlement. It would also save on costs, as there would be no need to involve third parties.

When it comes to streamlining payments, blockchain can help solve several problems, addressing such negative characteristics as:

- Slow and cumbersome process;
- Need for third-party involvement;
- Defaults on payment;
- High costs; and
- Time-consuming process.

*How to implement blockchain in streamlining payments*

There are multiple platforms you can use to achieve streamlined, more efficient payments, including:

- Blockchain platforms that support smart contracts. When making payments, the terms of the agreement can be encoded into a smart contract, automating the process.
- Blockchain platforms that support tokenization. With tokenization, payments can be made with digital tokens, which would be recorded on the blockchain.
- Blockchain platforms that support atomic swaps, a cryptocurrency exchange between two parties that wish to exchange tokens from different blockchains. With atomic swaps, two parties can exchange tokens without needing a third party.
- Blockchain platforms that support off-chain payments. Off-chain transactions occur on a cryptocurrency network that moves the value outside the blockchain.
- Blockchain platforms that support both smart contracts and tokenization. With this combination, payments can be made with digital tokens, which would be recorded on the blockchain.

These are just some of the ways to implement blockchain in streamlining payments. There are many other ways to do so, and the best way would depend on the specific needs of the parties involved.

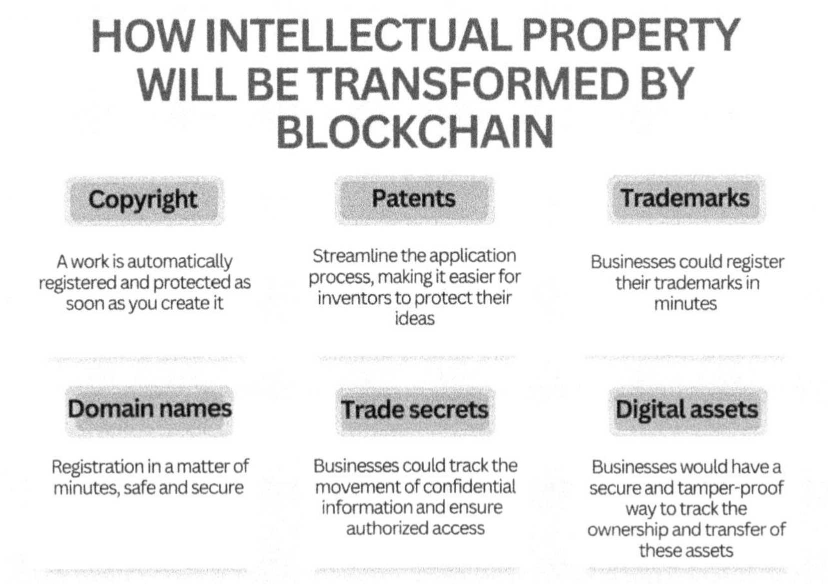


*Figure 3: How intellectual property will be transformed by blockchain.*

## Application 3: Intellectual property will be transformed

The way we think about intellectual property will be transformed by blockchain technology. For example, the registration and enforcement of copyrights could change. Additionally, new types of intellectual property, such as digital art and music, could be protected by blockchain-based smart contracts.

Some commentators have even suggested that the concept of ownership could be called into question by blockchain-based platforms allowing users to sell or lease digital assets. For example, on a platform like Ethereum, users can create and trade digital tokens representing ownership of physical assets like real estate, art, or other objects.

So far, these kinds of applications are still in their early stages. But, as technology matures, we can see a significant shift in how we think about intellectual property.

### *1. Copyright*

Your work is automatically copyrighted the moment you create it. To enforce your copyright, however, you must register it with the government. This process can be costly and time-consuming.

With a blockchain-based copyright system, your work can be automatically registered and protected as soon as you create it. Therefore, if someone tries to steal or plagiarize your work, you could use the blockchain to prove that you are the rightful owner.

Recently, IBM and Sony announced a partnership to develop a blockchain-based system for registering and protecting copyrights. The system is still developing, but it could one day be used by artists, musicians, and other creators to protect their work.

### *2. Patents*

The patent system is designed to protect inventors from having their ideas stolen or copied. But the traditional process of applying for a patent can be expensive and time-consuming.

A blockchain-based patent system could streamline the application process, making it easier for inventors to protect their ideas. The United States Patent and Trademark Office is already exploring using blockchain technology to store and share patent information.

In the past, some patent holders have been reluctant to share information about their inventions, fearing the loss of their competitive edge. With a blockchain-based system, however, patent holders could choose to share information with only the people or companies they trust, protecting their competitive advantage while collaborating with others.

Imagine a world where you could instantly register and share your ideas with the click of a button. That world is not so far off, thanks to blockchain technology.

### *3. Trademarks*

Trademarks protect brand names and logos from being used by other businesses. Like patents, applying for a trademark can require much time and money.

With a blockchain-based trademark system, businesses could register their trademarks in minutes. Because the blockchain is immutable, they could be confident that their trademarks would be safe from tampering or fraud.

The Trademark Office is also exploring using blockchain technology for storing and sharing trademark information, planning to implement it one day soon.

### *4. Domain names*

Domain names are used to identify websites and email addresses. Instead of spending hours or even days trying to register domain names, businesses could safely and securely register them in a matter of minutes with the help of blockchain.

During the registration process, businesses could specify the terms under which their domain names could be transferred or sold. Giving businesses greater control over their domain names could also help to prevent cyber-squatting.

So far, a few companies have begun exploring blockchain for domain name registration. For example, Unstoppable Domains is working on a decentralized domain name system powered by the Ethereum blockchain.

A few start-ups use blockchain to create new top-level domains (TLDs). For example, Blockstack has created a technology stack TLD that can only be used with applications built on the Blockstack platform.

While the use of blockchain for domain name registration is still in its early stages, it can streamline the process and give businesses more control over their domain names.

### *5. Trade secrets*

The phrase "trade secrets" refers to confidential information used in business. This information includes customer lists, recipes, manufacturing processes, and marketing strategies.

Because trade secrets are valuable, they are often the target of theft or espionage, and if a trade secret is leaked, it can significantly damage a company.

With a blockchain-based system for trade secret management, businesses could track the movement of confidential information and ensure that it is only accessed by authorized individuals. This would help identify and prevent trade secret theft and make it easier to prosecute those who engage in espionage.

A few start-ups have already recognized the potential of blockchain-based solutions for trade secret management. For example, the company Intellishare has developed a platform that uses blockchain to track the movement of confidential information. Additionally, the company Enigma is working on a decentralized trade secret management system powered by the Ethereum blockchain.

As more businesses become aware of the risks associated with trade secret theft, the need for solutions like this will likely grow.

### *6. Digital assets*

Digital assets are any type of assets – e.g., cryptocurrency, e-books, and music files – that exist in digital form.

With a blockchain-based system for managing digital assets, businesses would have a secure and tamper-proof way to track the ownership and transfer of these assets. Lawyers could use blockchain to track the ownership of legal documents. This would help to prevent fraud and make it easier to prove ownership in court.

A secure and tamper-proof way to track digital assets would be a significant advantage for businesses. As more and more business is conducted online, the need for such a system will only grow.

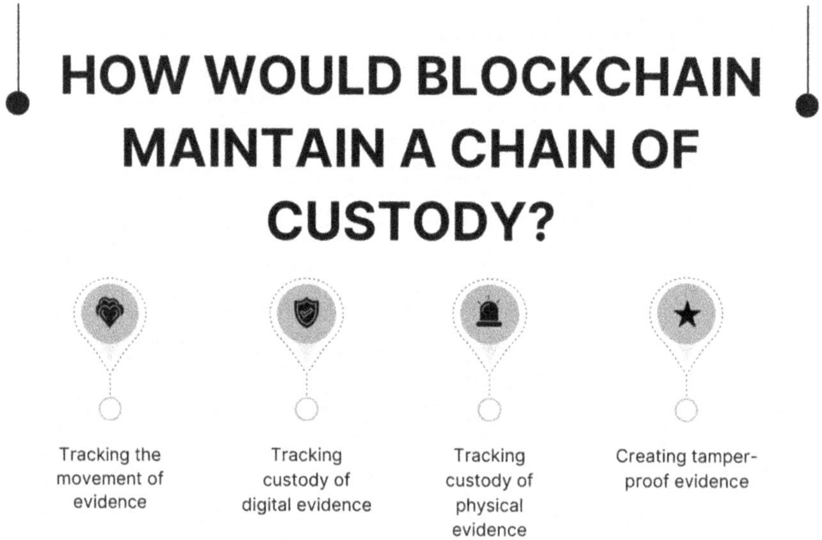


*Figure 4: How would blockchain maintain a chain of custody?*

### Application 4: Chain of custody

One of the most critical responsibilities of the law industry and court cases is maintaining a clear custody chain. This involves having a clear and well-documented record of who possessed what evidence at what time. This can often be difficult, especially if many people are involved in the case, or the evidence changes hands.

However, it would be much easier to maintain a complete and straightforward chain of custody with blockchain technology. Each time the evidence changed hands, that transaction could be recorded on the blockchain, creating a clear and immutable record of who possessed the evidence at what time. This would make it much easier to track down any potential issues or discrepancies in the chain of custody.

*What is a chain of custody in law?*

A chain of custody – a record of who had possession of what evidence at what time – is vital in law cases because it helps to ensure that evidence is not tampered with or lost. Your case may be thrown out if there are any issues with the chain of custody.

*What are the benefits of a blockchain-based chain of custody?*

Some of the many benefits of using blockchain for a chain of custody include:

- *Improved security.* Each transaction is securely recorded and cannot be altered. It is much more difficult for someone to tamper with evidence if the chain of custody is stored on a blockchain.
- *Increased transparency.* With blockchain, each transaction is recorded publicly. This means that anyone can view the chain of custody and see who had possession of the evidence at what time, simplifying the process of tracking any potential issues or discrepancies.
- *Improved efficiency.* Maintaining a chain of custody can be time-consuming and must be completed manually. However, blockchain can automate this process to save time and resources.
- *Reduced costs.* Automating the chain of custody process with blockchain would also reduce costs since you'd no longer have to manually pay someone to keep track of the chain of custody.

*How would blockchain maintain a chain of custody?*

There are many ways that blockchain could be used to maintain an effective chain of custody, including:

- *Tracking the movement of evidence.* Blockchain could create a record of each time evidence changes hands. This would create a clear and immutable record.
- *Tracking custody of digital evidence.* In many cases, the evidence is digital files. Blockchain could be used to track the custody of these digital files, ensuring that the files are not tampered with or lost.
- *Tracking custody of physical evidence.* Blockchain could also track the custody of physical evidence. For example, if the evidence is a piece of jewelry, blockchain could be used to track the custody of that jewelry. This would ensure that the jewelry is not lost or stolen.

- *Creating tamper-proof evidence.* One of the benefits of blockchain is that it is tamper-proof. This means it cannot be altered once something is recorded on the blockchain. This would be beneficial for creating tamper-proof evidence.

*What are some potential issues with using blockchain for a chain of custody?*

While there are many benefits to this use of blockchain, there are also some potential issues that should be considered, including:

- *The potential for human error.* While blockchain is tamper-proof, it is still susceptible to human error. For example, if someone incorrectly records the chain of custody, that error will be recorded on the blockchain and cannot be altered.
- *The reliance on technology.* Since blockchain relies on technology, a technical issue or outage could impact the chain of custody.
- *The need for consensus.* For a transaction to be recorded on the blockchain, it needs to be verified by a majority of the network. This means that any disagreements on the chain of custody could impact the accuracy of the record.

While there are some potential issues, the benefits of using blockchain for a chain of custody outweigh the theoretical drawbacks. Blockchain provides a clear, fixed record of who possessed evidence and when. This would make tracking any potential issues or discrepancies much easier.

Additionally, using blockchain-based solutions to automate maintaining a chain of custody makes the technology even more appealing due to the time and resources that could be saved.

## Application 5: DAOs

Decentralized autonomous organizations (DAOs) are one of the most hyped applications of blockchain technology. A DAO is a company or organization run by an algorithm rather than humans. The organization's rules are encoded in software, and the organization is thus run by code. There are no human managers and no need for trust between members because the rules of the organization are objectively enforced by the code.

This may sound like a recipe for disaster, but there are, in fact, DAOs that have already been successfully implemented. The most well-known example is the Ethereum Foundation, a DAO that has been running since

2014. The Ethereum Foundation is responsible for developing the Ethereum blockchain, and its rules are encoded in smart contracts.

The advantage of DAOs is that they are much more efficient than traditional organizations. They can be run entirely autonomously without humans needing to make decisions. As a result, DAOs can operate 24/7, considering options and making decisions much faster than traditional organizations.

Some of the other noticeable benefits of such organizations include the following:

### *1. Increased transparency*

When it comes to traditional organizations, there is often a lack of transparency. This is because humans are involved in the decision-making process and tracking each person's actions and thoughts is difficult. With DAOs, all the organization's actions are transparent and easily trackable on the blockchain.

Imagine a world where all organizations are DAOs. There would be no need for transparency reports or annual general meetings. All the information about the organization would be available on the blockchain, and anyone could see how it is run.

### *2. Reduced costs*

Another advantage of DAOs is that there is no need to pay humans to make decisions. All the work can be done through code, which is much more cost-effective than paying people.

In addition, DAOs can eliminate the need for traditional middlemen like lawyers and accountants, further reducing the costs of running an organization.

### *3. Improved security*

DAOs can improve security because all the data about the organization is stored on the blockchain, which is secure and tamper-proof. DAOs can use smart contracts to enforce the organization's rules, making it difficult for anyone to cheat.

### *4. Better governance*

DAOs can also improve governance. This is because the organization's rules are encoded in software and can be enforced automatically, removing humans – and their potential for corruption – from the equation. In the law industry, DAOs can create legal entities governed by smart contracts, run entirely by code, and do not need human managers.

### *5. Increased efficiency*

DAOs can also increase efficiency by operating 24/7 and making decisions faster than traditional organizations. This could mean resolving legal disputes much faster in the law industry, as human lawyers would not need to negotiate a settlement.

## New opportunities for lawyers

In the past few years, blockchain has been hailed as a revolutionary technology that will upend entire industries. As the underlying technology of cryptocurrencies such as Bitcoin, blockchain enables trustless peer-to-peer transactions without needing third-party intermediaries.

As blockchain technology becomes more widespread, new opportunities for lawyers will emerge. For example, lawyers will be able to create and enforce smart contracts, self-executing contracts that use blockchain technology to enforce the terms of an agreement automatically.

Blockchain can also create immutable records of contracts and other legal documents, streamlining the discovery process in litigation. In addition, blockchain-based identity management systems could be used to verify the identities of clients and witnesses, helping to prevent fraud and reduce the risk of identity theft.

As blockchain technology's popularity and possible uses grow, so will opportunities for lawyers to use it in their practice. By staying up to date on the latest developments in blockchain technology, lawyers can identify instances when it could be used to their advantage.

Blockchain technology is still in its infancy, and it remains to be seen how it will ultimately be used in the legal sector. However, it is clear that blockchain has the potential to revolutionize the practice of law. Lawyers who are early adopters of this technology will be well-positioned to take advantage of the new opportunities that it creates.

This exciting new industry can offer you a chance to completely change your career and become a leader in this unexplored territory.

### Relatively easy entry

Blockchain and smart contract experts are extremely rare, despite the industry's high demand for these professionals. With some practice and experience, you can quickly enter the industry and become highly successful. The relative newness of the technology means that the industry is not already saturated with professionals adept at handling blockchain and smart contracts. In addition, becoming an expert is relatively easy in this industry as it is still developing and is not yet too complex for a determined person to master. You can help shape and even lead its development. Finally, the industry is relatively easy to enter, as it does not have any legal requirements such as licenses or certifications for you to become an expert in the different elements of the business.

### Digitized assets

Digital assets are now common, especially with the role of the internet in our daily lives. The information collected from browsing and social media is an extremely important aspect of the advertising industry. Blockchain technology is a great asset for handling these types of digital assets as it allows for the distribution of digital information. It is the structure of a new form of the internet. This is the future of technology, and you do not want to be left out when this industry blows up.

### It pays

The lack of professionals in the industry means that existing experts receive significant remuneration. Professionals in this industry are already paid much higher than those still using typical financial structures. If you consider entering this industry, you can expect competitive pay. This is probably the most compelling reason why you should enter these industries. As you become an expert, you can expect your salary to continue to increase. More jobs but few workers allow you to negotiate competitive pay.

### It is a brave new world

Blockchain technology has revolutionized the internet in ways likely to have major economic benefits. Initially created to deal with online currencies, blockchain technology has completely changed how economic and financial transactions are conducted today. This technology has also changed how information is handled, opening up opportunities for dealing with digital data. A perceptive lawyer can take advantage of this and explore these new benefits. After becoming an expert, you can become a leader in a new industry, which can be very financially rewarding. For individuals interested in new technologies, blockchain is the industry for you.

### Long-term industry

The blockchain and smart contracts industry will likely last a very long time and will only expand in use. The technology is based on similar concepts as those that support the internet, meaning that it has the potential to survive for many years. The internet has been around for at least 30 years, with new uses being identified daily. This industry will likely provide you with ongoing work for numerous years. Being an early entrant can place you in the perfect position to take advantage of opportunities in this relatively new industry. The fact that the industry is diversified means you can get opportunities for a long time.

### Increased flexibility

The blockchain industry is highly flexible and easy to adapt. The information blocks are not stored in one central area and are not easy to manipulate. In addition, the technology can be adapted to numerous industries, making it very flexible. The flexibility stems from this technology, allowing you to work anywhere and with anyone. This is in line with the global work trend of working online and can allow you to select when and how you will work. Private businesses are also using the technology, making it even more flexible.

### Diverse work opportunities

The industry has many exciting employment opportunities for interested individuals. Numerous new companies in the industry require staff to handle the high demand for these businesses. Marketing, law, finance, and information technology staff are in high demand in the blockchain industry. In addition, individuals capable of solving arising issues or identifying new opportunities are highly sought after. As a lawyer, your talents cannot lack a home within the blockchain technology industry.

Although it can be an intimidating idea to switch from a legal career to an entirely new industry, the blockchain industry is a great choice for any lawyer willing to make a bold move. The brave attorneys who transition to the blockchain industry now, while it's still relatively new, will be rewarded with exciting work opportunities, relatively high compensation, and the chance to be a part of something incredible.

So, if you're a lawyer looking to stay ahead of the curve, keep an eye on blockchain. It just might be the next big thing in the legal industry. Who knows? You might even be the one to create the next killer app.

Part III:
# Broader issues in legal tech

# Chapter 12: Technology and the legal profession – what's legal ethics got to do with IT?

*By Jan L. Jacobowitz, founder and owner, Legal Ethics Advisor*

It's physical, only logical, a new direction, that leaves many dazed and confused, thinking about their own protection, and scared to be feeling this way. Yes, it's a riff on a Tina Turner classic but also an apt description of technology's penetration into the legal profession and the profession's reluctant embrace.[1]

In fact, the legal profession's use of technology implicates many of the legal ethics rules, not the least of which are competence, communication, and confidentiality – three of the rules that underly the fundamentals of effective representation and the loyalty required in an attorney–client relationship. So, let's briefly place the relationship between technology and the legal profession in historical context, then explore the relevant rules with some timely examples.

## Historical context

Although the proliferation of technology in the digital age serves as a catalyst in the current evolution of the practice of law, the legal profession's well-documented ambivalence about technology began in the analog age. For example, in the 19th century, male scriveners who refused to adopt the "new technology" known as the typewriter left the profession thereby creating the opportunity for female typists.[2] Law firms later scorned a more dynamic invention, the telephone, deeming it both unprofessional and a threat to client confidentiality.[3]

In fact, communication technology serves as a terrific vehicle by which to journey through the legal profession's historical hesitation to adopt technology. Although the landline became a mainstream means of communication, each new iteration of the telephone – from the portable cordless, to the cellular, to the smart phone – resulted in ethics opinions that analyzed the permissibility of use in the practice of law.[4]

Lawyers engaged in the same type of cautious analysis in connection with the telefax and email.[5] Interestingly, in 1999, the initial evaluation of email in an American Bar Association (ABA) Opinion found communication via email to be acceptable. However, in 2017, the Opinion was modified in ABA Opinion 477R. Opinion 477R suggests that today a lawyer's duties of confidentiality and competence require more caution when communicating via email and emphasizes the duty to conduct a threat analysis and consider the use of encryption.[6]

Between the 1999 and 2017 ABA Opinions, as technology continued to proliferate, the ABA amended the explanatory notes to ABA Model Rule of Professional Conduct 1.1 Competence. The new language defines a competent lawyer as one *who understands the benefits and disadvantages of technology.*[7] As of the writing of this chapter, approximately 40 states have adopted this comment to their competence rule.[8] Numerous state bar ethics opinions have also addressed the need for technology competence in the context of cloud computing.[9]

If the legal profession's growing acknowledgement that tech savviness had become a necessary component of ethics, and effective representation needed a nudge, then the COVID-19 pandemic lockdown of 2020 provided it. The pandemic required the legal profession to embrace technology as a means of survival. In fact, both early data and anecdotal evidence indicates that "five to ten years of technological advances [took] place [in the legal profession] over a mere two months".[10]

Remote workstations and video conferencing designed to facilitate meetings, depositions, and court hearings sprang up seemingly overnight. In fact, several commentators identified the pandemic as the "black swan" that catapulted the legal profession squarely into the digital age.[11]

One commentator observed, "The Coronavirus has harnessed the potential of underutilized tools and alternative work paradigms long resisted by the legal establishment. Entrenched ways of doing things have been altered with astonishing speed, ease, and acceptance."[12]

## Legal context for the use of technology and the legal ethics implications

No doubt, as the legal profession continues to emerge from the pandemic environment, technology remains an integral part of the practice of law. Many lawyers continue to work remotely, and video conferencing has become a core component of lawyering. What are the legal ethics implications of all this technology? A lawyer's traditional answer, "It depends", comes to mind.

What does it depend upon? The answer may be found in the evaluation of the legal context in which technology is employed. Three primary contexts for analysis are individual use, outsourcing of legal services, and social networking. While these contexts somewhat overlap, they also provide clarification in understanding the application of the legal ethics rules.

## Individual use

### Fundamental legal ethics requirements

The ABA competence language requiring the understanding of the benefits and disadvantages of technology essentially requires lawyers to learn how to use technology. When The Florida Bar adopted the ABA language, it not only required an additional three CLE technology credits each cycle, but also added this language:

> *"Competent representation may also involve the association or retention of a non-lawyer advisor of established technological competence in the field in question. Competent representation also involves safe-guarding confidential information relating to the representation, including, but not limited to, electronic transmissions and communications."*[13]

Florida's language clarifies that an individual lawyer's use of technology not only directly implicates the competence rule, but also dovetails with the duty of confidentiality and other rules of representation. Individual use differs from outsourcing because a lawyer directly engages with the technology instead of retaining an outside vendor to do so. (Think sending an email or link to a client or opposing counsel, e-filing court documents, or logging on to a Zoom hearing, as opposed to retaining an eDiscovery company or outsourcing legal research to a third-party vendor.)

### Understanding the benefits

Although the legal ethics headlines often highlight lawyers' ethical mishaps on technology, it is important to note that understanding the benefits of technology can play a significant role in contributing to the competent, successful practice of law. For example, technology can contribute to a lawyer's duties of competence, diligence, confidentiality, and billing practices. Software programs are available to manage a lawyer's calendar – including court dates, client meetings, and filing deadlines. Billing programs allow for time to be instantaneously recorded, and invoices may be created, reviewed, and sent on a timely basis. Document filing programs and cloud computing provides the opportunity for electronic storage and enhanced confidentiality.

In other words, for a lawyer who embraces office technology, gone are the days of the incomplete or misplaced paper calendar, forgotten or incomplete billing pads, and huge filing cabinets where the filing system is only as good as the last person who reached into the cabinet. Current tech legal company offerings generally include online tutorials as well as opportunities for individual training and assistance. A lawyer's understanding need not be instantaneous; rather it can be garnered over time with educational support.

Beyond basic legal tech software offerings, artificial intelligence companies are working to further streamline and support the practice of law. Imagining the future practice of law, William Davis suggests the following possibilities:

- *Focus.* A partner about to enter a client meeting verbally asks the computer to bring up the last few invoices. The verbal interface saves the attorney what would normally require several, rather distracting, navigational clicks. He or she is now focused on what needs to be done rather than searching for what needs to be done.
- *Expenses.* As a lawyer closes the door to an Uber ride that dropped him or her off at the client site, an AI application scans the attorney's inbox for the receipt and automatically enters it as a line-item expense.
- *Calendaring.* Near the end of an hour-long client meeting, the attorney and client agree to a follow-up meeting the next week. An AI application has been passively listening to the conversation – with legal consent – in the background and automatically reviews each party's calendar and proposes a new meeting time that's mutually beneficial.
- *Intake.* During new client intake, an AI application is listening in the background and automatically begins searching for potential conflicts. In the meantime, another algorithm continuously narrows down sources of legal research relevant to the legal matter at hand, as the intake form is completed, or files are added to the case.
- *Predictive analysis.* An AI application combs through the massive data set in a law firm's case management and practice management system – and compares that data to public sources such as newsfeeds and stock exchange data to make a prediction, for example: "In the next 12 months, this practice area, or this type of company, represents a growth opportunity for the firm; look for new lateral hires with this expertise".[14]

Both the current opportunities and future possibilities of legal tech may enhance a lawyer's ethical responsibilities and the efficient practice of law. Of course, as the note to the competence rule explains, a lawyer's obligation includes not only understanding the benefits, but also the disadvantages of technology to thereby avoid the ethical landmines that await the uninformed lawyer.

## Understanding the disadvantages

Ethical missteps that occur when a lawyer does not understand how to use technology range from major discovery mishaps and cybersecurity breaches to appearing in court behind a cat filter, failing to unplug a smart device, or using an insecure coffee shop internet connection.

The viral occurrence of "Sir, I am not a cat," evidenced the early challenges of lawyers appearing in court via Zoom. The lawyer appeared behind a cat filter and did not have the tech know-how to remove it. Fortunately, the event illustrated not only the importance of competence but also the value of professionalism as the judge and opposing counsel both handled the mishap with civility and compassion.[15]

Examples of fundamental tech competence that also implicates confidentiality include knowing to unplug a smart home device and avoid unsecured WIFI networks. Smart devices are always listening and unsecure networks at places such as hotels, coffee shops, and airports become easy targets for hackers.[16]

Confidentiality also intersects with the duties of competence and diligence in the contexts of discovery and cybersecurity. (More on the ethical implications of hiring vendors in these areas in the next section.) The Alex Jones case provides a recent example of legal ethics issues arising in the context of discovery. Apparently, Mr Jones' lawyer produced the entire contents of Mr Jones' phone to opposing counsel instead of only the documents subject to production.[17] Confidential and privileged material was included. Moreover, production was not timely, occurring 12 days before the documents were used at trial. ABA Model Rule 3.4,[18] Fairness to Opposing Counsel, requires that relevant evidence not be withheld.

Additionally, Rule 4.4, and most state rules, provide that a lawyer has a duty to notify opposing counsel upon receipt of inadvertently produced documents. Although Texas did not adopt that rule, the plaintiff's counsel did notify Mr Jones' lawyer; however, he took no action to retrieve the inadvertently produced documents. Subsequently, the plaintiff's counsel used some of the documents when he cross-examined Mr Jones in court.

Additional documents that contained confidential medical records pertaining to a different, but related, Sandy Hook case in Connecticut were also impermissibly released.[19] The medical records were subject to a protective order and the Connecticut court subsequently held a hearing to determine how the Connecticut attorney sent the documents to Mr Jones' Texas counsel and how he then sent the documents to the Texas plaintiff's counsel.[20] The Connecticut counsel invoked the Fifth Amendment, but the Texas counsel testified. Texas counsel indicated that he had only requested documents pertaining to Alex Jones from the Connecticut counsel. Texas counsel was unaware of the confidential plaintiffs' records on the computer drive that he received.[21] Moreover, he explained that one of his assistants mistakenly sent the wrong link to Texas plaintiff's counsel.[22] While he did instruct the assistant to deactivate the link, he took no further action until he realized that the documents were being used in the Texas trial.[23]

The Texas attorney's explanation in the Connecticut court not only reinforces the legal ethics rules mentioned above, but also adds the supervision rules to the mix. Model Rules 5.1-5.3 require that lawyers establish procedures in their offices to ensure that lawyers and non-lawyer employees conduct themselves in accordance with the applicable state code of professional conduct. One should query whether the Texas counsel had reasonable supervisory protocols in place to avoid his assistant's error. Of course, the fact that he took no other immediate action upon learning of the mistake takes us full circle back to the need for fundamental competence and confidentiality.

Competence, confidentiality, and communication also come into play when considering cybersecurity. Cybersecurity is a broad term that may be applied to the sole practitioner working remotely as well as to a large firm. In the small home office context, ensuring security may involve understanding the use of a VPN, encryption of devices and documents, and communicating with a client about their own protocols when interacting with the lawyer or otherwise managing their case. In one recent example where client education would have been helpful, a client inadvertently destroyed the attorney–client privilege by having a hotel front desk clerk print email correspondence from the client's former in-house lawyer.[24]

In a large firm context, it gets more complicated as law firms have become targets in cyberspace. Communication with clients is essential so that everyone is on the same page as to the security required by the client and the firm's cybersecurity efforts. While many law firms have been hacked, one of the most dramatic occurred in 2016. A cyberattack on a Panamanian law firm resulted in the disclosure of millions of confidential documents. Referred to as the Panama Papers, the leak exposed illegal conduct throughout the world.[25]

Another costly, high-profile attack in 2017 involved the law firm DL Piper. The firm disclosed in 2018 that it had paid 15,000 hours in IT overtime to recover from the cyberattack.[26]

While acknowledging that it is virtually impossible to absolutely secure information from all cyber criminals, the legal ethics rules and advisory opinions do require that reasonable measures are taken to protect information.

Regardless of the size of the practice, the confidentiality rules in most states provide guidance that defines reasonable measures consistent with the comment to ABA Rule 1.6:

> *"Factors to be considered in determining the reasonableness of the lawyer's efforts include, but are not limited to, the sensitivity of the information, the likelihood of disclosure if additional safeguards are not employed, the cost of employing additional safeguards, the difficulty of implementing the safeguards, and the extent to which the safeguards adversely affect the lawyer's ability to represent clients (e.g., by making a device or important piece of software excessively difficult to use). A client may require the lawyer to implement special security measures not required by this Rule or may give informed consent to forgo security measures that would otherwise be required by this Rule."*[27]

Similarly, ABA Opinion 477r provides a seven-step threat analysis that may be conducted in connection with employing reasonable measures to secure client information. The analysis involves determining:

1. The nature of the threat;
2. How client confidential information is transmitted and stored;
3. The use of reasonable electronic security measures;
4. How electronic communications should be protected;
5. The need to label client information as privileged and confidential;
6. The need to train lawyers and non-lawyer assistants in technology and cybersecurity; and
7. The need to conduct due diligence on vendors who provide technology services.[28]

The message of the legal ethics rules and ethics advisory opinions is clear; lawyers in any legal office setting must develop tech competence to comply with their ethical duties to clients. Becoming tech-savvy may also enhance the efficiency and ultimate success of a lawyer's practice. Moreover, it may be necessary to hire experts or outsource the use of technology to third-party vendors; however, outsourcing legal services creates additional legal ethics considerations.

## Outsourcing of legal services

Technology has provided numerous opportunities for the legal profession to streamline the practice of law by outsourcing aspects of a legal practice for increased efficiency and cost. In fact, legal outsourcing covers a wide range of services that include, but are not limited to, back office administrative tasks, document (cloud) storage, legal research, eDiscovery, drafting documents, and client billing. Some of these tasks are accomplished using online software programs or, alternatively, sending information to third-party vendors for processing. In some cases, a third-party vendor may offer artificial intelligence (AI) to create documents or conduct research.[29]

A discussion of the technical functionality and utility of each of these outsourcing vehicles is beyond the scope of this chapter; however, the ethical implications of outsourcing legal services remain central to the discussion. Fortunately, several ethics advisory opinions provide guidance.[30] The ABA Committee on Ethics and Professional Responsibility released Formal Opinion 08-451 in 2008, which incorporated the advice of several state bars that had already addressed outsourcing in opinions during 2006-2007.[31] The combined opinions include topics such as employing both international and domestic vendors to outsource legal research, document review, and the drafting of pleadings. In 2015, the New York City Bar Association issued an opinion focused on the permissibility of outsourcing a law firm's administrative or "back office" functions.[32]

Generally, the opinions advise that outsourcing legal services must be conducted in compliance with the rules of professional conduct.[33] Competence, diligence, communication, confidentiality, and the supervision of non-lawyer assistance not only comprise the fundamental rules of the ethical practice of law, but also, not surprisingly, appear as the primary focus of outsourcing guidelines.[34] In 2012, the ABA reinforced the application of the rules to outsourcing by enacting additional comments to Rule 1.1 Competence and Rule 5.3 Responsibilities Regarding Nonlawyer Assistants.[35] The comments explain that lawyers not only need to understand technology, but also should obtain client consent before outsourcing an aspect of a client's case.[36]

Obtaining client consent also implicates Rule 1.4 Communication. Some clients may require both the reasoning for outsourcing and the functionality of a specific type of technology. However, regardless of the depth of a client's queries, lawyers must thoroughly vet outsourcing companies. Confidentiality, a fundamental concern, should be addressed in a confidentiality agreement that binds both the vendor and its employees. The agreement may be a standalone document or incorporated into a service agreement; it should include a description of the vendor's data security protocols.[37] Security protocols include the measures used to protect data, the location of the vendor, and the relevant privacy laws in the vendor's jurisdiction.[38]

The vetting process should also include a review of the qualifications of the vendor's employees, and confirmation of a conflict-checking mechanism. Conflict checks prevent adversarial parties or parties to a transactional matter from retaining the same vendor.[39]

Other legal ethics considerations involve prohibiting a third party's interference with a lawyer's professional judgment[40] and avoiding the assistance of non-lawyers in the unauthorized practice of law.[41] The outsourcing opinions address these concerns by requiring a lawyer to review a vendor's work; the vendor's work product must only be a consideration in a lawyer's complete analysis and decision-making in a case.[42] In other words, a lawyer cannot ethically file a pleading that has been researched and drafted by a non-lawyer or third-party vendor unless the lawyer has carefully reviewed and analyzed both the quality of the research and the accuracy of the pleading.

Finally, it is important to note that when a lawyer obtains a client's consent to outsourcing, in accordance with Rule 1.5, the lawyer must bill only the net costs of outsourcing to the client unless the client agrees to pay additional charges. Nonetheless, the lawyer may be able to charge an additional fee for their time to supervise the third-party and review the work product.[43]

## Social networking, ethics, and technology

Perhaps a hybrid between the contexts of individual use and outsourcing, social networking has nonetheless infiltrated the practice of law, implicating the legal ethics rules in its wake. Social networking is user-driven, meaning one travels on the networks by directly accessing a social network platform. Thus, fundamental user competence becomes key in avoiding ethical landmines.

However, the platforms also have their own security and user protocols, not completely unlike the third-party vendors discussed above. So, it becomes critical for a lawyer to understand both how the platforms work and how a lawyer may ethically use social networks in the practice of law.

While a description of all the current social network programs and their functionality is beyond the scope of this chapter, the ethical implications of lawyers using social networking is worthy of discussion. While a discussion of the ethical implications of both the use of social media in the practice of law and the repercussions of posting negative commentary could fill an entire book, it is included here, much like cybersecurity, to enhance an awareness of the importance of considering the legal ethics rules when engaging with the growing use of technology in the legal profession.

### Social networking in the practice of law

Lawyers often access social media to investigate a case, establish jurisdiction, accomplish substitute service of process, obtain evidence, and investigate judges and jurors.[44] Each of these activities implicates any number of the rules of professional conduct ranging from competence and diligence to the obligations of filing meritorious actions, candor to the tribunal, fairness to opposing counsel, and avoiding misconduct.[45]

The following list contains many of the legal ethics rules cited in the ethics advisory opinions offering guidance for the use of social media as a litigation tool. The sheer number of rules evidences their vast reach in this area of technology.

- *Competence Rule 1.1:*[46] As discussed earlier, the ABA's 2012 amendment to the comments defines a component of competence as understanding both the benefits and disadvantages of technology.
- *Diligence Rule 1.3:*[47] A lawyer must act with "reasonable diligence and promptness in representing a client". The comment to the rule warns about the negative impact of procrastination. Procrastination in the realm of social media investigations may not only damage a case, but also may evidence a lack of competence. Social media posts that are initially available may be removed or hidden behind a privacy wall as a case proceeds, thereby preventing access to evidence or even the knowledge that it exists. Therefore, it is not uncommon to find that social media ethics opinions often link diligence with competence.[48]
- *Confidentiality Rule 1.6:*[49] Confidentiality, a fundamental component of an attorney– client relationship, creates the trust required for effective representation.[50] Moreover, confidentiality includes all information that a lawyer learns during a representation. In the words of one judge, "If you post a tweet, just like if you scream out of the window, there is no reasonable explanation of privacy. There is no

proprietary interest in your tweets, which you have now gifted to the world."[51] Thus, a posting lawyer may breach the duty of client confidentiality; a posting client may waive the attorney–client privilege.

- *Rule 3.1 Meritorious Claims and Contentions*[52] *and Rule 3.3 Candor to the Tribunal:*[53] Rule 3.1 requires that lawyers only file actions based in law and in fact. Rule 3.3 prohibits lawyers from presenting false evidence in court. In the realm of social media, these rules require a lawyer to ensure that their client's social media presence does not belie the client's case. A social media investigation may cause a lawyer to adjust the allegations in a client's case or, in a worst-case scenario, a lawyer may be compelled to refuse a representation or withdraw if the representation has already begun.[54]
- *Rule 3.4 Fairness to Opposing Party and Counsel:*[55] Fairness to opposing party and counsel has caused lawyers tremendous difficulty in the social media context. Failure to identify and produce social media discovery may result in court-ordered sanctions, fees, and in state bar disciplinary action. In fact, one lawyer's license was suspended for five years based largely on his improper handling of social media evidence.[56]
- *Rule 4.1 Truthfulness in Statements to Others,*[57] *Rule 4.2 Communication with Person Represented by Counsel,*[58] *Rule 4.3 Dealing with Unrepresented Person,*[59] *Rule 4.4 Respect for Rights of Third Persons:*[60] These four rules relate to interactions with individuals who are not a lawyer's client. Using social media to contact witnesses and opposing parties or using their accounts to obtain useful information implicates these rules.[61] Of course, when a party is represented, direct contact remains prohibited unless the represented party's counsel consents.[62] Regarding unrepresented individuals, the ethics opinions require transparency and honesty. In other words, the person initiating contact should disclose their identity and the reason for the contact.[63]
- *Rule 5.1 Responsibilities of a Partner or Supervisory Lawyer,*[64] *Rule 5.2 Responsibilities of a Subordinate Lawyer,*[65] *Rule 5.3 Responsibilities Regarding Nonlawyer Assistance:*[66] Social media use also implicates the supervisory rules. There are varying degrees of social media savvy among lawyers and non-lawyers in a legal office. Nonetheless, lawyers remain responsible for the conduct of their paralegals, law clerks, and other non-lawyer assistants – if one of them crosses an ethical line on social media, the state bar will likely hold the supervising lawyer responsible.[67]

- *Rule 8.4. Misconduct:*[68] The misconduct rule incorporates violations of any of the other rules and 8.4 (c) specifically prohibits conduct "involving dishonesty, fraud, deceit or misrepresentation". Rule 8.4 is often included with the other relevant rules in disciplinary complaints. In a social media context, 8.4 (c) often rides tandem with both the supervisory rules and the rules pertaining to dealing with others. Thus, if a lawyer or a non-lawyer assistant impermissibly contacts a party or witness on social media, then Rule 8.4 (c) will appear in the corresponding disciplinary complaint.[69]

### Ethical landmines for lawyers' general use of social networks

Another area of growing ethical concern for lawyers is the posting of negative or impermissible commentary on social media. Three main categories for discussion are commenting on current events, discussing a client's case, and responding to negative online reviews.[70] Each of these categories have resulted in negative repercussions for lawyers that range from reputational damage or job termination to state bar disciplinary action.[71]

The lawyers who have suffered reputational damage or loss of employment have often violated their employer's stated values or social media policies.[72] The lawyers who have been subject to disciplinary prosecution and punishment have generally breached their duty of confidentiality by discussing the client's case (without client consent) or being unable to resist the urge to respond to a client's negative online review without revealing the client's confidential information.[73] The takeaway here is that lawyers need to pause and consider the possible repercussions before posting commentary on social media.

## Conclusion

Technology continues to rapidly evolve and affect every aspect of society. The legal profession has slowly come to terms with technology's impact on the practice of law. The COVID-19 pandemic demonstrated the power of technological advances that allowed the legal profession not only to survive, but also to thrive. The bottom line – awareness of the ethical parameters within which to travel on the legal technology highway is the key to success for the future practice of law.

*Change is the law of life. And those who look only to the past or present are certain to miss the future.*
John F. Kennedy[74]

*References*

1 https://genius.com/Tina-turner-whats-love-got-to-do-with-it-lyrics.
2 Jan L. Jacobowitz and John G. Browning, *Legal Ethics and Social Media – A Practitioner's Handbook* 1 (2017) (citing M.H. Hoeflich, From Scriveners to Typewriters: Document Production in the Nineteenth Century Law Office, 16 *Green Bag 2D*. 395, 396 (2013).
3 Jan L. Jacobowitz and Danielle Singer, The Social Media Frontier: Exploring a New Mandate for Competence in the Practice of Law, 68 *Univ. of Miami L. Rev*. 1, 4-6 (2013) (citing Richard L. Marcus, The Impact of Computers on the Legal Profession: Evolution or Revolution? 102 *Nw. U. L. Rev*. 1,827, 1,855 (2008)).
4 See Jan L. Jacobowitz and Justin Ortiz, Happy Birthday Siri! Dialing in Legal Ethics for Artificial Intelligence, Smartphones, and Real Time Lawyers, 4 Tex. *A&M J. Prop. L.* 407, 409 (2018).
5 Jacobowitz, Social Media Frontier, *supra* note 3 at 450. The fax machine was an invention of the 19th Century but did not gain popularity in American offices until the 1980s.
6 See Jacobowitz and Ortiz, *supra* note 4, at 431-432; ABA Comm. on Ethics & Prof'l Responsibility, Formal Op. 99-413 (1999); ABA Comm. on Ethics & Prof'l Responsibility, Formal Op. 477R (2017).
Today, email may be considered by some to be "old school" technology, but email remains a central part of the legal landscape. In fact, both civility and ethics issues abound as evidenced by high profile incidences of the infamous reply to all email; See Christopher B. Hopkins, *The Misguided Practice of CC'ing Clients on Emails to Opposing Counsel*, PBCBA Bulletin (January 2020) https://secureservercdn.net/198.71.233.184/d7f.2f7.myftpupload.com/wp-content/uploads/2020/01/2020-cc-clients-emails.pdf?time=1577988628; Robert A. Barrer, *Ethical Implications and Best Practices for Email*, NY Legal Ethics Reporter (2016), www.newyorklegalethics.com/ethical-implications-best-practices-for-use-of-email/; Debra Cassens, Reply All Email By Miffed Federal Appeals Court Judge Tells Colleague He Isn't Paid to Save the Planet, *ABA Journal* (2019) www.abajournal.com/news/article/reply-all-email-by-miffed-federal-appeals-judge-tells-colleague-he-isnt-paid-to-save-the-planet; Joe Patrice, Biglaw Partner So Peeved By Pro Bono Assignment He Hits Reply All To Whine About It, Above the Law (4 May 2020) https://abovethelaw.com/2020/05/biglaw-partner-so-peeved-by-pro-bono-assignment-he-hits-reply-all-to-whine-about-it/.
7 Model Rules of Prof'l Conduct R.1.1cmt. (2020) (emphasis added).
8 Robert Ambrogi, Law Sites www.lawsitesblog.com/tech-competence.
9 Cloud Ethics Opinions Around the US, ABA, Joshua Lenon, A List of All Ethics Opinions on Cloud Computing for Lawyers, Clio, 20 July 2021 www.clio.com/blog/cloud-computing-lawyers-ethics-opinions/.
10 Andrea Solan, The Impact of COVID-19 on the Legal Industry, in Numbers, Maryland

State Bar Association (13 May 2020) www.msba.org/the-impact-of-covid-19-on-the-legal-industry-in-numbers/.

11 *See for example*, Chuck Lundberg, Legal Ethics and Risk Management in the Time of Pandemic, Bench & Bar of Minnesota 16 May/June (2020); Jake Evans, The 2020 Black Swan – COVID-19 and Its Impact on the Practice of Law, Law.com Daily Report (13 April 2020) www.law.com/dailyreportonline/2020/04/13/the-2020-black-swan-covid-19-and-its-impact-on-the-practice-of-law.

12 Mark A. Cohen, COVID-19 and the Reformation of Legal Culture, Forbes, (14 April 2020) www.forbes.com/sites/markcohen1/2020/04/14/covid-19-and-the-reformation-of-legal-culture/#28f8f4ca171d.

13 Florida Supreme Court, No. SC16-574 In Re: Amendments to Rules Regulating the Florida Bar 4-1.1 and 6-10.3 (29 September 2016).

14 William Davis, *How AI's Opportunities Will Augment Rather than Replace Lawyers*, LegalTech News (5 October 2017) www.law.com/legaltechnews/almID/1202799657613/ (https://perma.cc/4GQJ-5WYM).

15 www.nbcnews.com/news/us-news/i-m-not-cat-video-shows-lawyer-can-t-turn-n1257168.

16 See Jacobowitz & Ortiz, *supra* note 4.

17 Jonah E. Bromwich, Why the Sharing of Alex Jones' Text Messages is Really Wild, (*NYTimes*, 4 August 2022) www.nytimes.com/2022/08/04/us/why-the-sharing-of-alex-joness-text-messages-is-really-wild.html; Ishe Marathe, *Inadvertent Disclosure in the Alex Jones Trial Leaves e-Discovery Experts Flabbergasted*, Legal Tech News (4 August 2022) www.law.com/nationallawjournal/2022/08/04/inadvertent-disclosure-in-alex-jones-trial-leaves-e-discovery-experts-flabbergasted/.

18 Herein after, all references to a "Rule" will be to an ABA Model Rule of Professional Conduct.

19 *Ibid.*

20 Christine DeRosa, Alex Jones Atty Pleads 5th at Sandy Hook Data Leak Hearing, Law360 (25 August 2022).

21 *Ibid.*

22 *Ibid.*

23 *Ibid.*

24 Nhan T. Ho, Printing While Traveling Leads to Waiver of the Privilege, American Bar Association Litigation News, (12 August 2022); *Fourth Dimension Software v. Der Touristik Deutschland GMBh*, 19-cv-05561-CRB (AGT) (N.D. Cal. 14 September 2021).

25 Will Fitzgibbon and Michael Hudson, Five Years Later, Panama Papers Still Having a Big Impact, International Consortium of International Journalists, (3 April 2021) www.icij.org/investigations/panama-papers/five-years-later-panama-papers-still-having-a-big-impact/.

26 Ry Crozier, DLA Piper Paid 15,000 hours of IT Overtime After NotPetya Attack, ITNews (8 May 2018) www.itnews.com.au/news/dla-piper-paid-15000-hours-of-it-overtime-after-notpetya-attack-490495.

27 Model Rules of Prof'l Conduct r. 1.6 (Am. Bar Ass'n 2020).

28 *See* Peter Geraghty, *ABA Formal Opinion 477R: Securing Communication of Protected Client Information*, ABA (June 2017) www.americanbar.org/publications/youraba/2017/june-2017/aba-formal-opinion-477r—securing-communication-of-protected-cli.html.

29 Jan L. Jacobowitz, Chaos or Continuity? The Legal Profession: From Antiquity to the Digital Age, the Pandemic, and Beyond, 23 *Vanderbilt Journal of Entertainment and Technology Law* 279, 293-295 (2021), Jan L. Jacobowitz, Happy Birthday Siri! Dialing in Legal Ethics for Artificial Intelligence, Smartphones, and Real Time Lawyers, 4 Tex. A&M J. Prop. L. 407, 414-420 (2018).

30 *See* ABA Comm. on Ethics & Prof'l Resp., Formal Op. 08-451 (2008); State Bar of Cal. Comm. on Prof'l Resp. & Conduct, Formal Op. 2004-165 (2004); Colo. Bar Ass'n, Formal Op. 121 (2009); Fla. State Bar Prof'l Ethics Comm., Ethics Op. 07-2 (2008); NC State Bar, Formal Op. 2007-12 (2008); NY State Bar Ass'n Comm. on Prof'l Ethics, Ethics Op. 762 (2003); NYC Bar Ass'n Comm. on Prof'l & Jud. Ethics, Formal Op. 2006-3 (2006); Ohio Supreme Court Bd. Of Comm'rs on Grievances & Discipline, Advisory Op. 2009-06 (2009); San Diego Cty. Bar Ass'n, Ethics Op. 2007-1 (2007); LA Cty. Bar Ass'n Prof'l Resp. & Ethics Comm., Op. No. 518 (2006); DC Bar, Ethics Op. 362 (2012).

31 *Ibid.*

32 NY City Bar Ass'n Comm. on Prof'l & Judicial Ethics, Formal Op. 2015-1 (2015).

33 *See* Jacobowitz & Browning, 6-8 *supra* at note 2.

34 *Ibid.*

35 Model Rules of Prof'l Conduct r. 1.1 cmt. 6 (Am. Bar Ass'n 2020); Model Rules of Prof'l Conduct r. 5.3 cmt. 3-4 (A. Bar Ass'n 2020).

36 *Ibid*. It is important to note that if a lawyer opts to outsource to an AI vendor, clients may need additional explanation as to how AI may be used for legal work, why a lawyer has opted to use AI, and what the relative cost will be for the client. *See* Jan L. Jacobowitz and Justin Ortiz, Happy Birthday Siri! Dialing in Legal Ethics for Artificial Intelligence, Smartphones, and Real Time Lawyers, 4 Tex. A&M J. Prop. L. 407, 414-420 (2018).

37 Model Rules of Prof'l Conduct r. 1.6 (Am. Bar Ass'n 2020).

38 Model Rules of Prof'l Conduct r. 1.3 (Am. Bar Ass'n 2020).

39 Model Rules of Prof'l Conduct r. 1.7 (Am. Bar Ass'n 2020).

40 Model Rules of Prof'l Conduct r. 5.4 (Am. Bar Ass'n 2020).

41 Model Rules of Prof'l Conduct r. 5.5 (Am. Bar Ass'n 2020).

42 Model Rules of Prof'l Conduct r. 5.3 (Am. Bar Ass'n 2020).

43 Model Rules of Prof'l Conduct r. 1.5 (Am. Bar Ass'n 2020).
44 *See* Jacobowitz & Browning, *supra* at note 2.
45 *Ibid.*
46 Model Rules of Prof'l Conduct r. 1.1 (Am. Bar Ass'n, 2020).
47 Model Rules of Prof'l Conduct r. 1.3 (Am. Bar Ass'n, 2020).
48 *See, e.g.*, NYC Bar Ass'n, Formal Op. 2012-2 (2012) www.nycbar.org/member-and-career-services/committees/reports-listing/reports/detail/formal-opinion-2012-2-jury-research-and-social-media.
49 Model Rules of Prof'l Conduct r. 1.6 (Am. Bar Ass'n, 2020).
50 *See* Jan L. Jacobowitz and Kelly Rains Jesson, Fidelity Diluted: Client Confidentiality Gives Way to the First Amendment & Social Media in Virginia State Bar, ex rel. *Third District Committee v. Horace Frazier Hunter*, 36 Campbell L. Rev. 75, 80 (2014).
51 *People v. Harris*, 949 NYS. 2d 590, 591–92 (NY Crim. Ct 2012).
52 Model Rules of Prof'l Conduct r. 3.1 (Am. Bar Ass'n 2020).
53 Model Rules of Prof'l Conduct r. 3.3 (Am. Bar Ass'n 2020).
54 *See* NY Cnty Lawyers' Ass'n, Formal Op. 745 (2013) ("[I]f a client's social media posting reveals to an attorney that the client's lawsuit involves the assertion of material false factual statements, and if proper inquiry of the client does not negate that conclusion, the attorney is ethically prohibited from proffering, supporting or using those false statements").
55 Model Rules of Prof'l Conduct r. 3.4 (Am. Bar Ass'n 2020).
56 *Allied Concrete Co. v. Lester*, 736 SE 2d 699 (Va. 2013); *See* Final Order, *Lester v. Allied Concrete Co.*, Nos. CL08-150, CL09-223 (Va. Cir. Ct. 21 October 2011).
57 Model Rules of Prof'l Conduct r. 4.1 (Am. Bar Ass'n 2020).
58 Model Rules of Prof'l Conduct r. 4.2 (Am. Bar Ass'n 2020).
59 Model Rules of Prof'l Conduct r. 4.3 (Am. Bar Ass'n 2020).
60 Model Rules of Prof'l Conduct r. 4.4 (Am. Bar Ass'n 2020).
61 See Phila. Bar Ass'n Prof'l Guidance Comm., Formal Op. 2009-02 (2009) www.philadelphiabar.org/WebObjects/PBAReadOnly.woa/Contents/WebServerResources/CMSResources/Opinion_2009-2.pdf (hereinafter Phila. Formal Op. 2009-02); NY St. Bar Ass'n, Formal Op. 843 (2010) www.nysba.org/Content/ContentFolders/EthicsOpinions/Opinions826900/EO_843.pdf; NYC Bar Ass'n, Formal Op. 2010-2 (2010) www.nycbar.org/ethics/ethics-opinions-local/2010-opinions/786-obtaining-evidence-from-social-networking-websites ("There are boundaries to allowing a lawyer to "friend" an unrepresented party, but they are not crossed when the lawyer uses "only truthful information"); NH Bar Ass'n Ethics Comm., Advisory Op. 2012-13/05 (2013) www.nhbar.org/legal-links/Ethics-Opinion-2012-13_05.asp.
62 See San Diego Cnty Bar Ass'n, Formal Op. 2011-2 (2011) www.sdcba.org/index.cfm?pg=LEC2011-2.
63 *Supra* at note 57.

64 Model Rules of Prof'l Conduct r. 5.1 (Am. Bar Ass'n 2020).

65 Model Rules of Prof'l Conduct r. 5.2 (Am. Bar Ass'n 2020).

66 Model Rules of Prof'l Conduct r. 5.3 (Am. Bar Ass'n 2020).

67 *See Robertelli v. New Jersey Office of Atty Ethics*, 224 NJ 470 (NJ 2016).

68 Model Rules of Prof'l Conduct r. 8.4 (Am. Bar Ass'n 2020).

69 *See*, *e.g.*, Phila. Formal Op. 2009-02, *supra* note 25.

70 Jan L. Jacobowitz Ms., Negative Commentary – Negative Consequences: Legal Ethics, Social Media, and the Impact of Explosive Commentary, 11 *St. Mary's Journal On Legal Malpractice & Ethics* 312 (2021).

71 *Ibid.*

72 *Ibid.*

73 *Ibid.*

74 www.brainyquote.com/quotes/john_f_kennedy_121068.

# Chapter 13:
# Access to justice

*By Natalie Anne Knowlton, co-founder, Access to Justice Ventures*

## Introduction

Our justice system is not delivering on its core aspirations. Increasing numbers of people are being excluded from meaningful engagement with the system, to the point that the efficacy of the system itself should be called into question. Traditional providers are meeting the needs of fewer and fewer legal consumers. The justice gap as a concept does not begin to convey the human costs of this market failure. As the gap widens, however, legal technology solutions are pouring in to fill it. This chapter will explore how these solutions are enhancing the ability of certain consumer segments to better participate in the justice system.[1]

The chapter provides context and scope, exploring definitions of *access to justice*, detailing the justice gap as it has manifested in the "PeopleLaw" sector – legal services for individuals and small businesses[2] – and discussing what *legal technology* means in this context. We discuss the diversification of stakeholders who are developing, implementing, and deploying access to justice technologies before exploring various trends in today's consumer-facing technology solutions – specifically, tech's facilitation of accessible *and deployable* legal information, document assembly and automation, end-to-end case management services, productized legal services, and improvements to the user experience.

The chapter concludes with a few of the issues regarding the increasing technology undercurrent in access to justice solutions. Some of these issues include increasing digital divides, implications on traditional processes and providers, and regulatory uncertainties.

## Access to what? What is justice?

There are almost as many definitions of *access to justice* as there are people and organizations working in the field. The term is used so frequently, in so many different contexts, that some argue it has been relegated to buzz-word status. But the term *does* intuitively convey certain notions about rights and obligations, fair outcomes, the rule of law, and access to legal and related services. In the United States, some advocates use the term to mean specifically access to legal services.[3] A more restrictive variation on this theme limits the scope even further to mean access to an attorney.

This chapter takes a far more expansive view on what constitutes access to justice. The US Institute of Peace defines the concept in a way that reflects this broader scope:

> *"Access to justice is defined as the ability of people to seek and obtain a remedy through formal or informal institutions of justice for grievances in compliance with human rights standards. There is no access to justice where citizens (especially marginalized groups) fear the system, see it as alien, and do not access it; where the justice system is financially inaccessible; where individuals have no lawyers; where they do not have information or knowledge of rights; or where there is a weak justice system."*[4]

There is also a component to the definition offered by Bob Glaves, executive director of the Chicago Bar Foundation, that conveys an important point: "Access to justice includes both substantive and procedural elements, and they are interdependent".[5] As will be discussed further below, existing access to justice tools are serving both functions.

## The (access to) justice gap

There is an argument to be made that the US justice system is working exactly as intended – designed to serve the wealthy, the white, the privileged.[6] But even if we rely on an aspirational vision, a fair, impartial, and accessible system that serves all is still a distant blip on the radar. There are many ways in which our system is failing to deliver access to justice – and failing to deliver justice itself. This chapter focuses specifically on the growing disconnect in the PeopleLaw sector between what traditional providers are offering and what legal consumers are using,[7] and how technology solutions are pouring into this justice gap.

Our justice system is a system of gatekeepers. It was designed by judges and attorneys, for judges and attorneys. But in most state civil courts today, attorneys are not the predominate court user.[8] National figures suggest approximately three in four civil and family cases involve at least one person who does not have a lawyer.[9] US civil courts today are "lawyerless".[10] These court users face complicated procedures and rules full of Latin and legalese. Through a growing body of empirical evidence, we know that outcomes are affected when people do not have legal help.[11] People lose their homes or custody of their children, are forced into bankruptcy, and experience other serious consequences.

The justice gap disproportionately affects those living in poverty, and it perpetuates poverty. But it is not just low-income individuals who have trouble accessing justice. The Legal Services Corporation (LSC) income eligibility requirements include households with income at or below 125 percent of the US Department of Health and Human Services Federal Poverty Guidelines (FPG).[12] Under the 2022 FPG, this corresponds to annual incomes below $17,500 for an individual and $34,500 for a family of four. But there are substantial numbers of people living on just the other side of these income levels who are no more able to afford legal help.

The 2022 LSC *Justice Gap* report affirms this reality. Just under half (45 percent) of low-income study respondents felt confident in their ability to find a lawyer they could afford.[13] The numbers rise to 59 percent and 73 percent for those between 125 percent and 400 percent of the FPG and for those at or above 400 percent of the FPG, respectively.[14] The fact that 41 percent of individuals living between 125 percent and 400 percent of the FPG were not confident they could find an affordable attorney highlights the dangers of assuming that access to justice is only a *low-income issue*. This is where we meet the justice gap's Missing Middle – middle class individuals and families who have issues finding affordable legal help but for whom subsidized legal services are not available.

Further, there are many interrelated factors driving legal consumers to opt out of traditional legal services – or opt out of the civil justice system entirely. The cost of legal services is a major factor.[15] Affordability, however, is a nuanced concept. People make choices about how to prioritize the resources they have available. Income is a poor proxy for one's ability to afford legal services, as this figure does not reflect debts and liabilities. Beyond financial considerations, other reasons drive people to decline attorney help, including perceptions of attorneys,[16] personal preferences, and/or confidence in navigating the process alone. Viewed in this broader context of consumer behavior, the issue of choice in legal services providers becomes an important piece of access to justice.

The justice gap is incredibly complex and notoriously difficult (if not impossible) to measure, in large part because there are so many ways of defining the issue. The discussion above mentions just a few ways in which the gap is contextualized; there is much more work to be done. What *is* clear from existing research is that massive gaps exist in people's ability to meaningfully engage with our justice system.

## Using legal technology to narrow the gap

Like access to justice, the term *legal technology* is similarly amorphous. As this chapter sits within a broader handbook on legal technology, it is likely that any number of definitions have been presented. Many of these likely refer to solutions being used by lawyers and law firms.

The internal tools that private and public attorneys use to create efficiencies in practice are incredibly valuable to legal consumers. Legal aid providers, for example, are leveraging technology in impressive ways to streamline case intake, triage, case management, and other internal operations.[17] Suffolk University Law School's Legal Innovation and Technology Lab is working with the legal aid community to provide AI-powered issue-spotting through Spot API.[18] Private companies like Paladin are creating efficiencies in connecting lawyers to pro bono work. These technologies do support access to justice outcomes.

This chapter, however, will focus on the tools used by members of the public to participate in the legal process – consumer-facing technologies. Professor Rebecca Sandefur, in her 2019 American Bar Foundation report on the Survey of US Legal Technologies, refers to:

> *"Tools that non-lawyers may use to diagnose, understand, or take action on legal problems, whether those nonlawyers are using the tools to work on their own problems or are working to assist others with justice problems, for example in their work as staff of community organizations, courts, or social services providers."*[19]

Technology solutions targeted to these user groups include tools designed specifically for the legal and judicial sectors. They also include cross-sector technologies that are used for tasks in the legal domain (messaging apps, for example). Finally, this chapter includes those technologies that are classified in the emerging *justice tech* sector. The Justice Technology Association (on whose Board of Advisors I sit) defines justice tech as "innovative technology designed to improve access to one's legal rights, improve outcomes for justice-involved individuals, or more equitably administer a legal system".[20]

## Stakeholders

The proliferation of access to justice technologies is diversifying the stakeholder ecosystem.

State courts are on the frontlines of the deepening market failure in the PeopleLaw sector. By sheer necessity, the traditional court role is evolving into one focused on delivering (neutral) resources to people without attorneys. (This is not universal. Some state court systems are resistant to making even the most basic information or court forms available to the public.) Even so, courts generally do not operate at the cutting edge of consumer-facing technology. But new partnerships with institutions and private companies are supporting the development of more sophisticated court technologies.

Academic institutions have become active developers of access to justice technology. Some institutions have schools, labs, and incubators dedicated to exploring how technology can increase access to justice. On a smaller scale, individual educators are teaching students about the interplay between technology and access. Certain institutions work directly with court systems and legal services providers to develop and test technology solutions for the public.[21] For example, a new program at Georgetown Law is taking a unique approach to court modernization by placing justice innovation fellows within courts to build data infrastructure, simplify processes, and improve usability of services.[22] The Filing Fairness Project is a multi-jurisdictional effort to simplify court filing processes and enable high-quality form tools for lawyers and litigants. Stanford Law School's Deborah L. Rhode Center on the Legal Profession and Legal Design Lab are partnering with several state court systems on the project.[23]

Whether in partnership with traditional stakeholders or as independent market participants, consumer-facing technology companies are proliferating. The newly formed Justice Technology Association and its member companies are working to "grow, shape, and organize the emerging justice tech market to demonstrate how technology can provide affordable, accessible solutions to people facing everyday legal issues".[24] Access to justice organizations are even starting to invest in these kinds of companies.[25]

The relationships between these diverse stakeholders are not always harmonious. Some attorneys are skeptical of legal technology companies; others are downright hostile. Still other lawyers and law firms are partnering with or building their own technology solutions. As noted above, the long-standing relationship between courts and private attorneys is also changing. It is not uncommon for bar associations to oppose court efforts to make forms and self-help information available online. Not all lawyers and courts have acknowledged the fact that the tide has turned on attorney dominance in state courts.

While judges and courts are increasingly turning to legal technology companies to build out in-court tech capabilities, it is far rarer for courts to enter into outward-facing partnerships with and/or endorse specific companies.[26]

## Trends in today's access to justice tech solutions

### Accessible and deployable legal information

Access to justice advocates have long focused on making legal information readily accessible, and the internet today is packed with it. While few would find general information to be a substitute for bespoke legal advice, attorney services *are* being disintermediated by the proliferation of online information (however imperfect that information is). Today, search engines are among the – if not *the* – most used resources for people seeking legal help, whether or not they intend to hire an attorney.

As is true with online content in general, though, not all legal information is created equal. Thanks to pioneering research on the online behavior of legal consumers and on how laypersons digest legal information (or do not), we now know that accessibility is only part of the equation. The other part is *deployability*.[27] Even the most accessible legal information is of no use if a person cannot understand it and use it to advance their issue. As our understanding of the needs of legal consumers evolves, technology is supporting a shift away from the static website.

Evolutions in modern website design and thoughtful information architecture are creating a new generation of online legal resources. Thoughtful content hierarchies and staged information allow users to customize their journey. Workflows and other guiding information create a clear path from information to action. Providers are repackaging written content into videos – a strategy that many courts adopted during the pandemic[28] – and using other multimedia to provide users with multiple entryways to information. There are even tools that gamify parts of the court process to increase the deployability of information. RePresent, for example, simulates legal proceedings as a game in order to teach people how to represent themselves in civil cases – a sort of virtual moot court for self-represented litigants.[29]

Finally, just as the static page of legal information was, at one time, a notable development in access to justice, advances in machine learning are promising (or threatening, depending on one's perspective) to further change the way legal information is delivered online. At the time of writing, generative artificial intelligence is all anyone can talk about. Within the legal community, OpenAI's ChatGPT has written a law review article, passed the bar exam, and probably authored countless law school essays by now. While the information ChatGPT provides is imperfect and sometimes wrong (as is legal information online generally), future iterations of generative AI tools promise to be far more sophisticated. As utility and reliability increase, these tools will offer new ways for legal consumers to quickly and easily access deployable legal information – and even legal advice.[30]

## Document assembly and automation[31]

Deployment becomes immediate when technology automates certain pieces of the process.

From a consumer-facing standpoint, forms, filings, and other paperwork have been the most obvious targets of automation. Court forms are a particularly problematic piece of the process for people without attorney help. People make mistakes, omit necessary information, or submit the wrong form altogether.[32] Clerks frequently have to return forms to litigants and people can go through several iterations before having their documentation accepted. An increasing number of tools are using guided interviews with simple, clear, plain-language questions to help people fill out necessary forms.

The Utah State Courts, for example, developed the Online Court Assistance Program to assist unrepresented litigants with preparing court documents. Users select and complete the interview that corresponds to their document needs, and the program creates their documents.[33] LawHelp Interactive (LHI) is a website that helps individuals locate state legal documents in a variety of civil case types.[34] Questionnaires guide users through the document assembly and, in some instances, users can e-file directly with the court. LHI has generated more than 2.6 million documents in the last ten years.[35]

## End-to-end case management services

People navigating the legal system on their own must complete a dizzying array of tasks. It is easy for system insiders to simplify the process, but the complexity is not lost on the court user. It is not just substantive case preparation, which can be incredibly time consuming for people who rarely have even a base-level understanding of the legal and court process. When you add administrative and logistical tasks such as printing and notarizing forms, finding childcare, and traveling to the courthouse, it can add up to hundreds of hours for even a simple matter.

In 2016, the Institute for the Advancement of the American Legal System at the University of Denver conducted qualitative empirical research on the experiences of self-represented litigants in family cases. One study participant noted:

> *"It felt very much like wandering through a room with no lights on, and you'd bump into something, you'd ask somebody about it, and they'd shine a little flashlight and say, 'go that way.' … Nobody ever turned the lights on in the whole room to give us an idea of exactly what it should look like and how the process should look."*[36]

Today, a new category of access to justice platforms is facilitating a user experience that involves broader case management services – pairing curated legal information with step-by-step process workflows. The Self-Help Guide to the California Courts, developed by the California Judicial Council, helps users navigate the various stages of their civil or family court case.[37] Across Maryland, the judiciary-supported Justice Passport provides users with a digital portfolio of information that can be used to track service applications, store documents, and organize case information.[38]

An increasing number of private technology providers, too, are developing these holistic case management solutions. Courtroom5, for example, navigates users through various stages of the process and provides relevant legal information, training, and tools along the way.[39] JusticeDirect, developed by Quest for Justice, is designed to embed directly into a court's self-help website to provide guided legal education, document generation, and trial preparation.[40] Erin Levine, founder of the online divorce platform Hello Divorce, has said, "Self-service tools along with a clear roadmap has been key to our success rate".[41]

### Productized legal services

The traditional model of legal services delivery is still the dominant practice – attorneys provide bespoke legal services on a one-to-one basis, usually face-to-face, and through an hourly billing fee structure (or a fixed-fee arrangement often based on the average number of hours it takes to handle a matter). Lawyers and other service providers cannot scale such time-based, one-to-one service models.

Furthermore, the traditional model reflects the profession's often-singular focus on providing clients with bespoke legal advice. This is understandable, of course. Attorneys are uniquely positioned to provide this expertise, and bespoke legal advice is the gold standard in legal services. But since an increasing number of legal consumers cannot or will not pay for legal services through this traditional model, innovative attorneys are looking beyond legal advice to the other segments of their expertise that can add value for legal consumers and that can be widely distributed online – legal information, general guidance, non-legal advice.

Simple no-code and low-code tools allow attorneys to develop and package content that has sufficient generality to be of use to a wide range of legal consumers – and that does not necessitate their direct involvement.[42] For example, LawGuides provides Coloradans with easy-to-digest, step-by-step information about the divorce and custody process. Developed by Lester Law, the downloadable guides include video tutorials and instructions, links to court forms, checklists, and worksheets.[43] Similarly, Hello Divorce integrates legal information with automated forms and options for one-on-one engagement with a legal services professional. These products and services benefit legal consumers because the price point is far lower than would be possible through a one-to-one, client-attorney relationship. These products also offer consumers a choice of service level that is more responsive to what they want and need, not just what they can afford.

This one-to-many service model is enabling attorneys to reach people at different stages of their justice journey – and to reach people online who have no intention of hiring an attorney. Father-son team Richard Susskind and Daniel Susskind talk about this shift in the context of reintermediation. While online legal information has disintermediated attorneys to some degree, "some innovative professionals are seeking to reintermediate themselves, that is, to insert themselves in new places in the supply chain".[44] In a sense, these providers are maintaining their relevance while removing themselves from the delivery of their expertise.

### Improvements to the user experience

The strategy of meeting legal consumers where they are has not been one with which the legal industry has historically spent much time. Before virtual interfaces and remote services became a necessity during the pandemic, many of our nation's courts had not yet thought of court as a service (as opposed to a place). Now, some innovative courts are looking beyond practices like virtual hearings and asking how else the justice system can better integrate into the channels and places where users already are.

Here are some examples:

- The Salt Lake City Justice Court is using Doodle to coordinate between parties to schedule hearings, which has dramatically reduced failure to appear rates.[45]
- The CourtConnect app in Ohio's Cuyahoga County Domestic Relations Court sends users notification for filing deadlines and hearing scheduling and postponement.[46]
- Michigan Legal Help developed its What's Next Text program to improve the delivery of legal information via automated text messaging to those who are not eligible for traditional legal aid programs.[47]

In Jefferson Parish, Louisiana, Judge Scott Schlegel has deployed a number of tools designed to be responsive to user needs and to deliver necessary resources at the time people need them. Court users can schedule appointments with him directly through an online scheduling platform and those with questions can engage with Judge Schlegel's digital assistant – two separate chatbots (one for civil and one for criminal) powered by LawDroid. Finally, Judge Schlegel has an app that can be downloaded from a QR Code on his website, through which court users can schedule hearings, attend court online, and perform other functions related to their case.[48]

Interestingly, courts and legal services providers are also using technology solutions to reach court users who lack access to technology or a reliable internet connection. A2J Tech, a social enterprise that builds technology to improve access to justice, and Minnesota Legal Services partnered to create the Minnesota Legal Kiosks project.[49] The project installed a network of over 250 legal kiosks across the state in a variety of court, agency, non-profit, and community locations. Through these kiosks, Minnesotans can access legal information, connect with legal aid services, print forms, and even attend court hearings.

Private attorney services, too, are being delivered directly to clients at the time a legal issue arises. In the criminal justice space, TurnSignl is an on-demand, real-time service providing 24/7 legal guidance from an attorney while the camera on the user's smartphone records the interaction.[50] The company's attorneys are trained to de-escalate potentially volatile encounters. Similarly, at the time of writing, Dispatch Justice was beta testing a platform that virtually dispatches a live, local attorney to observe contact with police during stops.

## Challenges in redesigning tomorrow's tech-enabled justice system

### Shifts from processes and providers to outcomes

The integration of technology into legal systems and services is raising new questions about underlying processes and traditional providers.

Legal processes and court procedures are complex – very often unnecessarily so. If the same procedures just get incorporated into a technical solution, the result is just an unnecessarily complicated process with a digital interface. Former Colorado Supreme Court Justice Rebecca Love Kourlis refers to this practice as "paving the cow path". Automation magnifies inefficiencies.

Golden Krishna, head of design strategy, platforms and ecosystems at Google, suggests in his book *The Best Interface Is No Interface*, that somewhere along the way the disciplines of UI (user interface) and UX (user experience) blurred together. He writes that in creating technology experiences in the consumer marketplace, "instead of pursuing the best, most creative, inventive, and useful ways to solve a problem, we started solving problems with screens. … When we saw problems, we slapped an interface on it."[51] Consumers do not want an interface; they want an outcome.

A related theme emerges in literature on behavioral economics and choice architecture. In his book *Simpler: The Future of Government*, Cass Sunstein proposes that, "For governments, the goal should be to ensure that if people do nothing at all, things will go well for them. And if people are required to take action, government should make the process … as simple and automatic as possible."[52] But the human costs of doing nothing in the justice system can be severe, and the system does little to adequately (and proactively) inform people that there is something to be done.[53]

As courts and private providers develop direct-to-consumer tech solutions, there is a considerable opportunity to create tools that hide complexities, remove unnecessary interfaces, and focus the user experience on outputs and outcomes instead of inputs and processes. There is interesting work being done on this front in efforts to simplify court forms. At the time of writing, Stanford Law School's Deborah L. Rhode Center on the Legal Profession and Legal Design Lab are trying to scale filing simplification through the Filing Fairness Project. The project seeks to simplify the collection and filing of legal data, to create the standardization necessary to support sustainable, cross-jurisdiction technology solutions.[54] This effort and others are laying the foundation for a future move beyond court forms. After all, forms are not outcomes. They are merely vehicles through which to achieve a desired outcome – getting court user data into court systems.[55]

Of course, this shift to outcome-based thinking is also impacting the role of traditional legal services providers. Legal futurist Richard Susskind issued a candid warning to legal professionals in his book *Online Courts and the Future of Justice*:

> *"The disconcerting message here for all professionals is that clients do not really want them. They want the outcomes that professionals bring … and when these outcomes can be reliably delivered in new ways that are demonstrably cheaper, better, quicker, or more convenient than the current offering, we can expect the market to switch to alternatives."*[56]

This is precisely what we are seeing in the consumer legal services space. The disconnect between what traditional providers are offering and what legal consumers are buying is only growing. As more consumers shift to non-traditional providers (including technology solutions), there are far-reaching implications on legal education, professional licensure, and legal regulation.

## Regulatory uncertainty

Technology's role in legal services delivery and its exponentially increasing capabilities are converging at the edge of existing regulatory boundaries. Professional regulations and legal regulators are already unable (and sometimes unwilling) to keep pace with the changing realities of the legal services marketplace.

The regulation that most immediately impacts justice and legal technology companies is the prohibition on the unauthorized practice of law (UPL). Make no mistake, software today is capable of practicing law.[57] But this is less a testament to the sophistication of the technologies in the sector and more an indictment of the overly broad take on what constitutes the unauthorized practice of law.[58] The *practice of law* is poorly defined; as a result, what constitutes UPL is poorly defined.

All too often, UPL rules are used against legal technology providers by market incumbents – lawyers – and there is little evidence of actual consumer harm in enforcement actions.[59] Without new approaches, outdated regulations will continue to have a stranglehold on technology's capacity to deliver legal services. As technologies become more and more sophisticated, legal regulators will be forced to revisit the regulation of technology solutions – and specifically those that are delivering qualified, competent, and responsible legal services to consumers. It is critical that this conversation recognize the many shortcomings of the current consumer market.

The experience in Utah – where authorized entities in a regulatory sandbox can deploy software that practices law – suggests that, to date at least, providers are not in a rush to create technology solutions that obviate the need for human-provided advice.[60] The data collected through the sandbox will provide important insights on consumer harm as it relates to the technology solutions operating there. It will likely become increasingly difficult for traditional providers to maintain their monopoly on services that they are by and large not providing.

## Digital divides

At the same time that technology is creating more access than ever before, it is also creating new divisions.

Legal technologies are getting more sophisticated every day, but the transfer of voice, video, and data requires high-speed internet. Communities across the country – especially those in rural areas – often lack the broadband service necessary to meaningfully engage with this new technology ecosystem.[61] This issue is commonly referred to as the *digital divide* – although others suggest this term does not convey the gravity of the situation: "We are facing a digital chasm that will emerge if we do not act and the cluster of digital divides gets larger, longer-lasting, and harder to close."[62]

It is not just broadband access. Professor Tanina Rostain suggests there are other reasons that we need to temper our techno-optimism. Aspirations of self-help technologies being a great equalizer "overlook the cultural, material, and educational hurdles [people living in poverty] confront … when attempting to find legal help".[63] Rostain reminds us that, "For poor people, the struggle of dealing with chronic scarcity of money and food and lack of physical security makes it even more difficult to absorb and act on legal information". This is an important issue for the access to justice community. Rural communities contain some of the most vulnerable members of society; we risk them becoming even more so by excluding them from an increasingly tech-heavy justice system.

There is another digital divide of sorts playing out in states and counties. Individual judicial districts and judges enjoy a large degree of discretion on procedural issues, including decisions on how to manage courtroom processes and the integration of technology into those processes. As a result, there can be vast inconsistencies on virtual proceeding practices between regional court systems and even between courtrooms in the same courthouse. These divides seem to be deepening as courts make decisions on how to integrate pandemic protocols into permanent practices. Of course, these discrepancies are much broader than just practices on virtual proceedings. Judicial commitments to serving unrepresented persons varies wildly around the country. These inconsistencies in the administration of justice are troubling.

The major takeaway of these and related caveats is that technology alone is not going to solve the access to justice crisis. This does not, however, discount any of the technology developments discussed above. It *does* mandate additional efforts on behalf of justice stakeholders to create easily accessible alternatives, to ensure that broader communities are engaged in the service delivery process, and to support infrastructure building across the country.

## Conclusion

Overall, the future of legal technology to bridge justice gaps is bright – but this brightness is bounded by the limitations of technology, legal system capacity, intent, and legal practice. Technology is not the only solution, but in tandem with others it may well have the power to be transformative for the seemingly interminable access to justice crisis.

*The author would like to thank Dr Lachlan Deyong, former director of the Better Justice Lab, and Sam Glover, founder of Lawyerist and collaborator with do-gooders who want to build a powerful web presence. These colleagues and friends were instrumental in making the FFDF draft a little less FDF.*

## *References*

1 This chapter is by no means complete or exhaustive. It is impossible to cover all trends, opportunities, and pressing challenges in access to justice technologies in a single place. Furthermore, this chapter reflects the expertise and perspectives of one advocate. The field is rich with diverse voices; reading and consulting them will provide a more complete and holistic understanding of these issues.

2 The PeopleLaw sector is the sector serving individuals and small businesses. The justice needs of, and the technology tools available for, small businesses differ from those in the individual legal consumer space. Given the expertise of the author on individual legal consumers, this chapter will not cover small businesses.

3 *See, e.g.*, Chase Hertel, *Access to Justice: We Can Do Better*, Medium: Legal Serv. Corp. Emerging Leaders Council (7 March 2022) https://medium.com/justice-rising/access-to-justice-we-can-do-better-ee5af1d4921b ("I believe the phrase access to justice is inadequate, not because I don't believe in it as a call for action, but because the word justice doesn't align with what those who lack access are *actually* searching for – legal services.").

4 US Inst. of Peace, *Necessary Conditions: Access to Justice 7.8.1* www.usip.org/guiding-principles-stabilization-and-reconstruction-the-web-version/rule-law/access-justice (citations removed).

5 Bob Glaves, *What Do We Mean When We Say Access to Justice?*, Chi. Bar Found. (20 September 2018) https://chicagobarfoundation.org/blog/bobservations/what-do-we-mean-when-we-say-access-to-justice.

6 The author, among others, has made that argument. *See, e.g.*, Natalie Anne Knowlton, *Trusting the Public's Perception of Our Justice System*, IAALS (27 August 2020) https://iaals.du.edu/blog/trusting-public-s-perception-our-justice-system.

7 Within the PeopleLaw sector, access to justice scholarship gives quite a bit of attention to what is called the "knowledge gap", denoting the vast numbers of people who do not know their problems have a legal remedy. This chapter will focus solely on the justice gap, although technology promises to be disruptive for this broader market as well. *See, e.g.*, Daniel W. Linna Jr., *The Future of Law and Computational Technologies: Two Sides of the Same Coin*, MIT Computational L. Report (6 December 2019)

https://law.mit.edu/pub/thefutureoflawandcomputationaltechnologies/release/2 ("AI and pattern matching technologies can help catalyze the development of proactive approaches to identify potential legal problems and prevent them from arising, or at least mitigate their risk.").

8 The US criminal justice system is in crisis. There are pervasive and systemic access to justice issues in nearly all facets of the system. This chapter focuses on pieces of access to justice in the civil justice system, only because of the author's expertise. Some of the technology solutions discussed herein, however, reach people dealing with criminal issues as well as those dealing with civil issues.

9 Nat'l Ctr for State Courts and Inst. For the Advancement of the Am. Legal Sys., The Landscape of Domestic Relations Cases in State Courts 20 (2018); Nat'l Ctr. For State Courts, The Landscape of Civil Litigation in State Courts iv (2015).

10 *See* Anna E. Carpenter et al., *Judges in Lawyerless Courts*, 110 Geo. L.J. 509 (2022).

11 *See* Ellen Degnan et al., Trapped in Marriage, 10 (23 October 2018) https://papers.ssrn.com/sol3/papers.cfm?abstract_id=3277900 (finding that "lawyers unquestionably made a difference, an enormous difference, to low-income would-be divorcees in Philadelphia"); *Access to Counsel*, Nat'l Immigrant Justice Ctr. https://immigrantjustice.org/issues/access-counsel ("Immigrants who are not detained and have attorneys are five times more likely to pursue relief and are nearly five times more likely win [sic] their cases than those without attorneys.... Detained immigrants are 11 times more likely to pursue relief when they have legal counsel and are twice as likely to obtain relief than detained immigrants without counsel.").

12 Legal Serv. Corp., *What is Legal Aid?* www.lsc.gov/about-lsc/what-legal-aid.

13 Legal Serv. Corp., The Justice Gap: The Unmet Civil Legal Needs of Low-Income Americans, Section 5: Comparing Income Groups (2022) https://justicegap.lsc.gov/resource/section-5-comparing-income-groups/.

14 *Ibid*.

15 The costs associated with becoming a lawyer and running a law practice, of course, affect the rates attorneys charge clients. Professor Gillian Hadfield suggests that "[t]he real question is not whether lawyers earn too much but whether law costs too much. These are very different questions." Gillian K. Hadfield, Rules for a Flat World: Why Humans Invented Law and How to Reinvent It for a Complex Global Economy 177 (2017).

16 Innovation for Justice, Leveraging Regulatory Reform to Advance Access to Justice: January 2023 Prototype Draft (2023) https://docs.google.com/document/d/1064M_OpQwgm7CFBqIkiv9A0W_nh6QvSTr_KLG5wc1hw/edit (finding that the consumers involved in Innovation for Justice's research "tend to trust someone who has received legal training but not a JD as their legal advocate more than they trust an attorney. In fact, consumers are more likely to try to solve their legal problems on their own than seek assistance from an attorney.").

17 The Legal Services Corporation Technology Initiative Grant (TIG) Program is supporting many of these developments. *Technology Initiative Grant Program*, Legal Serv. Corp. www.lsc.gov/grants/technology-initiative-grant-program.
18 *The Legal Innovation and Technology Lab's Spot API*, Suffolk L. Sch. https://spot.suffolklitlab.org.
19 Rebecca Sandefur, Legal Tech for Non-Lawyers: Report of the Survey of US Legal Technologies 5 (2019) www.americanbarfoundation.org/uploads/cms/documents/report_us_digital_legal_tech_for_nonlawyers.pdf.
20 Justice Tech. Ass'n https://justicetechassociation.org.
21 *See also* Margaret Hagan, *Justice Innovation with Law School Design Labs*, Dialogue (15 June 2018) www.americanbar.org/groups/legal_services/publications/dialogue/volume/21/spring-2018/iolta-design-labs/?login.
22 *The Judicial Innovation Fellowship Program*, Geo. Law www.law.georgetown.edu/tech-institute/initiatives/georgetown-justice-lab/judicial-innovation.
23 *Filing Fairness Project*, Stan. L. Sch. https://law.stanford.edu/filing-fairness-project.
24 *About JTA*, Justice Tech. Ass'n https://justicetechassociation.org/about.
25 *E.g.*, *Innovating Justice Fund*, HiiL www.hiil.org/innovating-justice-fund.
26 An exception in a few courts are co-parenting tools in family court cases. Some individual judges will detail in the parenting agreement specific providers that parents must use.
27 *See* Margaret Hagan, *The User Experience of the Internet as a Legal Help Service: Defining standards for the next generation of user-friendly online legal services*, 20 Va. J. L. & Tech. 395, 401 (2016) ("Simply putting legal information and resources online will not by itself increase laypeople's access to it. The information must be presented in usable and user-friendly ways so that it will be of value to people beyond experts like lawyers and law librarians."). *See also* J. David Griener et al., *Self-Help Reimagined*, 92 Ind. L.J. 1119, 1123 (2017), ("Self-help materials cannot be successful unless two conditions are met: (1) the lay would-be user can find materials in a timely manner (are self-help materials *accessible?*), and once found, (2) the lay would-be user can successfully use the materials to advance his or her cause (are the self-help materials *deployable?*).").
28 *See, e.g.*, Michael Houlberg & Janet Drobinske, Pandemic Positives: Extending the Reach of Court and Legal Services (2020) https://iaals.du.edu/sites/default/files/documents/publications/pandemic_positives.pdf.
29 RePresent www.representgames.org/about.
30 As to whether legal consumers *should* be using ChatGPT to seek out legal answers is a separate issue from whether legal consumers *will* be using ChatGPT. The latter scenario is absolutely foreseeable, no matter what one thinks about the former question.
31 There is much more to be said on document assembly and automation as an

important access to justice tool. Readers can learn much more in another section of this handbook.

32 *See*, *e.g.*, Natalie Anne Knowlton et al., Cases Without Counsel: Research on Experiences on Self-Representation in U.S. Family Court 32-33 (2016) https://iaals.du.edu/sites/default/files/documents/publications/cases_without_counsel_research_report.pdf.

33 *Utah Online Assistance Program*, Utah State Courts www.utcourts.gov/en/self-help/services/ocap.html#accordion-1efc14234c-item-914e5c3b3e.

34 LawHelp Interactive https://lawhelpinteractive.org.

35 Claudia Johnson, *Document Assembly: An Essential Building Block for the Access to Justice Ecosystem*, Self-Represented Litig. Network (2016) www.srln.org/node/848/document-assembly-essential.

36 Knowlton et al., *supra* note 32, at 178.

37 *Self-Help Guide to the California Courts*, Judicial Branch of Cal. https://selfhelp.courts.ca.gov/.

38 Maryland Justice Passport www.mdjusticepassport.org.

39 Courtroom5 https://courtroom5.com.

40 Quest 4 Justice www.q4justice.com.

41 Erin Levine, *Stop Lawyer-splaining: What We've Learned About What Legal Consumers Actually Want*, Medium (24 October 2022) https://erinlevinepace.medium.com/stop-lawyer-splaining-what-weve-learned-about-what-legal-consumers-actually-want-68e763c0bc23.

42 Richard Susskind and Daniel Susskind discuss this evolution in the context of "the knowledge engineering model." Richard Susskind and Daniel Susskind, The Future of the Professions: How Technology Will Transform the Work of Human Experts, 221-22 (2015).

43 LawGuides https://colawguides.com.

44 Susskind & Susskind, *supra* note 42, at 121-22.

45 Houlberg & Drobinske, *supra* note 28, at 4.

46 Cory Schaffer, *Cuyahoga County Domestic Relations Court's new smartphone app meant to bring courtrooms to palms of users' hands*, Cleveland.com (8 August 2019, 4:05 PM) www.cleveland.com/court-justice/2019/08/cuyahoga-county-domestic-relations-courts-new-smartphone-app-meant-to-bring-courtrooms-to-palms-of-users-hands.html.

47 *Michigan Legal Help Launches Testing Program to Improve Services*, Mich. Legal Help (27 January 2022) https://michiganlegalhelp.org/news/michigan-legal-help-launches-texting-program-improve-services.

48 Judge Scott Schlegel www.onlinejudge.us.

49 *Minn. Legal Kiosks*, A2J Tech www.goa2jtech.com/case-studies-new/minnesota-legal-kiosks.

50 TurnSignl www.turnsignl.com.

51 Golden Krishna, The Best Interface Is No Interface: The Simple Path to Brilliant Technology 47 (2015). I have applied Krishna's framework in thinking about whether certain online dispute resolution (ODR) tools are merely slapping an interface on traditional mediation practices. Natalie Anne Knowlton, *Slap An Interface On It: Rethinking Our Approach to Tech Integration in Our Courts*, Medium (26 August 2019) https://medium.com/swlh/slap-an-interface-on-it-72b152eaa5e3.

52 Cass R. Sunstein, Simpler: The Future of Government 100 (2013).

53 *See, e.g.*, Natalie Anne Knowlton, *When Nothing is Something: Building Better Choice Architecture in Our Courts*, Medium (16 October 2020) https://medium.com/@natalalleycat/when-nothing-is-something-7092e2db8278.

54 *History and Theory of Change*, Stan. L. Sch. https://law.stanford.edu/filing-fairness-project/#slsnav-history-and-theory-of-change.

55 From here, it is not outside the realm of possibility that consenting users can have relevant data flow directly to court systems – bypassing them entirely. *See, e.g.*, Sunstein, *supra* note 52, at 123 (describing a Department of Education initiative that allowed key information like tax data held by the IRS to be automatically transferred to Free Application for Federal Student Aid applications).

56 Richard Susskind, Online Courts and the Future of Justice 48 (2019).

57 *See infra* note 58.

58 Consider *In re Patterson* and *In re Crawford* in the US Bankruptcy Court for the District of Maryland which involved Upsolve, a non-profit providing low-income Americans with free software in Chapter 7 bankruptcy proceedings. The Bankruptcy Court initiated its own inquiry into Upsolve's software, raising several issues including UPL. Despite applauding Upsolve for its mission and good intentions, and despite there being no consumer harm at play, the court found that Upsolve's tool *did* constitute the unauthorized practice of law. Specifically at issue: the software self-populated an exemption statute onto a schedule in the Chapter 7 filing. In re Renee Peterson, No. 19-24045 (Bankr. D. Md. 2022) www.govinfo.gov/content/pkg/USCOURTS-mdb-1_19-bk-24045/pdf/USCOURTS-mdb-1_19-bk-24045-0.pdf. This and other cases demonstrate how simplistic some of the software functions are that have triggered UPL enforcement actions.

59 *See, e.g.*, Deborah L. Rhode and Lucy Buford Ricca, *Protecting the Profession or the Public? Rethinking Unauthorized-Practice Enforcement*, 82 Fordham L. Rev. 2587 (2014).

60 The Utah sandbox is focused specifically on business models that seek to innovate around UPL rules and Rule 5.4's restrictions on fee-sharing and co-ownership. With a few exceptions, the authorized software is performing standard document completion functions. Office of Legal Serv. Innovation, Utah Sup. Ct. https://utahinnovationoffice.org.

61 This can be both an access issue and/or an affordability issue.

62 Jonathan Sallet, *America's Broadband Moment*, Benton Inst. for Broadband & Soc'y www.benton.org/blog/broadband-moment.

63 Tanina Rostain, *Techno-Optimism and Access to the Legal System*, Dædalus 93, 94 (2019); *see also* Sendhil Mullainathan & Eldar Shafir, Scarcity: The New Science of Having Less and How It Defines Our Lives (2013); Daniel Kahneman, Thinking, Fast and Slow (2011).

# Chapter 14:
# Adoption of legal tech by law firms

*By Zach Abramowitz, founder, Killer Whale Strategies*

## Introduction

Over the past few years, law firm tech businesses, sometimes called law firm subsidiaries, "New Law", or captive ALSPs, have generated quite a bit of buzz.[1] The attention is well deserved. For years now, panels of in-house thought leaders at industry conferences have lamented the lack of technology and innovation from their outside counsel to the agreeing nods of audience members. Mary O'Carroll's 2019 CLOC keynote[2] delved into what she described as the "disconnect" between the legal ops community and law firms. Tech start-ups can often be heard complaining,[3] even finger-wagging, about long law firm sales cycles and tech-averse attorneys (aka dinosawyers).

So, it is deservedly buzzworthy that a significant number of BigLaw firms have actually moved forward and become more intentional about technology, in some cases going so far as to dedicate a separate entity.

Is it time to be truly bullish about law firm tech businesses? I think the answer is yes, albeit we're likely a few years away from the hockey-stick growth that will convince the skeptics. Let's go on a tour of the surprisingly sturdy foundations upon which these businesses are being built.

## Law firms venturing into adjacent businesses

A 2020 study by Baretz + Brunelle[4] identified 35 firms in the AmLaw 100 and 57 firms in the Global 100 with their own captive ALSP (noting that "dynasties protect their own turf. And not just in sports.").

Because the Baretz + Brunelle study aims to highlight the competition between law firms and ALSPs, it uses a slightly different definition for captive ALSP than I do here for law firm tech business. To qualify for the Baretz + Brunelle study, the service offered must include technology and people. In addition, the focus is limited to the world's very biggest law firms, the AmLaw 100 and Global 100. Several of these businesses report generating tens of millions in annual revenue and a client roster filled with Fortune 500 companies.

As further evidence of market maturation, two firms have already had micro-exits for technology they built – Chapman and Cutler sold Closing Rooms (now SetBuilder) to NetDocuments,[5] and Litera Microsystems acquired a digital disclosure tool from Gilbert + Tobin, a 500-lawyer law firm based in Australia.[6] Hoping to give birth to similar initiatives, Mishcon de Reya's MDR Labs and Denton's Nextlaw Labs have each invested in full portfolios of start-ups, not to mention the cohort of firms that have invested in Reynen Court.

Law firm tech businesses come in all shapes and sizes. Some are structured as wholly-owned entities. Some sit within the firm but are independently branded. Some intend to take on external funding; some are embedded inside the firm. And some have been spun out completely or sold, as was the case with Bryan Cave Leighton Paisner and Lawyers on Demand.[7]

The way in which firms are engaging with technology, and hence the offerings, are not always the same. SixFifty, which is a subsidiary of Wilson Sonsini, has built a pure subscription technology business, whereas MDR Labs, which is owned by UK-based Mishcon de Reya, has built a legal-focused investment arm. Other subsidiaries are establishing deep partnerships with tech companies. For example, KP Labs, the subsidiary of the California-based law firm Keesal Young & Logan, designs workflows for in-house departments through its partnership with Mitratech.[8]

Similarly, in addition to its eDiscovery business and technology consulting, Gravity Stack, which is a subsidiary of Reed Smith, built a deep partnership with contract-review start-up Heretik (acquired by Relativity) to serve as the foundation for its contract intelligence and LIBOR repapering solutions. Gravity Stack also partnered with translation behemoth Lionbridge to develop an application that streamlines the translation process for eDiscovery and contract review.

## Tech businesses not just for BigLaw

To the extent that the trends described above are new, it's new only to BigLaw. In fact, many of the most successful legal technology start-ups of the past ten years were launched inside of a law firm or legal service provider. One of the best examples is cloud-based eDiscovery provider CS Disco, which announced[9] a $60m financing round in 2020 (bringing the total raised to $185m), and appears to be the primary challenger to market leader Relativity. But CS Disco actually started out inside the Houston-based litigation boutique Camara & Sibley, with the "CS" serving as an homage to its beginnings.[10]

CS Disco does not shy away from this messaging, it embraces it.[11] Likewise, eDiscovery software competitor Logikcull started out as Logik Systems, Inc., a brick-and-mortar eDiscovery service provider. Ultimately, however, it transformed into a SaaS company because it could see the opportunity of building better technology to heavily automate a labor-intensive process.[12] While both Camara & Sibley and Logik Systems were profitable as people businesses, the economic opportunity of converting their businesses to tech companies was exponential.

It is also worth noting that this pattern of origin story can be found in start-ups with a PeopleLaw focus. For example, Hello Divorce founder Erin Levine originally started her company as part of her law firm, the Levine Family Law Group, and only later spun it out as a separate company.[13] And although I have focused on law firms, I would be remiss if I didn't mention the 2019 Axiom reorganization that separated Axiom's business into staffing company Axiom, managed service provider Factor, and contract review tech company Knowable. There are even examples of legal departments that have birthed technology companies, such as Ford's and British Tobacco's joint venture / spin out of IP Docketing company Anaqua.[14]

The common origin story of these companies is no coincidence. Tech companies that start out as people businesses have (1) a better path to product/market fit, (2) a de-risked go-to-market strategy, and (3) perhaps most importantly, engaging with them requires little to no change in habits from the buyer.

It's worth diving into the specifics of each advantage.

## Better path to product/market fit

In one of his much-ballyhooed essays, Y Combinator founder Paul Graham says that he looks to fund start-ups where the founder is solving a personal problem ("The way to get start-up ideas is not to try to think of start-up ideas. It's to look for problems, preferably problems you have yourself.").[15]

It is almost cliche to say it at this point, but many start-up founders tend to build technology in search of a problem. When the founder experiences the problem themselves, it is a strong indicator that the problem itself is real and probably applies to more than just the founder.

That does not necessarily mean that legal start-ups must be created in a law firm lab, but it is certainly a huge advantage to diagnosing real problems that need tech-driven solutions. As Bryon Bratcher, managing director of Gravity Stack (a subsidiary of Reed Smith), put it, "Everything we build is demand-led based on our experience and our collaboration with subject matter experts".[16]

Indeed, I have followed this logic in my portfolio of legal tech investing. The primary motivating factor behind my own decision to invest in LegalMation, an AI company focused on the automation of litigation tasks, was that the product started inside LTL Attorneys, an LA-based litigation firm.

Originally, founders James Lee and Thomas Suh were trying to automate the ability to respond to complaints because it was tedious, low-margin work that no one in the firm wanted to do. Eventually, they realized that their technology solved a major problem, not just for the lawyers at their firm but for some of their clients like Walmart, who needed a better way to handle high-volume litigation. So, LTL launched a tech company, LegalMation, with Walmart as a customer.

From an investor perspective, it was also a significant signal to me that Lee and Suh thought there was a bigger economic opportunity in the software they were building than the already lucrative business they were running. To be fair, the success of a legal business does not depend upon a connection to a law firm or other legal service provider. There is a list of successful companies, including Casetext,[17] Paladin, and Ironclad (to name just a few) whose founders were solving a personal problem, but doing it outside the confines of their law firm. I would have been wise to invest in all three.

## De-risked go-to-market strategy

Another strength of starting as a people business is the go-to-market strategy. Some of the most successful investors specifically advise tech start-ups to layer in consulting services at the early stages.[18]

Venture capitalists will often scoff at services revenue because it is not recurring (so no 10× multiples on revenue to determine the company's valuation). The counterpoint, however, is that services revenue gives the founders more runway, which in turn gives them more time to achieve product/market fit without having to beg investors for more money. Law firms and service providers that morph into, or spin out technology companies, already have the consulting services in place; their challenge is to layer in technology.

This skepticism toward services revenue is even more pronounced in the legal industry, where top-flight venture capital firms already shy away from investing in legal start-ups. Yet, this tends to overlook a second enormous advantage of a legal services business – getting meaningful user adoption and feedback is incredibly difficult with lawyers who are often on time-sensitive assignments and do not have the patience to try new technology platforms. Sometimes, the better path is not to push a new user experience on lawyers, but instead for the law firm to use the technology themselves and sell the better result.

InCloudCounsel is a good example of a legal start-up company that has succeeded as a technology-powered people business. Its customers are benefiting from the technology that InCloudCounsel bakes into its offering without ever actually having to use the technology themselves. There are tech start-ups that I believe would have significantly more traction if they were not hell-bent on selling their SaaS, and instead were focused on delivering a better customer outcome.

### Minimal change to customer habits

The legal technology ecosystem has figured out that change management can be a real challenge. No one wants to learn how to use new technology. Not lawyers. (Not anybody, but especially not lawyers.) As a result, technology companies are building products that require very little change in user habits. More tools are built with Microsoft Word in mind, as that is where lawyers spend their days. The goal is to embed AI into current lawyer behavior. Thus, Blackboiler,[19] an automated contract markup tool, has a feature that allows users to email a document to the Blackboiler AI engine, which then sends back a first-pass review of the agreement. Obviously, this is designed to resemble how senior attorneys actually work when they send an agreement to a junior attorney.

But perhaps not enough attention has been paid to the purchasing habits of clients. If someone really likes donuts, why try and sell them a croissant? Legal departments are experts at engaging outside counsel services, but not necessarily buying technology. Therefore, it can actually be easier for a legal department to purchase technology through a letter of engagement with a law firm than it is to buy the technology itself.

Indeed, the obstacles facing the legal department are significant. Foremost, though hugely valuable to the company, law departments are cost centers and thus often lack technology purchasing power within their organization. Second, many in-house teams do not have their own tech budget and must work through IT and procurement in order to buy new tech. Yes, the Fortune 500 are buying more and more new technology each year, but that does not necessarily trickle down to legal. Corporate innovation teams are looking for technology that is core to the business and offers them a competitive advantage – and document automation tools are unlikely to be high on the list, particularly if the general counsel is an ineffective champion.

This is not to say that it is impossible to sell legal technology directly to corporations – the success of matter management companies demonstrates that pretty clearly.

Yet, law firm engagements have enormous built-in advantages, as they do not typically require sign-off from IT and sensitive data is protected under attorney–client privilege. In short, an in-house team might have an easier time engaging a law firm that will use AI to improve their process rather than having their own people adopt the technology internally. Enter the AmLaw 100 and their shiny new tech subsidiaries.

## The argument against law firm tech businesses

Dissenters to law firm-based legal tech will point to the failures of Atrium and Clearspire, both law firm technology hybrids.[20] A separate chapter could be written on the differences between Atrium and Clearspire, but they do share one thing in common – the tech portion of their businesses did not emerge organically from a pre-existing legal people business, they launched as hybrids. That is not to say that this go-to-market approach is inherently flawed. But while there are many examples of firms spawning a successful tech business, far fewer examples come to mind of successful start-ups that launched as hybrids, presumably because the former has an existing client base and brand and the latter has to build one. Still, if a start-up approached me to invest and a hybrid model was part of its go-to-market, it would check a box for me. Nonetheless, the advantages of the law firm hybrid are even more compelling.

Others argue that law firms that try to get too deep into the tech game may be going outside their lane. In 2019, for example, Greenberg Traurig Chairman Richard Rosenbaum shared his skepticism on law firms venturing outside their core competencies, saying:

> *"For a US law firm to say we are going to keep up with public companies, private equity-backed companies and other major technology players that have access to greater amounts of capital for technology and other major capital outlays is not realistic. And by the way, nobody is doing it. Instead of law firms focusing on what they are best at – which is being great law firms – they are spending time trying to keep up with innovation. And that isn't even the business they're in."*[21]

This perspective definitely has some validity – essentially that law firm tech businesses will have difficulty scaling. But I would point to another dictum of Paul Graham, who observes, "One of the most common types of advice we give at Y Combinator is to do things that don't scale".[22]

Graham's core point is that start-up founders have to do an enormous amount of legwork before scaling ever becomes an issue, such as:

- Recruiting users;
- Navigating a period of fragility where testing ideas is more important the selling or garnering investment;
- Figuring out how to delight your customers;
- Making the user experience "insanely great";
- Conquering a niche market, which has the advantage of controlled growth; and
- For B2B start-ups, consulting in order to get closer to potential implementation issues.[23]

Israeli Prime Minister Shimon Peres once said about Middle East Peace, "We should use our imagination more than our memory". This is a useful reminder when trying to avoid the usual eye rolls about law firm innovation. At least reputationally, law firm innovation has historically been perceived as a marketing ploy. Plus, the return on investment from law firm tech businesses, while impressive, is still a blip on the radar of law firm revenues. But we should use our imagination more than our memory.

The trend of law firm tech businesses, whether in Biglaw, boutiques, A2J, or service providers, is built on solid foundations, and there is every reason to be bullish about their future.

*This chapter first appeared on the Legal Evolution blog and is reproduced with kind permission.*

### References

1 See, for example, Dan Packel, "Big Law Branches Out: Firm Subsidiaries Want a Piece of the $10B ALSP Market", 25 June 2020 www.law.com/americanlawyer/2020/06/25/big-law-branches-out-firm-subsidiaries-want-a-piece-of-the-10b-alsp-market/; Zach Warren, "The Future is Not Just About Innovation", 3 December 2020 www.law.com/2020/12/03/78229/; Vanessa Blum & Zack Needles, "Big Law Goes 'Alternative': Can Traditional Firms Disrupt the Disrupters?", 30 October 2020 www.law.com/2020/10/30/big-law-goes-alternative-can-traditional-firms-disrupt-the-disrupters/.

2 See "CLOC Institute 2019 – Opening Session with Mary O'Carroll", 15 May 2019 www.youtube.com/watch?v=vHjnY8NvYGM.

3 See, e.g., Jae Um discussing the pattern at www.legalevolution.org/2018/05/legal-innovation-is-an-extreme-sport-51/.

4 See "Home Court Advantage: The AmLaw 100's Move into Alternative Legal Services", October 2020 https://blog.baretzbrunelle.com/newlaw-news/newlaw-captive-alsp-report-home-court-advantage.

5 See "Chapman and Cutler: Sale of Closing Room to NetDocuments could just be the start", 12 November 2018 https://legaltechnology.com/2018/11/12/chapman-and-cutler-sale-of-closing-room-to-netdocuments-could-just-be-the-start/.

6 See "Role Reversal as Litera Buys Tech Product from Law Firm", Artificial Lawyer, 5 November 2020 www.artificiallawyer.com/2020/11/05/role-reversal-as-litera-buys-tech-product-from-law-firm/.

7 See Thomas Alan, "New Law pioneer LOD primed for growth as BCLP sells to buyout house", 30 May 2018 www.legalbusiness.co.uk/blogs/new-law-pioneer-lod-primed-for-growth-as-bclp-sells-to-buyout-house/.

8 "Keesal, Young & Logan and Mitratech Announce TAP Workflow Automation Partnership with the Launch of Keesal Propulsion Labs", 14 August 2018 https://mitratech.com/en_gb/resource-hub/pressreleases/keesal-young-logan-and-mitratech-announce-tap-workflow-automation-partnership-with-the-launch-of-keesal-propulsion-labs/.

9 "Legal Technology Leader DISCO Raises $60 Million", 15 October 2020 www.csdisco.com/pressrelease/legal-technology-leader-disco-raises-60-million .

10 Zach Abramowitz, "How A Law Firm Becomes A Software Company: Conversation With CS Disco's Neil Etheridge", 9 June 2016 https://abovethelaw.com/2016/06/how-a-law-firm-becomes-a-software-company-conversation-with-cs-discos-neil-etheridge/.

11 See Cat Casey, "Everything I Thought I Knew About DISCO Was Wrong – And Why That is a Good Thing", 9 April www.csdisco.com/articles/everything-i-thought-i-knew-about-disco-was-wrong.

12 Andy Wilson, "The 13-year-old startup: How we went from Logik Systems, Inc. to Logikcull.com", 12 July 2017 www.linkedin.com/pulse/13-year-old-startup-how-we-went-from-logik-systems-inc-andy-wilson.

13 Bob Ambrogi, "Erin Levine Is Taking Her Innovative 'Hello Divorce' Platform To All 50 States", 5 August 2020 www.lawnext.com/2020/08/erin-levine-is-taking-her-innovative-hello-divorce-platform-to-all-50-states.html.

14 "The keys to successful IP asset management", 15 February 2006 https://sciencebusiness.net/news/73950/The-keys-to-successful-IP-asset-management.

15 "How to Get Start-up Ideas", November 2012 http://paulgraham.com/startupideas.html.

16 Zach Warren, "The Future is Not Just About Innovation", 3 December 2020 www.law.com/2020/12/03/78229/.

17 "Casetext raises $12M to expand its AI-powered legal research platform" https://techcrunch.com/2019/02/06/casetext-raises-12m-to-expand-its-ai-powered-legal-research-platform/.

18 Mark Suster, "Seven Tips For Layering Professional Services Revenue Into Your Startup", 21 March 2013 https://techcrunch.com/2013/03/21/7-tips-for-layering-professional-services-revenue-into-your-startup/.

19 "Blackboiler raises $3.2M to automate tedious contract review process" https://techcrunch.com/2021/06/16/blackboiler-raises-3-2m-to-automate-tedious-contract-review-process/.

20 See, e.g., Josh Constine, "$75M legal startup Atrium shuts down, lays off 100", TechCrunch, 3 March 2020 (discussing failure of Atrium) https://techcrunch.com/2020/03/03/atrium-shuts-down; Mark Cohen, "The Clearspire Story", Legal Business World, 12 December 2017 (discussing failure of Clearspire) https://legalbusinessworld.com/single-post/2017/12/12/The-Clearspire-Story.

21 Roy Strom, "Greenberg Traurig Chair: Law Firms Struggle to Compete with ALSPs", 12 June 2019 https://news.bloomberglaw.com/us-law-week/greenberg-traurig-chair-law-firms-struggle-to-compete-with-alsps.

22 Paul Graham essays, "Do Things That Do Not Scale", July 2013 https://paulgraham.com/ds.html.

23 *Ibid.*

# Chapter 15: Humanizing legal tech adoption – fostering trust and innovation for a future-ready legal industry

*By Colin S. Levy, legal tech maven and director of legal, Malbek*

## A no-tech industry

When you first enter the world of legal tech, you are bombarded with terms such as AI, machine learning, and automation. Many of all stripes love to pump out content proclaiming the transformative potential of these technological advancements, highlighting how they will reimagine our daily lives in ways both anticipated and unforeseen. There is market demand for technology as we see countless start-ups bringing to market apps that strive to address unmet needs within the legal industry.

For a long time, the legal landscape appeared to be devoid of technology. Legal work was traditionally time-consuming and labor-intensive with lawyers and other legal professionals meticulously poring over documents, emails, and other work product before presenting them or relying on them. These efforts were seen as critical as even the slightest oversight could portend disaster. As someone who has personally navigated this treacherous terrain, I can attest to the sometimes-nerve-wracking nature of performing legal work. Today, technology has introduced a paradigm shift with legal professionals no longer burdened by having to manually check for errors or oversights. And now with the arrival of powerful AI-based tools and solutions, legal work is more and more data-driven and less and less reliant on history and tradition.

Yet there is a genuine risk of investing in technology only for it to end up underutilized or completely unused and promising software solutions become akin to dusty old law tomes, sitting on a shelf never to be glanced at again. The financial and other costs of shelfware are substantial. The expenses related to researching and purchasing the "right" solution and the time devoted to implementation and training can be high. Another cost of shelfware, however, is one borne by others as well as the purchaser of such shelfware – the impeding of adoption of legal technology. When legal teams and firms allocate substantial resources to acquire technological tools but fail to use them effectively, the consequences are threefold – financial, resource-based, and trust-related. From a financial perspective, when organizations squander valuable funds on tools that remain idle, they exacerbate the issue by neglecting to track usage metrics properly. In terms of resources, the efforts expended on implementing and integrating these tools by various departments, including security, development, and support, are rendered fruitless when the technology goes unused. Finally, the spread of shelfware erodes trust within the legal community, as lawyers become increasingly skeptical of the benefits of new technology. Addressing the issue of shelfware is therefore crucial to ensure that the legal sector, including those who consume legal services, can fully embrace and benefit from using technology-driven solutions.

### The challenge of adoption

The challenge of investing in legal tech is further complicated by the inherent difficulty of change. Humans, by nature, crave comfort, certainty, and familiarity; we prefer to adhere to established practices rather than venture into uncharted territory. This reluctance often manifests as a litany of excuses to avoid change, such as professing a lack of technological aptitude or claiming to be too busy to learn new skills. These justifications help mask a fundamental discomfort with doing things differently, particularly when adopting new technology. To optimize the benefits of legal tech investments and overcome the hurdles of shelfware and resistance to change, legal professionals must be willing to embrace innovation and adapt to new methods. By fostering a culture of continuous learning and recognizing the transformative potential of technology, the legal sector can overcome these challenges and unlock unprecedented efficiencies and opportunities for growth.

True adoption of legal tech extends far beyond mere technological solutions; it warrants engaging with stakeholders and users meaningfully, considering their comfort level with technology, their working habits, and their preferences in their day-to-day tasks. To achieve this, it is vital to listen attentively, allowing your users and stakeholders to define success on their terms. In essence, embracing legal tech is a dual-faceted endeavor, as much about the human element as it is about the technology itself. As we continue to forge ahead into an increasingly technology-driven future, the real challenge lies in striking the delicate balance between advocating for the use of new tools and acknowledging the human side of change. This balance requires empathy towards the concerns and reservations of your team and stakeholders, coupled with the understanding that the key to successful adoption lies in open communication, comprehension, and support.

There remains, though, the common question of how can we encourage change in those who are resistant to it? The answer begins with establishing trust. To cultivate genuine trust, it is crucial to ensure that users and stakeholders have faith in your judgment and the information you provide. One way to jeopardize trust-building, particularly with lawyers, is by insinuating that they are doing something wrong or suggesting that your approach is the sole viable option. To avoid being perceived as condescending or overly critical, strive to understand the current working methods of your users and stakeholders and the reasons behind them. The more insight you gain into their thought processes and motivations, the better equipped you will be to tailor your approach, helping them see that change is not only beneficial but also a natural step in their professional growth, rather than an imposition from an external source.

By fostering trust and showing a genuine interest in understanding your users' and stakeholders' perspectives, you create a foundation for change grounded in empathy and mutual respect. This approach paves the way for more successful adoption of legal tech, as it empowers individuals to see the value in embracing innovation and adapting to new methods. One key driver for change within the legal industry is understanding the relationship between technology and humanity. Getting someone to adopt legal tech doesn't happen out of the blue. Often adoption demands taking a slower, pragmatic, and human-centered approach. Sure, sometimes you can show someone a basic legal tech tool – say a document automation solution – and they can immediately start to use it. The more common case is when you need to show a group how they can be more productive, happier, and perhaps more valued by others that they work with by using a tech-based tool.

## A human-centered approach

Focusing on the human impact of technology can help overcome the challenges described earlier. When employees can see how legal tech can make their work lives easier and support their career goals, they are more likely to adopt new tools. Take document review, for example. It is a necessary but time-consuming task that requires a great deal of attention to detail. Assisted by AI-based technology, document review can be automated, making it faster and more accurate. By showing employees how a new AI tool can help them work more accurately, they can see how the technology will benefit them directly.

When introducing legal tech to your team, it's essential to frame it as a tool that will improve their work lives and support their career goals.

Projected users of a new tool are more likely to use them when they understand how they will benefit from them. Often this means focusing first on how use of the tool will be to their benefit, allowing them to work faster, easier, and more enjoyably. A user wants to use a new tool because they want to use it, not because someone is ordering them to use it. By highlighting the human impact of technology, you can make the benefits of legal tech both tangible and relatable. Of course, it is also critical to provide your users with all the support they need when they need it, including training and access so they can go about doing their jobs each day.

Creating a culture of innovation and continuous improvement is a long-term strategy but an effective one for supporting, encouraging, and enabling better adoption of new technologies. In practical terms, this means showing, especially from key leaders of the business, that teams can and should explore new technologies and share their experiences with each other. Give your team or users the freedom and autonomy to engage in experimentation and see what happens. I recall once being told by a manager to explore new tools to help manage a particularly sensitive yet time consuming and repetitive task. I had a chance to test out new tools. Most failed to do what I needed to do, but then the final one I tried worked as I had desired. I told my manager and showed them the tool. They then gave the go ahead for me to purchase, implement, and use the tool. This approach continued with other matters that I was tasked with, and I felt encouraged to do what I needed to do to accomplish my work productively. By creating such a supportive environment where employees feel comfortable trying new things, you can foster a culture of innovation that drives the adoption of legal tech. One example of someone who has engaged in this work quite successfully is Jason Barnwell.[1]

To facilitate better legal tech adoption, it's essential to prioritize open communication channels where feedback, concerns, and ideas can be shared openly and without fear of judgment. Encourage your team to ask questions, express their concerns, and share their experiences with new tools. As a leader, be receptive to feedback and incorporate it into the implementation process. Celebrate small wins and acknowledge the efforts made by individuals in embracing change, as this will contribute to a positive environment where innovation can flourish. Sharing success stories and positive experiences with new tools among colleagues can further encourage adoption. When individuals see their peers benefiting from legal tech, they are more likely to be open to using it themselves. I once tried out a new technology and saw the dramatic impact it had made upon my ability to automate the creation of a new document that was a document I needed to create again and again. I shared my experience with a colleague and we both started to use the tool more often and told others until the entire team and other business teams were using this tool. This example illustrates the power that user-led experimentation and storytelling can have to enable innovation and drive change. This approach fosters a supportive environment for change and innovation, promoting a culture that embraces legal tech adoption and ensures a more efficient and effective workplace. Enabling a culture that values learning and continuous improvement, you can help your team feel more at ease with the adoption of legal tech, ultimately leading to a more efficient and effective workplace.

*References*

1 See www.legalevolution.org/2021/11/legal-evolution-is-industrial-evolution-277/ for an overview of Jason's journey so far and www.colinslevy.com/post/jason-barnwell for more about his current work.

# Chapter 16: Environmental change and legal innovation ecosystem evolution

*By Richard Tromans, founder, Artificial Lawyer*

Why do things evolve? There are two main reasons. The first is that the environment changes in ways that allow only those that can adapt to prosper and suppresses those that don't. The second is that participants in the ecosystem change on their own, affording them advantages within their environmental niche.

In short, and in terms of organizations in the market, it's the "stick and the carrot". The "stick" is where the environment changes against the businesses there that have previously adapted to the old status quo. If they want to retain their hold on their niche, they have to adapt.

Luckily for humans, we don't have to wait for our physical DNA to mutate to adapt to something. We can analyze the situation, collect evidence, and then imagine a better way of doing things (i.e., innovate).

Then we can test that idea (the hypothesis), build tools to help and new ways of working and deploying our group's talent, and try to overcome the challenge. If we succeed, we secure our place in the niche. If we fail, we have wasted resources and perhaps have allowed rivals in the niche to take our place. *But if we don't try to innovate then we are almost certainly going to be out-adapted by rivals in the same environment.*

Then there is the "carrot". Again, in nature, DNA mutates each generation. In most cases we don't notice. But sometimes – and across large expanses of time – those mutations are truly positive and allow a species to take advantage of its environment, or expand its environment, in new ways, allowing it to grow as a group, avoid competition, and reach new resources. An example is the development of the ability to fly among reptiles.

For humans, as noted, we can go the innovation route if we want to benefit positively from this scenario, often by choice and for our own advantage. And one could argue the history of civilization has been largely steered by opportunistic steps forward in innovation. No one held the citizens of Manchester and the West Midlands in the UK at gunpoint, demanding they create the Industrial Revolution – certain people saw what could be done through innovation and they did what was possible with the technology and processes of the time. It changed the world.

## Environmental change in the legal world

It looks like we are now facing a period of rapidly increasing change in the legal market, driven by both environmental factors that many of the participants can do nothing about other than to:

- Try to resist; or
- Adapt to and prosper from;
- As well as increasing opportunities for "positive evolution" created from opportunistic developments.

So, what's changing? What follows are some of my thoughts, but first an updated map of what I call the Legal Innovation Ecosystem, which has been refreshed to include more aspects.

The map is here because that is where most of us are situated, and as is often the case in an ecosystem when one part of the system changes then the effects are felt in many other branches of this "meta-entity".

## A root cause: client change

Ever since the first panel was created, in-house legal teams have very slowly, very incrementally, been thinking more and more about how they procure legal services. In turn, the legal operations movement has seen those same teams consider how things operate internally. Meanwhile, and especially since the last financial crisis in 2008/09, the CFOs of larger companies have been looking at legal spend and asking a simple, but powerful, two-part question: "Why do we spend this much on legal needs? And is there anything that can be done to improve things while still providing the same level of protection?"

Another factor has been the advance of technology. For example, CLM systems are not new, but in the last few years they have arguably got a lot better, primarily because of improvements in software. For example, the provision of Natural Language Processing (NLP) capabilities to extract key data from both new and old contracts has helped companies to have better data visibility without having to rely upon thousands of people in a Legal Process Outsourcing (LPO) type of facility that is joined to the CLM provider. Add to this faster and smarter approaches to workflows and docu-

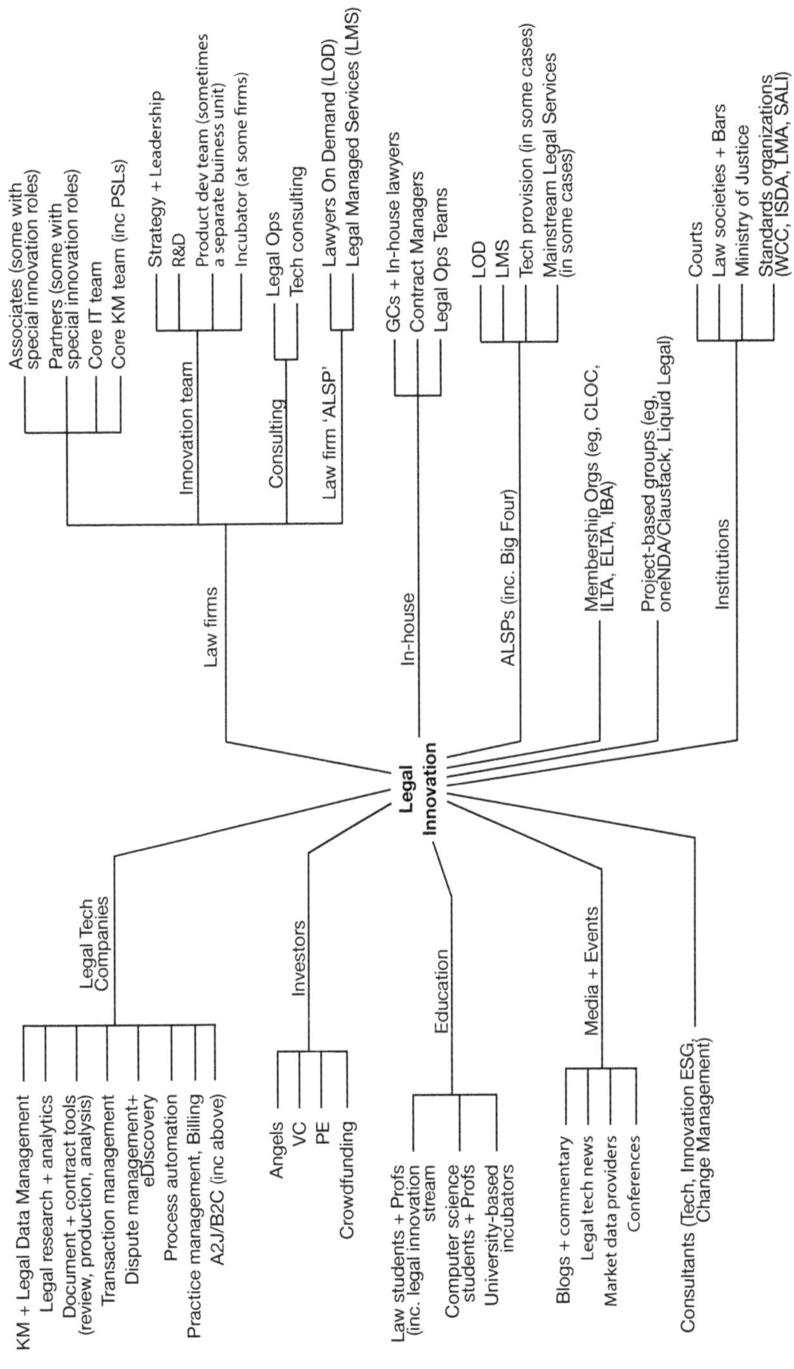


*Figure 1: Legal Innovation Ecosystem. © Artificial Lawyer, November 2022.*

ment automation, as well as building better-connected platforms that ferry information and documents back and forth across the legal team and to the business as a whole, and in-house teams have been able to leverage tech to gain plenty of benefits.

But the adoption of tech is not in itself the most profound change.

What really matters is that as in-house legal teams – with the encouragement of other parts of the business – rethink how legal work is handled, from triaging work streams to considering who should do what work and how, then the traditional relationships with external suppliers and internal clients evolve.

If you have more awareness of what you do, what it costs, how it helps or hinders your efforts to do higher value work, and that there is now real engagement from the rest of the business to have those insights and improvements, then in-house legal teams will change – and are changing, albeit at present still incrementally. However, *once new norms of behavior are established then change will accelerate. Then, upon those new norms will come further change and improvement*, as the GCs and other senior in-house lawyers, heads of contract management, as well as CFOs, gain a new appreciation of what can be done.

For law firms, the clients are in effect the "land that they live upon". If this environment changes then everything changes. So, what changes?

- Clients really start to expand their use of ALSPs, whether dedicated entities, or part of a law firm or Big Four firm, not just for long-established needs such as eDiscovery work, but for everything that can be determined to not be high risk or "cost irrelevant", and so service delivery can be significantly improved.
- Clients expect smoother service and longer-term relationships with providers. Where before "value add" meant seconding a junior associate to a client as a kind of "free gift" to keep the client sweet and loyal, things now are much more sophisticated. Clients will be expecting a suite of useful digital tools from providers. They will expect things like tech-based deal management support and on-demand knowledge services, e.g., expert systems, or perhaps an entire contract management system, whether built by the firm or provided by the firm via a third party.
- This will often be in tandem with consulting services, from legal ops to legal tech to special project management. Just expecting external providers to offer high risk, high value advice will become less and less common.

- As some law firms pull ahead here, others will be forced to adapt to keep up. Or perhaps give up on certain types of work. There will also be opportunities for some firms to rise in the ranks by providing the right mix of advice and process help. The market could well change plenty in the coming years because of this environmental shift.

However, there are some who may not change much – and will still prosper for now – and that in turn will reshape the market. Some US law firms, especially those working on "price-irrelevant" matters, e.g., for very large private equity funds, and where the associate hours and overall business model has been skewed to maximize profits at all human costs, are now breaking away from the rest of the market in terms of profits. *They have doubled down on the "traditional" super-inefficiency model and surprisingly many of their clients don't seem to care a jot about all the wasted money.* This group, often associated with the New York legal market, may of course find they are left high and dry one day in the future if their "cost-blind" clients have a change of heart. But it could go on like this for a long time.

We are already seeing now a split in the "elite" firm group, with the older model plus profligate clients creating stratospheric partner profits – but only for a very small group of firms.

Everyone else is having to adapt.

## The future direction

This topic could probably turn into a book.

*The key point here is that as the clients change so does everything else.*

If the clients change, then the law firms have to change. ALSPs see new niches in the environment open up and expand. The use of tech increases and opportunities for new tech solutions expands as well. The rethinking of processes accelerates. New approaches to staffing also arrive, or expand if already here.

In turn, legal education needs to change and so too the variety of jobs widens in this field. Organizations spring up and expand to support this change. And so on. Every branch of the ecosystem tree feels the effects.

As noted, this has not happened overnight. We can trace the first changes back to the earliest efforts to create panels, followed by what was called back then "the new normal", referring to GCs having to really explain why they did what they did to their CEOs and CFOs. Then we had the legal ops movement, the New Wave of legal tech since 2015, the much greater expansion of ALSPs and the Big Four, and generally a widening of knowledge and education around legal data and the economics of legal processes, to now a push to drive a more human-centric approach to the legal world, which embodies all of the above.

All in all, this amounts to environmental change, and that in turn will super-charge the legal innovation ecosystem, and in turn the legal market as a whole.

There is so much more to be said here, but it's been a fantastic experience and a privilege to have been a part of the journey up to this point. We are really now only just beginning what will be a much more rapid era of evolution in this market. Exciting times ahead!

# Further reading and resources

## General developments

- LawNext (formerly known as LawSitesBlog) – www.lawnext.com
- Legal Technology Hub – www.legaltechnologyhub.com
- Legal Tech Blog – https://legal-tech.blog/
- Law Technology Today – www.lawtechnologytoday.org
- Law Insider – www.lawinsider.com

## Thought leadership

- Legal Evolution – www.legalevolution.org/
- Artificial Lawyer – www.artificiallawyer.com
- CodeX – https://law.stanford.edu/codex-the-stanford-center-for-legal-informatics
- Law21 – www.law21.ca

## Podcasts

- Legal Geek Podcast
- Dear Legal Ops
- Technically Legal
- LawNext
- The Future Law Podcast

## Books

- *On Legal AI* by Joshua Walker

- *Artificial Intelligence for Lawyers* by Noah Waisberg and Dr Alexander Hudek
- *The Legal Team of the Future* by Adam Curphey
- *Legal Data and Information in Practice* by Sarah A. Sutherland
- *Working Smarter with Knowledge Tools* by Marc Lauritsen
- *The Handbook for Legal Innovation* by Nicola Shaver
- *Ethics, Law, and Technology Adoption* by Dr Steven A Wright

# About Globe Law and Business

Globe Law and Business was established in 2005. From the very beginning, we set out to create legal books that are sufficiently high level to be of real use to the experienced professional, yet still accessible and easy to navigate. Most of our authors are drawn from Magic Circle and other top commercial firms, both in the United Kingdom and internationally.

Our titles are carefully produced, with the utmost attention paid to editorial, design and production processes. We hope this results in high-quality publications that are easy to read and a pleasure to own.

In 2021, we were very pleased to announce the start of a new chapter for Globe Law and Business following the acquisition of law books under the imprint Ark Publishing. Our law firm management list is now significantly expanded with many well known and loved Ark Publishing titles.

We are also pleased to announce the launch of our online content platform, Globe Law Online. This allows for easy search and networked access across firms. Key collections include the Legal Content Collection (including a Private Client module) and the Law Firm Management Collection. Details of all titles included can be found at www.globelawonline.com. Email glo@globelawandbusiness.com for further details and to arrange a free trial for you or your firm.

We'd very much like to hear from you with your thoughts and ideas for improving what we offer. Please do feel free to email me on sian@globelawandbusiness.com. Happy reading and thank you for your time.

**Sian O'Neill**
Managing director
Globe Law and Business
www.globelawandbusiness.com